Which worldview best addresses the various specifics of arguably the thorniest philosophical problem of all? In this careful and thorough analysis, Campbell probes the most central cognate dilemmas in order to evaluate the ability of each perspective to provide the best insights without avoiding the toughest sub-issues. The chief benefit of this volume is being guided through the maze by an insider. Highly recommended.

—GARY R. HABERMAS, Distinguished Research Professor and Chair, Department of Philosophy, Liberty University

The problem of evil is perhaps the most difficult problem that Christian theism faces. In his impressive new book, *Worldviews and the Problem of Evil*, Ronnie P. Campbell Jr. takes a novel approach to the problem, addressing the broader theological and philosophical problem of evil as it relates to four prominent worldviews: naturalism, pantheism, panentheism, and theism. Without attempting to offer a full-blown theodicy, Campbell makes a compelling, clear, and insightful case that Christian theism offers a preferable framework for understanding and addressing the problem of evil. Along the way, Campbell carefully introduces and charitably engages a host of theological and philosophical issues, providing a well-written and easy-to-read treatment that will be of value to both introductory and more seasoned readers.

—JOHN C. PECKHAM, Professor of Theology and Christian Philosophy, Andrews University

In this fine work, Ronnie Campbell marshals some compelling arguments in defense of an explicitly Christian form of theism in the face of evil. Written in accessible and engaging prose, the book is also a robust work in comparative philosophical theology—one that considers both theistic and nontheistic perspectives. *Worldviews and the Problem of Evil* offers a lucid and refreshing engagement with this age-old problem.

—CHAD MEISTER is Professor of Philosophy and Theology at Bethel University and author of *Evil: A Guide for the Perplexed*

Amid the sea of books dealing with the problem of evil, Ronnie Campbell's work truly stands out. Impressively wide-ranging and unique in approach, Campbell offers a comparative study of the problem of evil in four (or five) distinct worldviews, assessing the resources of each to make sense of evil in the world. Especially noteworthy is the treatment of the problem of evil in pantheistic and panentheistic systems. By bringing to bear philosophy of religion, religious studies, and analytic theology, Campbell argues that a robust, "thick" Christian theism explains evil as well as or better than rival worldviews. I highly recommend this creative volume for philosophers and theologians alike, and indeed anyone troubled by the problem of evil (as we all should be).

—GARRETT J. DEWEESE, Professor at large, Talbot School of Theology, Biola University

T0327056

In this engaging, wide-ranging and thought-provoking book, Campbell offers an impressively comprehensive argument that the reality of evil should not cause us to reject theism but to embrace it as the most adequate view. Contemporary discussion of the problem of evil is helpfully developed through an interdisciplinary consideration of the way in which a specifically Christian theism can offer a uniquely satisfying response to both the intellectual and existential/pastoral problems of suffering.

     —JONATHAN J. LOOSE, School of Advanced Study, University of London

WORLDVIEWS & THE PROBLEM OF EVIL

WORLDVIEWS & THE PROBLEM OF EVIL

A COMPARATIVE APPROACH

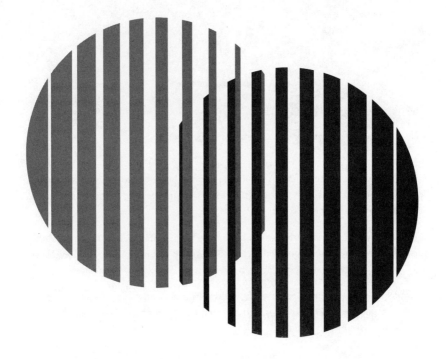

RONNIE P. CAMPBELL, JR.

LEXHAM PRESS

Worldviews and the Problem of Evil: A Comparative Approach

Copyright 2019 Ronnie P. Campbell Jr.

Lexham Press, 1313 Commercial St., Bellingham, WA 98225
LexhamPress.com

Print ISBN 9781683593058
Digital ISBN 9781683593065

Lexham Editorial Team: Douglas Mangum, Eric Bosell, Erin Mangum
Cover Design: Micah Ellis
Typesetting: ProjectLuz.com

To Dave Baggett:

Mentor, Colleague, Friend

CONTENTS

PREFACE

Has not much ink been spilt over this one topic already? Can anything new be said that has not already been said? In response, there are at least three reasons why this work on the problem of evil is needed.

First, while it is true that much has been written on this topic, even within the last thirty years or so, the problem of evil remains a significant challenge to Christian theism.[1] Evil affects every one of us in some way or another, and it is not just a challenge to Christianity, but to all worldviews. *Worldviews and the Problem of Evil* will consider how theism, and Christian theism in particular, compares with other broader worldview systems (naturalism, pantheism, and process panentheism) in making sense of evil in the world. While many Christian theists engage naturalists on the problem of evil, surprisingly few Christian works take seriously pantheistic

---

1. During the editing stages of this book, two other works on the problem of evil came out that I regret being unable to consider in this present work. The first is Greg Welty's *Why Is There Evil in the World (And So Much of It?)* (Fearn, Ross-shire: Christian Focus, 2018). Welty takes a serious look at the "Greater Good theodicy" (see pages 151–55 below) and provides the reader with reasons why he takes such an approach to be the best response to the problem of evil, over against other traditional theodicies. The second book, *Explaining Evil: Four Views* (London: Bloomsbury Academic, 2019), edited by W. Paul Franks, provides an all-star cast of philosophers, two theists and two non-theists, debating on the merits of whether theism stands given evil in the world. Because I find difficulties with Greater Good theodicies, Welty would have made for a good discussion partner on this important issue. On the other hand, the two non-theistic viewpoints from Franks' edited volume would have provided helpful insight into my discussion on naturalism, the metaphysics of good and evil, and human responsibility. Nevertheless, while both works would have been helpful to consider in this book, both are strikingly different. The primary focus of *Worldviews and the Problem of Evil* is to provide a comparative analysis of four worldview approaches to evil. Unlike Welty's book, which focuses on a singular theodicy, *Worldviews and the Problem of Evil* places emphasis on how Christian theism provides a more robust response to evil in the world than its metaphysical rivals—two different approaches. In contrast to *Explaining Evil*, *Worldviews and the Problem of Evil* goes beyond the debate between theists and atheists/naturalists to consider other worldview contenders, specifically pantheism and process panentheism.

and process panentheistic attempts at explaining evil. This work takes up that challenge. As will be argued, these other worldviews, when confronted with evil, have serious difficulties of their own. The upshot of such a comparative analysis is to show that, if Christian theism explains evil as well as or better than its metaphysical rivals, then there's no reason to reject Christian theism outright because of evil in the world.

A second purpose of this present work is to provide a uniquely Christian response to the problem of evil. Philosophers of religion in the analytic tradition have largely led the charge in confronting the intellectual challenges brought on by the various arguments from evil, along with some significant attempts at answering the existential problem from evil—though this latter area has not received nearly as much attention. Regarding the intellectual problem, Alvin Plantinga, in his monumental work, *God, Freedom, and Evil*, has largely put to rest the so-called logical problem of evil, so much so, that hardly anyone, including most atheists, accepts it as a real threat to theism.[2] Even its more modest cousin, the evidential problem of evil, has received significant attention by philosophers.[3] Surprisingly, there have been far fewer volumes written by theologians and biblical scholars on the topic in comparison to the work of philosophers. When they do touch on the topic of evil, often it is done without serious engagement with the work of these philosophers. That is not to say that no theologians or biblical scholars have given the topic of evil due consideration, but, in large part, they have been somewhat absent comparatively. Philosophers of religion, however, particularly those who are convinced of the truth claims of Christianity, are not entirely off the hook. Many of them have done their defense within the realm of a generic or minimalistic theism. But it doesn't seem that minimalistic theism provides the kind of robust answer to evil that is needed, and it certainly doesn't get us to the truth claims of Christian theism.

In this book I aim to move from defending minimalistic theism to defending a more robust, distinctly Christian theism in responses to evil (see especially chapters 6–8). In other words, *Worldviews and the Problem of*

---

2. See Alvin Plantinga, *God, Freedom, and Evil* (Grand Rapids: Eerdmans, 1977).

3. See, for example, the essays in *The Evidential Argument from Evil*, ed. Daniel Howard-Snyder (Bloomington, IN: Indiana University Press, 1996).

Evil is an attempt at what Richard Swinburne calls "ramified natural theology" (RNT), which he distinguishes from "bare natural theology" (BNT).[4] According to Swinburne, BNT can get us to a generic concept of God, which can be shared among most theists; however, it cannot move us from generic theism to particular religious claims as found in Islam or Christianity. RNT, then, is a natural extension of BNT.[5] The comparative approach taken in this book gives us a good angle for bridging the gulf and helping us to move from generic theism to Christian theism. In addition to being a work in RNT, *Worldviews and the Problem of Evil* is also an attempt at analytic theology. Because this work at times gets technical, I have included for the reader a glossary of key philosophical and theological terms used throughout, and those terms can be found throughout the text printed in bold italics (usually the first time the term is used in a chapter).

Third, and lastly, this book, especially in the last chapter, takes steps toward bridging the gap between the intellectual and existential problems from evil. Philosophers rightly understand these two problems as distinct and believe that we should approach them differently; however, they often do so at the risk of severing the two. While evil raises significant intellectual problems for the Christian theist, it is also a very real existential feature of reality that must be dealt with. For any worldview that seeks to confront the problem of evil, it must do so in a multi-dimensional way, not only by answering the intellectual demands raised by the problem of evil, but also by giving considerable attention to the existential dimension. As I argue, Christian theism points a way forward, offering, against other worldviews, a view of a God who loves his creature deeply and who acts in the world to defeat evil.

---

4. Richard Swinburne, "Natural Theology, Its 'Dwindling Probabilities' and 'Lack of Rapport,'" *Faith and Philosophy* 21 (2004): 533.

5. Ibid., 533, 536.

ACKNOWLEDGEMENTS

There are many people who made this book possible, and to them I owe my deepest appreciation. First, I am grateful for the folks at Lexham Press, especially my editor, Doug Mangum, who made this work all the better with his keen insights and good editing sense. I would also like to thank Brannon Ellis, Jesse Myers, and Todd Hains. Each of you played a significant part in getting this book project started and off the ground. Thank you!

I would also like to express my gratitude to several people who have read portions of this book. To my teachers and colleagues at Liberty University, Dave Baggett, Chad Thornhill, Leo Percer, Ed Martin, and Gary Habermas, thank you for helping me to think through many of these concepts and ideas. This book is the fruit from your labor and investment in me. To William Hasker, Greg Ganssle, and Jamie Dew, thank you for your encouragement and feedback, and for writing me a letter of recommendation to the publisher. Finally, I would like to thank the students from my Faith and Reason class at Liberty University, particularly Caroline Boozer, Joshua Anderson, Victoria Grant, Sarah Stewart, and Shane O'Neal, who met with me and discussed the content from this book. To each of you, I am deeply indebted.

Finally, I want to thank my wife, Debbie, who is an immutable source of strength and encouragement, and who is a daily reminder to me of God's goodness in this world.

CHAPTER 1
UNTANGLING THE KNOT

K nots come in many shapes and sizes and perform a variety of functions, as any Boy Scout or outdoors enthusiast knows. Understanding how to tie a knot may mean the difference between life and death. Some knots unravel easily, while others need persistent focus and attention in order to untangle. Working through the **problem of evil**[1] is much like untangling a knot that's both challenging and delicate. It's not merely an intellectual exercise, whereby one seeks to solve a problem, as one might do when working through a complicated math theorem or scientific theory, but a problem that affects each of us deeply and existentially.

We all experience evil in some way or another, and how one understands and responds to evil is deeply connected to one's **worldview** commitments, especially those worldviews that hold to the existence of God. As John Feinberg reminds us in *The Many Faces of Evil*, one's conception of God plays a significant role in how one answers the question of evil.[2] For not all concepts of God are equal. Even among people within the same general worldview, there are substantial differences between their ideas of God. Take, for example, the difference among theists. Unlike Jews or Muslims, who hold to God as one person, Christians believe that God is tri-personal. But what ultimate difference does it make if God is mono-personal or tri-personal?

---

1. Throughout this work I use "problem of evil" and "problem from evil" interchangeably. Technically speaking, one could argue that the phrase "problem of evil" is in reference to the problem that evil raises specifically for Christian theism. The "problem from evil," on the other hand, refers to the problem that evil raises in general, despite one's worldview.

2. John S. Feinberg, *The Many Faces of Evil: Theological Systems and the Problems of Evil* (Wheaton, IL: Crossway, 2004), 23-24.

The problem of evil not only affects theists of every stripe, but all people who have been confronted by the tragedies and horrors of evil in the world. Each worldview[3] must confront the reality and problems brought about by evil—problems that touch every tangent of our finite earthly existence. While each worldview provides an answer to such questions, not all worldview responses are on par with one another. Some worldviews provide a thicker response to the question of evil than others.[4] The problem of evil raises questions related to the meaning and purpose of life. Is there any meaning to our finite existence and the suffering we experience in the world, or is this life all there is? Should we have as our motto: "let us eat and drink, for tomorrow we die"?[5] As theologian Paul Tillich reminds us, each one of us stands in between being and nonbeing. We all teeter on the edge of life and death.[6] But even if this life is all that there is, can a person find meaning and purpose in the face of suffering? For a serious seeker, she must contend with the question of what constitutes a *thick* worldview response to evil and how such a response differs from a *thin* worldview response. What criteria should one use when analyzing worldview responses to evil in the world? Which worldviews are even live options in the face of evil?

Any adequate response to the problem of evil, then, must answer such questions as the ones raised above. How does Christian theism fare with such questions in comparison to other worldviews or metaphysical systems?[7] Does Christianity have within it, not only the resources to present a rational explanation for why evil exists and an answer to what God is doing about evil (or, at least, why he allows it), but also the capacity to provide

---

3. While worldviews are as prevalent as there are human persons, there are, nevertheless, general features that places people within the confines of a broader worldview, mostly in response to how a person answers the question of God and ultimate reality.

4. When philosophers speak of "thick" or "thin" with respect to possible worlds or worldviews, they have in mind the extent to which a person finds value, meaning, and purpose within that world. A "thin" world is one where there is no objective value, meaning, or purpose; whereas a "thick" world is one that is teaming with such attributes. For a fuller discussion, see J. P. Moreland, *Kingdom Triangle* (Grand Rapids: Zondervan, 2007), 26–29.

5. 1 Corinthians 15:32. Some consider Paul to have in mind Menander's comedy *Thais*.

6. Paul Tillich, *Systematic Theology*, vol. 2 (Chicago: Chicago University Press, 1957), 66–75.

7. I recognize that there are various ways of classifying worldviews. Here, I am classifying worldviews based on their metaphysical commitments on God and God's relationship to the world. Hence the terms "worldview" and "metaphysical systems" are used interchangeably.

a response to the existential dimension of evil in the world? This book is an attempt at providing a robust response to the problem of evil from a Christian perspective. In this book I argue that, in comparison to four other broad metaphysical systems—**naturalism, pantheism, process panentheism**, and **theism**—Christianity provides a thick response, not only to the intellectual problem of evil, but also to the existential/religious problem. In addition, I argue that Christian theism provides a thicker response than other theistic worldviews. Particularly, within the central teachings of Christian theism, especially the doctrine of the Trinity, Christians have the tools for providing a robust response to the problem of evil.

This chapter is the first of eight that seek to unravel the knot we call "the problem of evil." In this chapter I aim to do three things. First, I set my sights on clarifying key terms related to the problem of evil, especially as they bear on this book's overarching purpose. It is common for books, such as this one, to distinguish between the various types and kinds of evil (e.g., moral, natural, and gratuitous); however, few books make the important distinction between *pain* and *suffering*.[8] A key contribution of this chapter is to disambiguate the two. Other key terms considered include: the problem of evil, **theodicy**, and **defense**. Second, I aim to build a positive case for the classic Christian view that *evil is the privation of the good*. In recent years, the *privation view of evil* has fallen on hard times. Despite this, I seek to make some carefully nuanced clarifications on what Christians mean by privation in order to resuscitate this important Christian teaching. As will be discussed below, I do not expect other worldviews to adopt the privationist view of evil, though it is important to discuss in the chapter for a number of reasons. That evil is a privation of the good has been the primary Christian understanding since the early church. Yet, it is also the view most often criticized by non-theists. In their critiques, the privationist view is often misunderstood, taking privation to be primarily a metaphysical issue. In part, this chapter seeks to correct such a misunderstanding, showing that evil as privation has a moral dimension to it. Third, and finally, this chapter lays out the overall methodology and approach to this book.

---

8. Making the distinction between pain and suffering has significant implications for discussion in chapter 5 on theism's response to evil.

EVIL, KINDS OF EVIL, AND THE GOOD

When asked to define *evil*, our response might be like Augustine's about time: "If no one asks me, I know; but if I wish to explain it to one who asks, I know not."[9] Some have concluded that evil is indefinable, much like the word "person." We know a person when we see one, even if we cannot arrive at a clear or concise definition of what constitutes personhood. Perhaps the same is true of evil? Perhaps we don't have sufficient conditions for classifying something as evil? That doesn't mean we have no parameters or boundaries for considering just what it means to call something evil.

Before moving on to a discussion on the nature of evil, it would be helpful to make some preliminary distinctions between different kinds of evil. Philosophers and theologians recognize that evil comes in two forms: **moral evil** and **natural evil**. Moral evils are such that the evil produced is the result of a moral agent. Murder, rape, genocide, and bio-chemical warfare are all examples of evil produced by a moral agent. *Natural evils*, on the other hand, refer to those evils that come about through nonhuman means. When human (or animal) life has been devastated by such natural events as hurricanes, tornadoes, or tsunamis, such is classified as natural evil. Natural evils may also come about through disease. Some philosophers even classify certain unintentional actions brought by human agents as belonging to natural evil. An example might include a child injured due to dashing out in front of an oncoming vehicle. In such a case the driver would not be held morally culpable since the action was not intentional on the part of the driver.[10] It may also be helpful to consider that some evils, which appear to be a result of natural processes, are, rather, the result of moral agency. Examples of this variety include the evils of pollution or forest fires caused by humans. One final category is the notion of **horrendous evils** (or **gratuitous evils**). Horrendous evils are, as Marilyn Adams defines, "evils the participation in which (that is, the doing or suffering of which) constitutes prima facie reason to doubt whether the participant's

---

9. Augustine, *Confessions*, 11.14.

10. Bruce R. Reichenbach, *Evil and a Good God* (New York: Fordham University Press, 1982), xi.

life could (given their inclusion in it) be a great good to him/her on the whole."[11] Such evils are "worse than others," and include things like

> the rape of a woman and axing off of her arms, psycho-physical torture whose ultimate goal is the disintegration of personality, betrayal of one's deepest loyalties, child abuse of the sort described by Ivan Karamazov, child pornography, parental incest, slow death by starvation, the explosion of nuclear bombs over populated areas.[12]

Horrendous evils go beyond the physical or mental pain they cause, to the point where the individual becomes devalued and degraded, engulfing any positive value in the person's life, to which they are organically tied.[13]

Classifying evils as "moral," "natural," or "horrendous" sheds light on thinking about evil, but such a classification does nothing by way of telling us just what evil is. How should we understand the nature of evil? Christians have generally sided with Augustine's view that evil is *privatio boni*—the "absence" or "privation" of good.[14] In the *Enchiridion*, Augustine described *privatio boni* as follows:

> In the bodies of animals, disease and wounds mean nothing but the absence of health; for when a cure is effected, that does not mean that the evils which were present—namely, the diseases and wounds—go away from the body and dwell elsewhere: they altogether cease to exist; for the wound or disease is not a substance but a defect in the fleshly substance—the flesh itself being a substance, and therefore something good, of which those evils—that is, privations of the good which we call health—are accidents. Just in the same way, what are called vices in the soul are nothing but privations of natural good. And when they are cured, they are not transferred elsewhere: when they cease to exist in the healthy soul, they cannot exist anywhere else.[15]

---

11. Marilyn McCord Adams, *Horrendous Evils and the Goodness of God* (Ithaca, NY: Cornell University Press, 1999), 26.

12. Ibid.

13. Ibid.

14. Augustine, *Enchiridion*, 11.

15. Ibid.

As Augustine worked out his views on evil, he kept one eye on Neo-Platonic thought and the other on the narrative of Genesis. From Genesis, Augustine understood that God created all things good and that the whole, taken together, was "very good." Evil exists in reality; however, it does not have being of its own. Much like a parasite needs its host in order to remain alive, evil, for Augustine, could not exist apart from the good.[16] Working from within a Neo-Platonic framework, Augustine equated being with goodness. A thing that is a good without any evil is a "perfect good."[17] An example of such a good would be God, who is "supremely and unchangeably good."[18] Yet, because God is supremely or unchangeably good, he, unlike all created goods, is incapable of corruption. Goods that have been corrupted are "faulty" or "imperfect" goods.[19] But because God created all things good, as seen in the Genesis narrative, no particular thing can exist and be completely corrupt at the same time; otherwise, it would cease to be.[20]

Philosopher of religion John Hick, who also stands broadly within the Christian tradition, finds Augustine's view wanting. Hick, in *Evil and the God of Love*, seems to affirm the biblical teaching that God is supremely good, and that creation itself, too, is good, in a derivative way. Yet, he questions whether Augustine (and Aquinas) too readily accepts the Neo-Platonic equation of being with goodness, going beyond the simple affirmation of Scripture.[21] Augustine's defense of holding to the Neo-Platonic equation of good with being rests in his acceptance of the greater chain of being:

> the claim that certain characteristics, which are necessarily present in different degrees in every existent thing—principally "measure, form, and order"—are intrinsically good. To possess these characteristics is to be a part of the continuum of entities constituting the created universe, so that to exist is, as such, to be good.[22]

---

16. This perspective on evil is not new to Augustine, but was promoted by other Church Fathers, such as Athanasius, who saw evil as "non-being." Evil is, says Athanasius, "the negation and antithesis of good." See Athanasius, *On the Incarnation*, 1.4.

17. Augustine, *Enchiridion*, 13.

18. Ibid., 12.

19. Ibid., 13.

20. Ibid.

21. John Hick, *Evil and the God of Love* (New York: Palgrave Macmillan, 2007), 172.

22. Ibid., 171.

However, says Hick, Augustine provides no philosophical arguments for accepting this principle; rather, it is a holdover from the Neo-Platonic view of reality. Further, claims Hick, "there appears to be no basis within Christian theology for affirming the intrinsic goodness of existence in any other than the biblical sense that God wills and values the world that he has created."[23] For Hick, to affirm creation's goodness is only to affirm that it "is willed and valued by God."[24] But such an affirmation, says Hick, "does not entail any metaphysical doctrine of the identity of being and goodness; nor does there appear to be any adequate reason to adopt such a doctrine."[25]

So how ought we to think of evil? Hick believes that one must distinguish between the theological insight that "evil is the going wrong of something good," which he thinks follows from the Christian teaching on God and creation, and evil as "nothingness or nonbeing."[26] Augustine's approach inadequately captures evil's true nature in light of human experience. Hick doesn't doubt evil's reality. It is both a "positive" and "powerful" element of human experience. "Empirically," says Hick, "it is not merely the absence of something else but a reality with its own distinctive and often terrifying quality of power."[27] It takes little reflection to see the limitations and inadequacy of the privation understanding of evil as an empirical description. Hick argues,

> What we call evil in nature can, it is true, often be regarded as consisting in the corruption or perversion or disintegration of something which, apart from such disruption, is good. ... Volcanic eruptions, droughts, tornadoes, hurricanes, and planetary collisions can perhaps likewise be regarded as breakdowns in some imagined ideal ordering of nature. In all such cases the evil state of affairs can plausibly be seen as the collapse of a good state of affairs, and as tending toward non-existence, at least in the relative sense of the dissolution of a previously established arrangement of life or matter. But does such an account really lay bare that aspect of the

---

23. Ibid.
24. Ibid., 172.
25. Ibid.
26. Ibid., 180.
27. Ibid., 55.

event or of the situation that makes us call it evil? Do we regard a volcanic eruption, for example, as evil considered simply as a loss of a previous "measure, form and order"? Do we not, on the contrary, regard it as evil only if it causes harm to human, or at least to sentient life? Is the eruption of a volcano an uninhabited island, or (assuming it to be uninhabited) on Venus, an evil? Or again, is the natural decay of vegetation in virgin jungle to be accounted evil? Or the burning up of a star or the fragmentation of a meteor a million million light years distant from us in space? If not, the quality of evil is not attributed to physical disintegration as such, but only in so far as it impinges deleteriously upon the realm of the personal, or at least upon the sphere of animal life. It is in fact not loss of "measure, form and order" *per se* that is evil, but only this considered as a cause of pain and suffering.[28]

Tornadoes and tsunamis are not evils in and of themselves. The problem arises when such events move into the realm of the personal or the sphere of animal life, causing pain, suffering, and destruction. But even in those cases where evil is brought on by human agency, the privation view becomes all the more problematic. Evil is not merely the devaluation or absence of the good, but "it can be a terrifying positive force in the world."[29] Hick explains, "Cruelty is not merely an extreme absence of kindness, but is something with a demonic power of its own. Hatred is not merely lack of love, or malevolence merely in minimum degree of goodwill."[30] Moral evils, it would seem, go beyond "merely privations of their corresponding moral goods."[31]

Given Hick's critique of Augustine's view of evil, how might the privationist respond? In their essay, "Evil is Privation," Bill Anglin and Stewart Goetz argue that privationists are at least minimally committed to the belief that "evil is evil just insofar as there is a privation of something which

---

28. Ibid., 55–56.
29. Ibid., 57.
30. Ibid.
31. Ibid.

ought to be there."[32] This seems right, to me at least, but it does nothing by the way of answering Hick's objection that something like hatred seems to go beyond a *mere lack* of love. If a theist is going to maintain the privation view, it must, at least, be able to accommodate Hick's objection regarding the positive nature of evil in the world. Perhaps, reflection on the goodness of God and the goodness of creation will provide some insights here.

Most theists recognize that God is essentially good. This is especially the case for Christian theists. Christians hold to a further claim that all that God made is good. At the climax of the creation account in Genesis 1, we read that God pronounced all he had made was "very good."[33] Therefore, in working out a view of evil, Christians will want to preserve both God's goodness and the goodness of what God had made, something that the privation view does well. As noted earlier, God is essentially good; creation, on the other hand, is good in a derivative sense, in that it is contingently so. By saying that creation is "derivatively" and "contingently" good, I do not mean that God could have created something evil, but only that God, who is the creator of all things, is the only being who is good necessarily. Any other thing that exists is dependent on God for its existence, thus **contingent**. Those things that are derivatively good are so because they find their source in God, who is necessarily good.

But what is it that Christians mean by "good"? Thomas Morris suggests a twofold claim for understanding God's goodness. First, a theist might think of God as being *wholly good*. By this, the Christian theist means that God has no defects or blemishes. Furthermore, this understanding of God's goodness means that "God never does anything which is ultimately wrong or evil" and that "His character contains no flaw, and he is subject to no moral weakness."[34] Secondly, as previously noted, *God is necessarily good*.[35] To speak of God as necessarily good means that "God is so firmly entrenched in goodness, or alternately, that goodness is so entrenched in God, that it is strictly impossible for there to be in him any sort of flaw or

---

32. Bill Anglin and Steward Goetz, "Evil Is Privation," *International Journal for Philosophy of Religion* 13, no. 1 (1982): 4.

33. Genesis 1:31.

34. Thomas V. Morris, *Our Idea of God: An Introduction to Philosophical Theology* (Vancouver: Regent College Publishing, 1991), 48.

35. Ibid.

defect," that is to say, "he is utterly invulnerable to evil."[36] It follows that if God is essentially good, then those actions which God performs must also be good.[37]

But how are we to understand the goodness of creation? Biblical scholars and theologians often debate on whether interpreters should understand Scripture, on certain issues, as using "being" language or "functional" language. In his book, *The Lost World of Genesis One*, Hebrew and ancient Near Eastern scholar John Walton builds a case that the Genesis 1 narrative is one of "functional" **ontology** and not "material" ontology. When pondering existence, we can think of something as existing in more than one way, says Walton. For example, as I look at my coffee cup, I think of its material composition. I consider the various types of material used to compose my cup, the various elements within the paint, the smoothness of the edges, and so on. However, I can also look at my coffee cup and think in a different way on why it exists as it does. What is its purpose? Why is it shaped as it is? The former understanding of my coffee cup has to do with questions concerning *material ontology*; whereas the latter has to do with questions concerning its *functional ontology*. Walton argues that people from the ancient Near Eastern world were far less concerned about material existence than they were about functional existence. Much of the problem for modern interpreters has to do with how we moderns view ontology. Walton explains:

> When we speak of cosmic ontology these days, it can be seen that our culture views existence, and therefore meaning, in material terms. Our material view of ontology in turn determines how we think about creation, and it is easy to see how. If ontology defines the terms of existence, and creation means to bring something into existence, then one's ontology sets the parameters by which one thinks about creation. Creation of a chair would be a very different process than the creation of a company. Since in our culture we believe that existence is material, we consequently believe that to create something means to bring its material properties into

---

36. Ibid.
37. Reichenbach, *Evil and a Good God*, 133.

existence. Thus our discussions of origins tend to focus on material origins.[38]

However, "people in the ancient world," argues Walton, "believed that something existed not by virtue of its material properties, *but by virtue of its having a function in an ordered system.*"[39] By "ordered system," we are not speaking in scientific terms; rather, it has to do with "an ordered system in human terms, that is, in relation to society and culture."[40] Walton continues,

> In this sort of functional ontology, the sun does not exist in virtue of its material properties, or even in its function as a burning ball of gas. Rather it exists by virtue of the role that it has in *its* sphere of existence, particularly in the way that it functions for humankind and human society. ... In a functional ontology, to bring something into existence would require giving it a function or a role in an ordered system, rather than giving it material properties. Consequently, something could be manufactured physically but still not "exist" if it has not become functional.[41]

Walton's view of Genesis 1 is controversial since many theologians today still take Genesis 1 as having to do with material origins. My purpose is not to solve the debate between "functional" and "material" ontology in the ancient world; rather, it is to bring Walton's insight on ontology into our discussion on the nature of the goodness of creation.

When we think of the goodness of God's creation, perhaps much of what the biblical writers had in mind had to do with, not *merely* the substance of the thing made, which privationist theories have often placed emphasis on, but also the function given to the thing made. This insight, it seems, is one that those who promote the privation theory of evil often fail to emphasize. Evil doesn't have to do with the corruption of the thing *only* but also *a disruption to the order and function that God assigned to certain things within creation.*

---

38. John H. Walton, *The Lost World of Genesis One: Ancient Cosmology and the Origins Debate* (Downers Grove, IL: InterVarsity Press, 2009), 22–23.

39. Ibid., 24 (emphasis original).

40. Ibid.

41. Ibid.

So as not to equivocate on terms, confusing Walton's emphasis on function within an ordered system with how I'm going to use the notion in this book, it may be helpful to think of God establishing more than one order—or, perhaps better, distinctions within that one order—the *natural* order of creation and the *moral* order of creation. By *natural* order, I mean the order in which God established the world or universe to function in a certain way. Here, one might include such things as the laws of nature (or, more accurately, law-like regulating principles) and the normal goings-on of nature. If, indeed, God created the universe to operate in such a way, then, perhaps, when the text describes all that God had made as good, it may include such things. Now, surely, the biblical writers did not have a scientific worldview when they wrote about the goodness of creation, nor did they posit such things as law-like regulating principles behind the goings-on in the world (at least not as far as we know); nevertheless, they did understand that reality functioned in an orderly way, and this was the result of God's bringing it about to do so. The emphasis on goodness, then, is not so much on *how* God brought about order within creation (whatever that may include), but, rather, *that there is order to the way things are to function in the world that God has made.* That stones fall to the ground when dropped or waves crash into the shore of a beach are examples of the *goodness* of creation because these are part of the fabric of the natural created order as God intended.

Much of the same could be said with respect to the *moral* ordering of things. The moral order of creation has to do with God's establishing that some of his creatures with a capacity to perform certain morally significant actions are to function in a certain way within the larger framework of the natural order. There is a moral fabric that runs through the whole of God's intentions for these creaturely moral agents to operate within such a world. Goodness, then, refers to *the order in which moral agents are intended to function within the world that God has made.* When humans and, perhaps, angels too, comply with how God intended them to function as moral agents, then such is good, since these kinds of things line up with the fabric of the moral order God intended for creation.

Whether Genesis 1 establishes material origins is debatable, but Genesis 1 is not the only passage within Scripture emphasizing that the spatiotemporal universe came into existence *ex nihilo*.[42] Traditionally, Christians have held to the belief that God brought all things into existence out of nothing, using no pre-existing materials to make and form the universe, as Platonists thought and as process theologians today believe.[43] If God created all things, then that which God brought into existence is good. Otherwise, if God created something that was essentially evil, then God is to be held responsible for the origin of that evil. Further, if, as I have been arguing, goodness in creation refers to, not only the thing created, but also to the ordering of how things are to function, including how moral agents are to function within the larger universe, then an evil is not merely the privation of the good of some "thing" but can also be ascribed to the *absence of some good as it relates to God's intentions for the created order*, particularly the *moral* order.

Privation, then, would seem to be an important aspect of something being evil or having badness. On this point, Brian Davies hits the nail on its head.

> To say that something is bad or in a bad way assumes that we have a sense of what it would be like for it not to be so (just as to say that someone is ill assumes that we have a sense of what it would be like for someone to be well). If "good" is a logically attributive adjective …, it sets a standard for things as we describe them as being bad since its use depends on our understanding of a noun. We do not understand what is being said when told that something is a bad X unless we have a sense of what it would be to be a good X. If rotten apples were the norm, we would not understand what a bad apple is. So we are indeed complaining when calling something bad. … And

---

42. John 1:3; 1 Corinthians 8:6; Colossians 1:16–18; Hebrews 1:2–3, 10–12. Theologians have based the doctrine of creation *ex nihilo* on arguments from God's eternality. For an excellent defense of creation *ex nihilo*, see William Lane Craig and Paul Copan, *Creation Out of Nothing: A Biblical, Philosophical, and Scientific Exploration* (Grand Rapids: Baker Academic, 2005).

43. David Ray Griffin, *God, Power, and Evil: A Process Theodicy* (Louisville, KY: Westminster John Knox, 2004), 285–91.

in doing so we are, I think, always noting that something is not as good as it could or should be.[44]

The key in understanding the privationist view of evil is not so much in understanding that the privation of the good in view is the good's opposite, but, rather *that something is not how it should be*. It is out of sorts, so to speak.[45] So when Hick speaks of, say, hatred as not being merely a lack of love, he's right, since a lack of love might also include something like indifference or greediness. That is not to say, however, that when a person exhibits hatred toward another that nothing is lacking. As Davies rightly notes, we understand that something is a bad X because we have a sense of what some good X looks like. When a person exhibits hatred toward another person, it may be the case that love is lacking, but there might also be other qualities missing, such as a lack of kindness or a desire to bring about unity. But beyond these, hatred toward others breaks into a failure to maintain God's intentions in keeping with the moral order of creation. We know what it looks like for things like harmony and peace to be exhibited within creation. Hatred is in contrast to and brings about a lack in such an order.

Whether I have answered Hick's objection is left to the reader. Nevertheless, both Hick and the privationist account of evil recognize that evil is a reality in the world. Before finishing this section, it would be helpful to consider one final point. Certain religions like Zoroastrianism, and even some Christians, believe that reality consists of two eternal opposing forces, such as God and Satan—a view known as **cosmic dualism**. The Christian view has classically rejected this way of thinking, since as noted above, God alone is the creator of all things and a **necessary being**. Satan, who is a created being and contingent, owes his existence to God, along with any power that he may have. Christians thus reject any notion that evil is eternal or personal and that it is an entity equal to God.

In summary, we can draw four conclusions about the nature of evil from the Christian perspective: 1) evil is a part of reality and not just an

---

44. Brian Davies, "Reply to Mark Robson on Evil as Privation," *New Blackfriars* 94, no. 1053 (September 2013), 567.

45. Perhaps we too readily bifurcate between ontology and morality when it comes to a thing's goodness.

illusion; 2) evil is not a creation of God, nor is it a substance, person, or force; 3) evil cannot exist apart from the good (though it is true that good can exist apart from evil); and 4) evil is the absence, privation, or lack of some good, whether in a thing or in God's intentions for the moral created order.

PAIN AND SUFFERING

In the literature on the problem of evil, too often the words "pain" and "suffering" are used interchangeably. There are, as we shall see, important reasons for not equating the two. First off, Eleonore Stump rightly suggests that the problem from evil has more to do with suffering, and not so much natural evil, since, had there not been any sentient beings who are affected by things such as hurricanes or tsunamis, there would be no cause to raise question about the evils that occur in nature. Even with respect to moral evils, that which we are most concerned with is the suffering that results from the moral actions of human creatures.[46] So what is the difference between pain and suffering?

Pain can be construed in one of two ways: *physical pain* and *mental pain*. *Physical pain*, as I take it, has to do with our physical equipment and it can occur on a variety of levels or degrees. For example, pricking my finger does not amount to the same sensation of discomfort as breaking my leg. Both experiences result in pain, but not of the same sort or degree.

Mental pain, on the other hand, has to do with those pains that are more emotionally or psychologically oriented. A person can experience mental pain without having any physical sensation whatsoever. Modern day lepers are examples of people who experience mental anguish brought on because of their physical deformities, rejection by the people around them, or their inabilities to accomplish certain daily tasks, yet, they feel no bodily pain. Surgeon and leprosy specialist Paul Brand recounts in his book *The Gift of Pain* a story of a young girl named Tanya, whose rare genetic defect, commonly known as "congenital indifference to pain," resulted in her eventually having both legs amputated, the loss of most of her fingers, a lacerated tongue due to an obsessive habit of chewing on it, constant

---

46. Eleonore Stump, *Wandering in Darkness: Narrative and the Problem of Suffering* (Oxford: Oxford University Press, 2010), 4.

dislocated elbows, and chronic sepsis caused by ulcers on her limbs and appendages. Brand tells a story of Tanya's mother finding her as a young child doodling on a piece of paper with what seemed to be red liquid. But to her shock and horror, Tanya had bitten off the tip of her finger and was making designs out of her own blood, while all the time going on as if nothing had ever happened to her.[47] Tanya, and others similarly afflicted, cannot feel pain physically. Their nerve receptors do not function properly. When they do damage to their bodies, they are often not aware of it, resulting in certain deformities because of infection and gangrene, which requires the removal of the person's limbs or appendages. Yet, their inability to have the physical sensation of pain, nevertheless, causes much mental anguish. In his years of working with lepers, and others with nerve related complications, Brand has concluded that life without physical pain can bring about just as much suffering as a life with it. On this point Brand says, "If I held in my hands the power to eliminate physical pain from the world, I would not exercise it. My work with pain-deprived patients has proved to me that pain protects us from destroying ourselves."[48] This is not to trivialize the horrible effects of physical pain. Physical pain, if unchecked, "saps physical strength and mental energy, and can come to dominate a person's entire life." [49] Yet, for most people, says Brand, we live our lives somewhere between the two extremes of painlessness and chronic illness.[50]

Despite its often-debilitating effects, pain has a significantly important role in the way that we live our lives daily, without which we would not function properly in the world. Take, for example, something as seemingly trivial as shifting one's weight while standing. Those whose pain receptors are working optimally shift their weight often while standing or they change up their patterns when walking. Such shifting and changing are brought on by minor physical discomforts that the person experiences. Failure to make shifts while standing or to change one's pattern while walking can result in serious bodily complications, which is what happens to lepers when they do not consciously change their walking patterns or shift

---

47. Paul Brand and Philip Yancey, *The Gift of Pain: Why We Hurt and What We Can Do about It* (Grand Rapids: Zondervan, 1997), 4–5.

48. Ibid., 219.

49. Ibid.

50. Ibid.

their weight when standing. There are, however, other reasons to think pain is only prima facie bad. As Eleonore Stump argues:

> Furthermore, even pain is bad *only* prima facie, other things being equal; and other things are not always equal. To see this, consider that, for a variety of reasons, human beings voluntarily submit themselves to pain they could otherwise avoid—that is, pain that is not necessary for life or health. Perhaps the most obvious case in our culture has to do with athletics, where the best athletes put themselves through agonies in the interests of athletic excellence. We might suppose that in cases of this sort pain is only a necessary accompaniment to something that we would be glad enough to have without the pain if we could. But even if, contrary to appearances, this is true as regards athletics, not all cases in which people voluntarily accept pain they could forgo can be similarly explained away. Many women refuse anesthetics in childbirth, for example, although the baby would be born without the mother's pain just as well as with it.[51]

Yet, when people willing submit themselves to certain pains, we often do not consider such as an evil, as Stump continues,

> We are not inclined to raise the problem of evil in connection with the voluntarily accepted pains of childbirth, not only because the sufferer has in some sense chosen the pain, but also because it seems that, at least in the view of the women who have chosen to forgo anesthetics, the experience of so-called natural childbirth (that is, childbirth with its attendant pain) is, somehow, a great good.[52]

While the experience of childbirth can be extremely painful, it does not seem that such pains, when voluntarily chosen apart from anesthetics, are the kinds of pains that would raise the problem from evil, nor does it seem that it warrants justification or explanation.

It may be the case that both physical and mental pain might lead to suffering, but not all suffering is a result of pain. At the heart of suffering,

---

51. Eleonore Stump, *Wandering in Darkness*, 5–6.
52. Ibid., 6.

Stump argues, is the notion of what a person most cares about. There is both an objective and subjective side to it; but not only that, the nature of suffering itself is two-sided.[53] Regarding the objective side, "Every human person," says Stump, "has some care about what kind of person she is and about her flourishing as that kind of person. For that reason, part of what it is for her to suffer is for her to be kept, to one degree or another, from flourishing."[54] The subjective element, however, has to do with the desires of a person's heart. On this Stump says, "Although a thing that is a heart's desire for some person may (or may not) have considerable intrinsic value, the very great value it has for that person is a function of her commitment to it."[55] The value of a person's heart's desire is derivative from one's care and love for it. Suffering results when we lose or when we are denied those things that are most desirable to our hearts. Essentially, what is bad about suffering, according to Stump, can be formulated in the following way: "What is bad about the evil a human being suffers is that it undermines (partly or entirely) her flourishing, or it deprives her (in part or in whole) of the desires of her heart, or both."[56]

Stump thinks that making a connection between what a person most cares about and suffering helps to explain, for example, why a person who voluntarily goes through certain instances of pain, such as in the case of a woman going through childbirth apart from anesthetic or an epidural (though she has it available to her), does not seem to be an instance that would raise questions pertaining to the problem from evil. As Stump explains, ordinarily pains associated with childbirth do not undermine a mother's flourishing; moreover, if a mother so chooses voluntarily to give birth apart from medication or some other pain-reducing means, enduring such pain does not take away from her that which she cares most about. What makes suffering bad, then, "is that it undermines or destroys what the sufferer centrally cares about, her own flourishing or the desires of her heart or both."[57] However, it may not always be obvious to the sufferer that she is indeed suffering or that she even knows what her heart's desire is.

---

53. Ibid., 10.
54. Ibid.
55. Ibid.
56. Ibid., 11.
57. Ibid.

On the other side of it, she may not be aware that she is indeed flourishing or that she has obtained her heart's desire. Stump has us imagine a person who thinks that she is perfectly healthy, only to come down
with an illness and suddenly die. Yet, there may be a person who has had
cancer. This person may have gone through treatment, while the whole
time thinking that she still has the cancer, only to find out some time later
that she is now cancer-free. The period between treatment and finding
out she is cancer-free she thinks that she still has the cancer, when in fact
she is healthy. Such does not mean that a person *never* knows when she is
flourishing or when she has the desires of her heart; rather, all it implies
is that a person's views on her own flourishing or when she has the desires
of her heart are not infallible. Stump's conclusion regarding suffering is
that it is more like ill health than it is like pain.[58] On this last point she says,

> Unlike pain, the state of our bodily health is not a matter that is
> invariably known to us by introspection or to those around us by
> ordinary observation. In the same way, neither introspection nor
> observation is invariably sufficient to recognize suffering. Suffering
> can have an opacity that pain typically does not.[59]

Suffering, as I'll use it in this book, is concerned with that which occurs
in human creatures; it is that which depletes the soul, keeping a person
from flourishing or from having the desires of his heart. The suffering of a
person may be connected to pain, either physical or mental; however, that
need not be the case. If suffering has to do with a lack of flourishing or the
obtaining of the desires of one's heart, there are certain types of suffering,
then, that are not tied to pain.

PROBLEMS FROM EVIL, THEODICIES, AND DEFENSES

When contemplating the problem of evil, one must keep in mind that
there is more than one problem. We can distinguish between the exis-
tential/religious and the intellectual forms of the problem of evil. The
existential/religious (or pastoral) form of the problem is less concerned

---

58. Ibid., 11–12.
59. Ibid., 12–13.

with philosophical and theological inquiry and is more sharply focused on individual or personal suffering.[60] The intellectual problem of evil, on the other hand, comes in several forms, of which the most prominent are the logical and the evidential variety.

The logical problem of evil sets out to show that there is a logical contradiction between the following propositions: God is omnipotent; God is wholly good; and evil exists.[61] Most atheist philosophers today believe that theists have adequately shown no logical contradiction exists between the three propositions, and thus do not defend the logical problem.[62] Instead, they resort to its weaker cousin, the evidential problem from evil. Central to the evidential argument is the notion that, given the amount and intensity of certain kinds of evil in the world, it doesn't *seem* that there's any point to such suffering.[63]

In his 1979 article "The Problem of Evil and Some Varieties of Atheism," William Rowe set out to offer an argument for atheism that would rationally justify a person in believing that atheism is true based on the problem of evil.[64] According to Rowe, when we look in the world, we see occurring daily great amounts of intense human and animal suffering. Such instances of intense suffering would be justified if it leads to some greater good, that is, a good that could not have been attained otherwise. Rowe's argument is as follows:

1. There exist instances of intense suffering which an omnipotent omniscient being could have prevented without thereby losing some greater good or permitting some evil equally bad or worse.

---

60. For an extended discussion on this subject, see Feinberg, *Many Faces of Evil*, chapter 14.

61. J. L. Mackie, "Evil and Omnipotence," in *The Problem of Evil*, ed. Marilyn McCord Adams and Robert Merrihew Adams (Oxford: Oxford University Press, 1990), 25; Plantinga, *God Freedom, and Evil*, 1977), 13.

62. This is largely due to the work of Plantinga's work in *God, Freedom, and Evil*. For an example of an atheist who thinks Plantinga has successfully defended the logical problem, see David O'Connor, *God, Evil, and Design: An Introduction to the Philosophical Issues* (Malden, MA: Blackwell, 2008), 35–71.

63. William L. Rowe, "The Problem of Evil and Some Varieties of Atheism," in *The Evidential Argument from Evil*, ed. Daniel Howard-Snyder (Bloomington, IN: Indiana University Press, 1996), 5.

64. Ibid., 1.

2. An omniscient, wholly good being would prevent the occurrence of any intense suffering it could, unless it could not do so without thereby losing some greater good or permitting some evil equally bad or worse.

3. There does not exist an omnipotent, omniscient, wholly good being.[65]

No doubt the argument is valid. The question is whether it is sound; that is, are the premises of Rowe's argument true? As far as (2) is concerned, Rowe believes that atheists and theists alike would agree to this premise based on shared moral beliefs.[66]

In order to clarify what he means by an instance of intense suffering, Rowe gives the example of a fawn caught in a forest fire, suffers several days due to burns, and then dies (E1).[67] Another example Rowe provides elsewhere is of a little girl who was raped, beaten, and strangled, resulting in her death (E2).[68] "So far as we can see," says Rowe, such instances of intense suffering, as demonstrated by E1 (and E2), are "pointless."[69] He continues:

For there does not appear to be any greater good such as the prevention of the fawn's suffering would require either the loss of that good or the occurrence of an evil equally bad or worse. Nor does there seem to be any equally bad or worse evil so connected to the fawn's suffering that it would have had to occur had the fawn's suffering been prevented. Could an omnipotent, omniscient being have prevented the fawn's apparently pointless suffering? The answer is obvious, as even the theists will insist.[70]

65. Ibid., 2.
66. Ibid., 4.
67. Ibid., 2.
68. William L. Rowe, "The Evidential Argument from Evil: A Second Look," in *The Evidential Argument from Evil*, ed. Daniel Howard-Snyder (Bloomington, IN: Indiana University Press, 1996), 262.
69. Rowe, "The Problem of Evil," 4.
70. Ibid.

Rowe admits that the case of the fawn doesn't lead one to confirm or prove the truth of (1). Cases such as E1 and E2 provide rational grounds for accepting (1). Given one's experience and knowledge, one is in a position to make such judgments, and one is rational to accept such statements as true. Suppose someone were to show that some greater good is intimately connected to, say, E1, or that the prevention of E1 would have led to a worse evil, and that if one were to believe that one is rationally justified in holding both of these things concerning E1, what of all the instances of intense suffering in the world? Rowe states,

> It seems quite unlikely that *all* the instances of intense suffering occurring daily in our world are intimately related to the occurrence of a greater good or the prevention of evils at least as bad: and even more unlikely, should they somehow all be so related, that an omnipotent, omniscient being could not have achieved at least some of those goods (or prevented some of those evils) without permitting the instances of contents suffering that are supposedly related to them.[71]

Rowe's argument has force, and many abled philosophers have taken up the task of defending theism against his argument for atheism from evil. As important as Rowe's argument is (and other evidential versions like it), I do not take it up directly in this book, though I do address it in an indirect manner in two ways.

First, the problem of evil in the world is often couched as a religious or theological issue. Doubtless such is the case, but the problem of evil is also a metaphysical problem. According to Peter van Inwagen and Dean Zimmerman, the task of **metaphysics**, as a philosophical discipline, is to "get behind all appearances and describe things as they really are."[72] What we want to know is whether evil is a real feature of our world. Why is it here (if this can be explained)? Why is it the way that it is? Why is there so much evil in the world? What best explains the phenomena of evil? Granted, for theological systems this becomes complicated in a different way. We

---

71. Ibid., 5.

72. Peter van Inwagen and Dean W. Zimmerman, "Introduction: What is Metaphysics?," in *Metaphysics: The Big Questions*, ed. Peter van Inwagen and Dean W. Zimmerman (Malden, MA: Blackwell, 2004), 2.

want to know, given God, why evil? What is God doing about evil, if indeed God *is doing* or *can do* anything about evil? Yet, evil in the world is also a moral problem. Given a person's worldview, how should one respond to evil? Is there a moral obligation to respond to evil? Since theists are not the only ones who raise questions about the phenomenon of evil in the world and moral responsibility in the face of evil, it would seem reasonable to presume that all worldviews or metaphysical systems must contend with evil in the world (if there is indeed evil *in the world*).

A second reason that I do not take up Rowe's argument is that I believe he's mistaken on (2). I agree with Rowe that there seems to be instances of intense suffering that the world would be better off without, but it's not at all clear that God must always stop such instances of intense suffering in order to prevent some worse evil or to keep from losing some greater good. Many theists accept Rowe's (2) and adopt the view that God always brings about some greater good out of such instances of intense suffering. There are at least four reasons theists, and Christian theists in particular, should reconsider Rowe's premise and the greater-good principle in general. Such a view (1) demands an overly meticulous view of divine sovereignty, (2) leads to a concept of God that is consequentialist in nature regarding his interactions with his creatures, (3) makes evil necessary for God to bring about some greater good and to accomplish his purposes, and (4) takes away from human moral responsibility. To deny the greater good thesis doesn't mean, however, that God has no reasons for permitting the evils in the world that we see, nor does it mean that God is inactive in stopping evil, as I aim to show in later chapters. I cannot develop these four arguments here but will take them up in various ways throughout the book (especially chapter 5). What I'm mostly concerned with in this book is the broader theological and philosophical problem from evil and how it affects other worldviews.

Before ending out this section, let me say something about theodicy and defenses. A theodicy, says John Hick, is "a defence of the goodness of God in the face of the evil in His world."[73] Hick's definition is as good as any. Some philosophers make a distinction between defenses and theodicies,

---

73. Hick, *Evil and the God of Love*, 243.

claiming that a theodicy seeks to do too much.[74] Defenses, they claim, are more modest in nature, in that they do not claim to know God's reason(s) for allowing evil. All that's required is something like a story, which, for all we know, might be true, and which seems to be a real possibility as to why God allows evil in the world.[75] William Hasker, on the other hand, thinks this is misguided and suggests making a more nuanced distinction between a theodicy and defense, highlighting the strengths of each. A theodicy, claims Hasker, gives possible reasons for why God permits certain evils; whereas a defense is "any counterargument that attempts to defeat or neutralize an argument from evil *without* claiming to give God's reasons for allowing the evil in question."[76] This distinction seems right, and I believe it's perfectly acceptable for a theist to offer a theodicy as here defined by Hasker; however, that is not the aim of this book. My goal is less ambitious. The purpose of this book is to offer a general defense of Christian theism, suggesting that it provides a more robust response to the phenomena of evil in the world than its metaphysical rivals.

APPROACH AND METHOD

So how might one go about such a task of defending Christian theism in the face of evil? C. Stephen Layman offers four strategies for responding to the problem of evil: 1) offer a theodicy; 2) show that the arguments from evil against theism are flawed; 3) argue that, though evil counts against theism, natural theology and religious experience warrant theism and thus override the evidence of evil against theism; and 4) argue that though theism does not answer all of the evils that take place in the world, it provides an explanation that is as good or better than its metaphysical competitors. Layman calls this last approach "The Comparative Response."[77] In this book I focus on (4) as an argumentative strategy.

---

74. Plantinga, *God, Freedom, and Evil*, 28; Peter van Inwagen, *The Problem of Evil* (Oxford: Oxford University Press, 2008), 7.

75. For fuller discussion see van Inwagen, *The Problem of Evil*, 65–67.

76. William Hasker, *The Triumph of God over Evil: Theodicy for a World of Suffering* (Downers Grove, IL: InterVarsity Press, 2008), 20.

77. C. Stephen Layman, "Natural Evil: The Comparative Response," *International Journal for Philosophy of Religion* 54 (2003): 1. See also Jeremy Evans, *The Problem of Evil: The Challenge to Essential Christian Beliefs* (Nashville, TN: B&H Academic, 2013), 113–31.

As I understand it, the comparative response need not argue that theism explains all evils well; rather, all that is required is that theism on the whole explains evil as well as (or better than) its metaphysical rivals. But what would that accomplish? It would show that (1) evil is just as much a problem for theism's metaphysical rivals and (2) if theism explains evil better than its metaphysical rivals, then the phenomena of evil in the world does not give us any reason to accept theism's metaphysical rivals over theism.[78]

The comparative approach, as I shall employ in this book, is something akin to, or perhaps, a form of "inference to the best explanation" (IBE)—a type of abductive reasoning often used in law courts, forensics, AI, history, and archeology.[79] IBE seeks to choose the best hypothesis from a pool of possible alternatives to describe some phenomenon in question. The argument pattern can be described in the following way:

We begin with a set of data points—states of affairs or established facts, the aforementioned phenomena in question—and construct a pool of possible explanation candidates. On the basis of a principled set of criteria we winnow the list down to the best explanation among the possibilities, and then hopefully achieve sufficient warrant to infer to it as the likely true explanation. The inference does not settle the matter, but produces new opportunities to subject the explanation to critical scrutiny to assess its effectiveness at providing further explanation of additional observations. Three important components of such an inference pattern, then, are (1) the set of salient facts requiring explanation, (2) the list of explanation

---

78. C. Stephen Layman, "Moral Evil: The Comparative Response," *International Journal for Philosophy of Religion* 53 (2003): 1–2.

79. Abductive reasoning differs from both deductive and inductive reasoning. Abduction does not guarantee that the conclusion follows logically and formally from the premises if they are true, like deductive arguments do; rather, it is more like induction in that the conclusion is warranted, though not guaranteed. However, unlike induction, which emphasizes a movement from the particulars of some set to a generalization (as understood by Aristotle) or statistical probability (as understood in a modern sense), abduction is concerned more with plausibility. For a good discussion on the differences between the three types of reasoning, particularly the views of Charles Saunders Peirce on comparing the three, see Douglas Walton, *Abductive Reasoning* (Tuscaloosa, AL: University of Alabama Press, 2013), 2–17, 31–36.

candidates, and (3) the criteria by which we reduce the candidates down to the one that is the best.[80]

In our case, the salient facts include not only the types and kinds of evil in the world (moral and natural), but also the quantity and intensity of such evils, or, at least, how such evils appear to us, something of the phenomenology of encountering putative instances of evil. The candidates for explanation, as noted, include naturalism, pantheism, process panentheism, and theism. Others could have been chosen, but for economy's sake, these four hypotheses (metaphysical systems or worldviews) have the most potential as live possibilities for explaining evil in the world. Each was chosen based on (1) how the metaphysical theory provides a unique perspective on God and the God-world relation and/or ultimate reality and (2) the broadness of each metaphysical system, especially in how each can accommodate a variety of other perspectives that fall under those broader categories. Lastly, there are criteria by which one can judge between alternative hypotheses. Let us consider such criteria, especially in relation to evaluating metaphysical systems as hypotheses or theories.

A metaphysical theory is a type of theory such that it sets out to provide an explanation or response to a metaphysical question. Though not identical, metaphysical theories function much like scientific theories, seeking to unify our experiences and make them understandable.[81] Philosopher William Hasker provides three important criteria for evaluating metaphysical theories: factual adequacy, logical consistency, and explanatory power.[82]

Concerning factual adequacy, like any given scientific theory, metaphysical theories, too, are falsifiable, that is to say, such theories can be shown to be false. Moreover, just as scientific theories are built on the data that one knows to be true, so too are metaphysical theories. The problem, then, is this: when evaluating metaphysical theories, what are the facts that everyone agrees upon? For a first approximation, consider Hasker's idea in

80. David Baggett and Ronnie Campbell, "Omnibenevolence, Moral Apologetics, and Doubly Ramified Natural Theology," *Philosophia Christi* 15, no. 2 (2013): 338–39.

81. We might also compare the task of evaluating metaphysical theories to the task of the historian or the exegete. See Basil Mitchell, *The Justification of Religious Belief* (New York: Oxford University Press, 1981), 45–53; William Hasker, *Metaphysics: Constructing a World View* (Downers Grove, IL: InterVarsity Press, 1984), 25–26.

82. Hasker, *Metaphysics*, 26.

this regard. Hasker suggests that the facts used to construct a metaphysical theory "must be consistent with what you know by other means to be true, and a theory which is inconsistent with what everybody knows (if there is anything which is known to everyone!) cannot be acceptable to anyone."[83]

Hasker's second criterion, logical consistency, suggests that a theory cannot propose two logically inconsistent statements. While some inconsistencies are easy to spot, others are not always easy to identify. An example of logical inconsistency may be that God is both timeless and, yet, knows what is occurring *now* in the world, or that a loving God *seemingly* does nothing to stop evil from occurring in the world. To some, these may seem only prima facie inconsistent.[84]

Explanatory power, the last of Hasker's criteria, is important for any metaphysical theory in that it brings unity to the data. While all the data may be correct and in proper order, such is meaningless without some kind of explanation. Thus, when comparing metaphysical theories, it is not enough to have the data and logical consistency. Explanatory power is what helps the metaphysician to evaluate the various theories.[85]

Additional criteria for evaluating metaphysical systems—not mentioned by Hasker but which are nonetheless important—include the following: explanatory scope; ad hoc-ness present; plausibility; and livability. Explanatory scope refers to how broad a theory extends in explaining the data. When philosophers use ad hoc-ness as a criterion, they mean that the less artificial or contrived some theory is, the better.[86] Concerning plausibility, we want to know (1) how plausible of an explanation is the theory in itself? and (2) how plausible of an explanation the hypothesis is relative to the other hypotheses?[87] Lastly, what good is a theory if, after having shown that it explains the data well or that it is logically consistent, it proves not to be a hypothesis that one can live consistently with from

---

83. Ibid.

84. Ibid., 27. For an extended discussion on the debate over different notions of logical consistency, coherence, and the divine attributes, see Ronald H. Nash, *The Concept of God* (Grand Rapids: Zondervan, 1983), 12–14.

85. Hasker, *Metaphysics*, 27–28.

86. Baggett and Campbell, "Omnibenevolence," 113.

87. Walton, *Abductive Reasoning*, 241.

day-to-day? We want to know that a theory is livable and can be tested by our everyday experiences.

Not everyone will be on the same page about what criteria should be used. There will be disagreements over starting points or on what criteria should be included or excluded, but I agree with Stephen Layman that "one unavoidably makes controversial assumptions about a series of issues, e.g., the nature of explanations, how best to formulate theism and its rivals, the nature of good and evil, and so on."[88] Controversial premises shouldn't be a reason for rejecting the comparative response. Any well-argued philosophical position will come up against opposition, employing controversial premises not held by everyone.

The above criteria will examine four areas related to each major metaphysical system: life, consciousness, the metaphysics of good and evil, and human responsibility. Any metaphysical theory or worldview that's worthwhile must make sense of these four areas, especially as they relate to the problem of evil. Consider the following reasons. Regarding life, every worldview must explain: Why we are here? Why is there something rather than nothing? Moreover, why is there sentient life? Adherents of certain worldviews may not care all that much why there's something, but they nevertheless have an answer for why the universe exists as it does—even if their answer is that it's simply a brute fact. How and why life is as it is plays a significant role in how one answers the problem of evil. Atheists are going to answer this question far more differently than, say, a Hindu. As for consciousness, the problem of pain and suffering deeply affects those sentient beings, like ourselves, who are capable of thinking, knowing, and understanding the world, especially given our capacities for reflecting on our experiences of the world. It is conscious beings, after all, who experience pain and suffering. As living and thinking beings, who experience pain and suffering, there must be something in place that grounds goodness and badness. Moreover, how are we to make sense of ethics? To say that some experience or action is bad, there must be a standard in place by which we judge that experience or action. Each worldview must make sense of this if it is to take evil seriously. Finally, wrestling with the

---

88. Layman, "Natural Evil," 2.

concept of evil includes making sense of certain evils that are caused or produced by agents.

One final point concerning the comparative approach is in order. Christians have generally taken evil to be the privation of the good, as has been defended in this chapter, but not everyone accepts such an understating of evil. Therefore, when evaluating each metaphysical system, I'll use evil in a broad and general sense, consisting of the kinds of things we generally call evil.[89] What sorts of things count as "broad" or "general"? Michael Peterson suggests the following:

> The set of commonly recognized evils includes, at the very least, such things as extreme pain and suffering, physical deformities, psychological abnormalities, the prosperity of bad people, the demise of good people, disrupted social relations, unfulfilled potential, a host of character defects, and natural catastrophes.[90]

Such items on the list are commonly considered as evil, without having the negative effect of prejudicing the discussion. The list, suggests Peterson, indicates all the things to which the term "evil" applies (*extension*), without specifying all that the term implies (*intension*).[91]

MAPPING IT OUT

Having established parameters for thinking about some of the key concepts surrounding discussions on the problem from evil, the remaining chapters are as follows. Chapters 2 through 6 make a case for Christian theism. In these chapters I examine four broad metaphysical system (worldview) responses—*naturalistic, pantheistic, process panentheistic,* and *theistic*—to the phenomena of evil in the world. I consider how adherents of each metaphysical system explains evil according to their system's commitments to four areas: life, consciousness, the metaphysics of good and evil, and human responsibility.[92] Each area is evaluated by the criteria given above

---

89. Michael L. Peterson, *God and Evil: An Introduction to the Issues* (Boulder, CO: Westview Press, 1998), 10.

90. Ibid., 11.

91. Ibid.

92. Though I consider "the metaphysics of good and evil" and "human responsibility" to be separate categories, while evaluating each major metaphysical system, I take them together,

(factual adequacy, logical consistency, explanatory power, explanatory scope, ad hoc-ness present, plausibility, and livability). Having argued that theism best explains the phenomena of evil in the world and provides an overall thicker worldview response, I consider a significant weakness of minimalistic theism, namely that it cannot account for God's aseity and essentially loving nature without slipping into panentheism. For, if God is mono-personal and essentially loving, as some theists believe, then God would need something other to love, thereby making God dependent on something, namely creation, in order to exhibit the divine perfection of love. If God needs some "other," then God is not a necessary being, and therefore, not, following Anselm, "that-than-which-a-greater-cannot-be-thought."[93] Among the various live theistic options, Christian theism avoids this because God is a tri-unity of persons, thereby preserving both God's aseity and essentially loving nature. Having argued for Christian theism in the previous chapter, chapter 7 considers three live possibilities for the Christian theist: classical theism; neoclassical theism; and **open theism**. Having explained each, a version of neoclassical Christian theism will be defended. Finally, chapter 8 gives attention to Christianity's unique contribution to answering the problem of evil by exploring God's work to defeat evil, especially in the death and resurrection of the Son in conquering evil, while also taking into consideration the Holy Spirit's work in the life of the Church to combat evil in the world. The chapter ends with some reflection on Scripture's eschatological vision and God's final triumph over evil. Now that we've begun to unsnarl the knot, shall we turn to the comparative response?

---

since there is often an organic connection between the two.

93. Anselm, *Proslogium*, 3, in *Anselm of Canterbury: The Major Works*, ed. Brian Davies and G. R. Evans (Oxford: Oxford University Press, 1998), 88.

CHAPTER 2
NATURALISM—EVIL IN A WORLD WITHOUT GOD

In his ode to secularism, John Lennon invites his listeners to think of a world where there's no religion, no heaven, no countries, no killing, no possessions, and no hell. Instead of these things, we're spurred on to consider a world where people come together in brotherhood, sharing their possessions with one another, and living in universal peace.[1]

Many naturalists believe that something like Lennon's vision for the world is the kind of world we should hope and aim for. Take, for example, the words of the American naturalist philosopher, Daniel C. Dennett:

> I am inclined to think that *nothing could matter more* than what people love. At any rate, I can think of no value that I would place higher. I would not want to live in a world without love. Would a world with peace, but without love, be a better world? Not if the peace was achieved by drugging the love (and hate) out of us, or by suppression. Would a world with justice and freedom, but without love, be a better world? Not if it was achieved by somehow turning us all into loveless law-abiders with none of the yearnings or envies or hatreds that are the wellsprings of injustice and subjugation. It is hard to consider such hypotheticals, and I doubt if we should trust our first intuitions about them, but, for what it is worth, I surmise that we almost all want a world in which love, justice, freedom, and

---

1. John Lennon, "Imagine," from the album *Imagine*, Apple Records, 1971.

peace are all present, as much as possible, but if we had to give up one of these, it wouldn't—and shouldn't—be love.[2]

I am not here going to parse out what Dennett means by each of these virtues.[3] My only point is that he recognizes a world with such virtues as love, justice, freedom, and peace—especially love—is a world that's far superior than one without them.

In this chapter, what I want to wrestle with is whether such a utopian view of the world is achievable given *naturalism*. On the one hand, to have the kind of world pictured above, we must have an idea of what such virtues as love, justice, freedom, and peace look like, and there must be something that grounds them to our world. Yet, on the other hand, to call something "immoral," "wrong," or "evil" suggests that some sort of objective criteria or standard exists by which we judge these salient features of our world. Finally, to reach such a desired state, people must have the capacity for moral responsibility. Can we make sense of such things as good, evil, and human responsibility in a world where nature is all there is?

DEFINING NATURALISM

Among metaphysical alternatives in the West, perhaps naturalism is the greatest rival to theism. But what is naturalism? How should one understand the naturalistic conception of reality? To what extent does naturalism explain evil in the world? How does naturalism as an overarching worldview respond to evil in the world?

---

2. Daniel C. Dennett, *Breaking the Spell: Religion as a Natural Phenomenon* (New York: Viking, 2006), 253–54.

3. It seems that Dennett agrees with the apostle Paul that love is the greatest of virtues (see 1 Cor 13), but upon reading Dennett further, it becomes obvious that he and Paul have quite contrasting ideas on what they take love to mean. Dennett believes that love, in and of itself is not enough, and gives the following example to prove his point: "A world in which baseball fans' love of their teams lead them to hate the other teams and their fans that murderous war accompanied the playoffs would be a world in which a particular love, pure and blameless in itself, led to immoral and intolerable consequences" (Dennett, *Breaking the Spell*, 254). The Christian view of love, in contrast, doesn't allow for the kind of hate Dennett suggests. Take, for example, Paul's words in 1 Corinthians 13: "Love is patient, love is kind. It does not envy, it does not boast. It is not proud. It is not rude, it is not self-seeking, it is not easily angered, it keeps no record of wrongs. Love does not delight in evil, but rejoices with the truth. It always protects, always trusts, always hopes, always perseveres" (1 Cor 13:4–7, NIV; compare Rom 12:9–21).

Nailing down a definition of naturalism is not an easy task; this is in part due to how one thinks of the word "nature." As Stewart Goetz and Charles Taliaferro suggest, one might take in the older, broader sense of everything having a nature as being "natural." We may speak of humans, rabbits, rocks, angels, or God as all having a nature.[4] But that is not, of course, how most people in the West take the words "nature" and "natural" today, unless one is steeped in philosophy or has studied theology. Much of recent Western thinking has been shaped by the enterprise of scientific thinking, which has, in turn, shaped how we in the West have come to think of nature.

Science has become for many the primary tool by which we come to understand the world. Philosopher John Post outlines this train of thought well:

> According to a number of influential philosophers, the sciences cumulatively tell us, in effect, that everything can be accounted for in purely natural terms. The ability of the sciences to explain matters within their scope is already very great, and it is increasing all the time. The worldview this entails, according to many, is *naturalism*: Everything is a collection of entities of the sort the sciences are about, and all truth is determined ultimately by the truths about these basic scientific entities.[5]

All naturalists, to some extent, place a high emphasis on scientific inquiry; however, some naturalists, more so than others, take science to be not just one of many ways of understanding the world, but *the primary or only means by which we come to know things about our world*. Such an epistemology has come to be known as *scientism*.

Philosophers have rightly distinguished between **methodological naturalism** and **metaphysical naturalism**. Too often the two have been conflated, which is a mistake, since a conflation of the two leads to the false assumption that all naturalists are atheists. Methodological naturalism primarily concerns itself with a certain epistemology—a way of knowing the material world grounded in science; whereas metaphysical

---

4. Stewart Goetz and Charles Taliaferro, *Naturalism* (Grand Rapids: Eerdmans, 2008), 6.
5. John F. Post, *Metaphysics: A Contemporary Introduction* (New York: Paragon, 1991), 11.

naturalism, while accepting the epistemological view of methodological naturalism, goes beyond to accept certain metaphysical commitments and implications about the nature of reality. A methodological naturalist may hold to belief in God and yet be deeply committed to scientific exploration and inquiry, while rejecting scientific design arguments such as those put forth by adherents of Intelligent Design (ID). Further, a methodological naturalist may or may not be committed to materialism.[6] Nevertheless, scientific explanation, by its very nature, naturalists say, leaves out any appeals to the supernatural or religious; all explanations appeal to the purely physical.[7] While a worthy discussion in and of itself, our primary concern is not with methodological naturalism but metaphysical naturalism (henceforth abbreviated to naturalism), to which we shall now turn.

Metaphysical naturalists accept the conclusions of methodological naturalism but go beyond by concluding that physical reality is all that there is—a view known as "physicalist materialism," "physicalism," or "materialism."[8] Regarding materialism, naturalistic philosopher John Searle has this to say:

> There is a sense in which materialism is the religion of our time, at least among most of the professional experts in the fields of philosophy, psychology, cognitive science, and other disciplines that study the mind. Like more traditional religions, it is accepted without question and it provides the framework within which other questions can be posed, addressed, and answered.[9]

The universe, or nature (i.e., all physical reality), according to the naturalistic point of view, is a closed system of cause and effect. There is no ultimate cause for the universe, such as a god, gods, ground of being, or underlying force; rather, the universe as we know it is self-sufficient and

---

6. It should be noted that while methodological naturalists place a high view on science in their epistemology, not all are committed to scientism, nor are all materialists or moral relativists. For further discussion see Kathryn Applegate, "A Defense of Methodological Naturalism," *Perspectives on Science and Christian Faith* 65, no. 1 (2013): 37–45. For a critique of methodological naturalism, see Stephen C. Dilley, "Philosophical Naturalism and Methodological Naturalism: Strange Bedfellows?" *Philosophia Christi* 12, no. 1 (2010): 118–41.

7. Dilley, "Philosophical Naturalism and Methodological Naturalism," 119.

8. Post, *Metaphysics*, 11.

9. John Searle, *Mind: A Brief Introduction* (Oxford: Oxford University Press, 2004), 48.

arrived to where it is now through a series of blind, purposeless natural processes. Mental states, suggests Searle, if they do have real existence, "must in some sense be reducible to, they must be nothing but, physical states of some kind."[10] As Post suggests, such physicalist materialism reduces "all the properties of things to the properties of the basic physical entities."[11]

Following Layman, then, I take naturalism to mean *the view that there is a material reality that is essentially physical, that exists either necessarily, eternally, or by chance, that is self-organizing—that is to say, it is not organized by a deity or force of sorts—and that every ultimate explanation is inanimate.*[12] But to what extent can naturalism account for evil? How plausible is evil given naturalism?

NATURALISM AND LIFE

If naturalism is to succeed at explaining evil, then it seems that naturalism must, at least, be capable of explaining life.[13] The naturalistic understanding of life begins with the Big Bang, by which the entirety of the universe, including all space, time, and matter, exploded into existence some 13.8 billion years ago. Resulting from the Big Bang, galaxies, stars, and planets all formed. On one small planet—earth—life emerged from non-life out of a pre-biotic soup through evolutionary processes. As philosopher J. P. Moreland describes it,

> the process of evolution, understood in either neo-Darwinian or punctuated equilibrium terms, gave rise to all the life forms we see including human beings. Thus, all organisms and their parts exist and are what they are because they contributed to (or at least did not hinder) the struggle for reproductive advantage, more specifically, because they contributed to the tasks of feeding, fighting, fleeing, and reproducing.[14]

10. Ibid.

11. Post, *Metaphysics*, 11.

12. Layman, "Moral Evil," 7.

13. I am following closely certain aspects of Layman's format and method when considering all four views, though Layman only contrasts naturalism and theism.

14. J. P. Moreland, "The Ontological Status of Properties," in *Naturalism: A Critical Analysis*, ed. William Lane Craig and J. P. Moreland (New York: Routledge, 2000), 76.

Given naturalism's grand story, how surprising is life? As Stephen
Layman argues, there can be no life unless the universe has been "fine-
tuned" for life to exist.[15] Layman is referring to the **anthropic principle**,
which states that the universe has certain fundamental features that if they
were slightly different, there could be no life in the universe as we know
it.[16] But how likely should we expect the anthropic principle to be, given
naturalism? It does not seem likely. If the universe came into existence at
a finite point in time, as the Big Bang model of cosmology suggests, then
one might always ask why the laws of nature turned out as they did. Why
these laws? Why this universe?[17] Perhaps, one might reply by saying that
there was something in place prior to the Big Bang? But as John Barrow
and Frank Tipler suggest with respect to the Big Bang singularity, "At this
singularity, space and time came into existence; literally nothing existed
before the singularity, so, if the universe originated at such a singularity,

---

15. Layman, "Moral Evil," 14.

16. Astrophysicists often make a distinction between the Weak Anthropic Principle (WAP)
and the Strong Anthropic Principle (SAP). John Barrow and Frank J. Tipler define the two
as follows:

> Weak Anthropic Principle (WAP): the observed values of all physical and cosmo-
> logical quantities are not equally probable but they take on the values restricted by
> the requirement that there exists sites where carbon-based life can evolve and by
> the requirement that the Universe be old enough for it to have already done so. ...

> Strong Anthropic Principle (SAP): the Universe must have those properties which
> allow life to develop within it at some stage in its history. (Barrow and Tipler, The
> Anthropic Cosmological Principle [Oxford: Oxford University Press, 1986], 16, 21)

Of the two, SAP is the more controversial. Virtually no one denies that something like
WAP is true, though there are various definitions of it. For our concerns, we have something
more like WAP in mind. See also Patrick Glynn, God the Evidence: The Reconciliation of Faith
and Reason in a Postsecular World (Rocklin, CA: Forum, 1997), 26–31; Robin Collins, "A Scientific
Argument for the Existence of God," in Reason for the Hope Within, ed. Michael J. Murray
(Grand Rapids: Eerdmans, 1999), 47–75, especially 49.

17. Paul Davies asks a similar question,

> Whatever initial conditions gave rise to our universe, one can always ask: Why
> those? Given the infinite variety of ways in which the universe could have started
> out, why did it start out in the way it did? Is there something special, perhaps,
> about those particular initial conditions? It is tempting to suppose that the ini-
> tial conditions were not arbitrary, but conformed to some deep principle. After
> all, it is usually accepted that the laws of physics are not arbitrary, but can be
> encapsulated in neat mathematical relationships. Might not there exist a neat
> mathematical "law of initial conditions" too? (Davies, The Mind of God [New York:
> Touchstone, 1992], 89–90)

we would truly have a creation *ex nihilo*."[18] In other words, there was no mechanism in place prior to the Big Bang that would assure the laws to turn out just as they did in our universe. As a self-organizing reality, the universe surely could have existed in a variety of forms.[19] Without something in place, it seems highly improbable that the universe just churned out such principles and regularities that are necessary for the existence of life in our universe. Robin Collins gives the following example of just such a principle:

> The force of gravity is determined by Newton's law $F = Gm_1m_2/r^2$. Here G is what is known as the *gravitational constant*, and is basically a number that determines the force of gravity in any given circumstance. For instance, the gravitational attraction between the moon and the earth is given by first multiplying the mass of the moon (m_1) times the mass of the earth (m_2), and then dividing by the distance between them squared (r^2). Finally, one multiplies this result by the number G to obtain the total force. Clearly the force is directly proportional to G: for example, if G were double, the force between the moon and the earth would double.[20]

Collins goes on to explain:

> Some calculations indicate that the force of gravity must be fine-tuned to one part in 10^{40} in order for life to occur. What does such fine-tuning mean? To understand it, imagine a radio dial, going from 0 to $2G_0$ where G_0 represents the current value of the gravitational constant. Moreover, imagine the dial being broken up into 10^{40}—that is, ten thousand, billion, billion, billion, billion—evenly spaced tick marks. To claim that the strength of gravity must be fine-tuned to one part in 10^{40} is simply to claim that, in order for life to exist, the constant of gravity cannot vary by even one tick mark along the dial from its current value of G_0.[21]

---

18. Barrow and Tipler, *Anthropic Cosmological Principle*, 442.
19. Layman, "Moral Evil," 14.
20. Collins, "A Scientific Argument," 67.
21. Ibid.

The example given here by Collins is just one of many recognized constants.[22] Not all naturalists agree that the Big Bang is the final stop. In order
to explain the anthropic principle, some naturalists have turned toward
multiple universe theories. Such theories stress a multitude of distinct
physical universes that exist (or could have existed), and, for all we know,
there could be (have been) an infinite number of such universes.[23] One
such model is the oscillating Big Bang model, by which the universe, at
random, expands and contracts, perhaps ad infinitum. If such a process
of exploding and collapsing has been going on for all eternity, then eventually we should expect the coming about of such a fine-tuned universe
as our own. While such a theory may increase the probability of one or
more universes eventually producing life,[24] it nevertheless complicates
the naturalistic hypothesis by adding a further feature, going merely from
a self-organizing reality to a mechanism that generates a large (perhaps
infinite) number of universes at random.[25]

The oscillating model is by no means the only model available. There are
a variety of other multiverse scenarios. Despite the model taken, as physicist Paul Davies suggests, the multiverse hypothesis merely shifts the problem elsewhere. Such a theory requires many assumptions. He explains:

> First, there has to be a universe-generating mechanism, such as
> eternal inflation. This mechanism is supposed to involve a natural,
> lawlike process—in the case of eternal inflation, a quantum 'nucle-
> ation' of pocket universes, to be precise. But that raises the obvious
> question of the source of the quantum laws (not to mention the
> laws of gravitation, including the causal structures of spacetime
> on which those laws depend) that permit inflation. In the standard
> multiverse theory, the universe-generating laws are just accepted
> as given: they don't come out of the multiverse theory. Second, one

---

22. Hugh Ross, *The Creator and the Cosmos: How the Greatest Scientific Discoveries of the
Century Reveal God* (Colorado Springs, CO: NavPress, 1995), 118–21.

23. Layman, "Moral Evil," 14.

24. Though, even here there are questions as to whether or not one is playing fast and
loose with probability, given that such other universes are incapable of being compared and
studied empirically. See Paul Davies, *The Cosmic Jackpot: Why Our Universe is Just Right for Life*
(New York: Houghton Mifflin Company, 2007), 170.

25. Layman, "Moral Evil," 15.

has to assume that although different pocket universes have different laws, perhaps distributed randomly, nevertheless laws of some sort exist in every universe. Moreover, these laws are very specific in form: they are described by mathematical equations (as opposed to, say, ethical or aesthetic principles). Indeed, the entire subject is based on the assumption that the multiverse can be captured by (a rather restricted subset of) mathematics.[26]

Even if one were to couple the multiverse scenario with something like string/M theory, explains Davies, such mathematical specifications must be accepted as a given. But even here there could be other different unified theories, such as N theory, that one could propose. Davies questions such theories, because theorists often choose their theories based on the theory's elegance. He goes on to argue,

> But this is to import a new factor into the argument—questions of aesthetics and taste. We are then on shaky ground indeed. It may be that M theory looks beautiful to its creators, but ugly to N theorists, who think that their theory is the most elegant. But then the O theorists disagree with both groups.[27]

NATURALISM AND CONSCIOUSNESS

Despite the difficulty of the presence of life given naturalism, there are still yet other problems with the naturalistic paradigm as it relates to the question of evil. Such difficulties include the notion of consciousness, the metaphysics of good and evil, and human responsibility. We begin with the problem of consciousness.

If naturalism is to explain either moral or natural evil, then it must also be capable of explaining the presence of sentient creatures that are capable of suffering. Yet, in order to do this, it must also explain the presence of creatures with consciousness. How successful is naturalism in this respect?[28]

---

26. Davies, *Cosmic Jackpot*, 204.
27. Ibid., 205.
28. Layman, "Natural Evil," 23.

Granting something like evolutionary theory, naturalists have reason to expect life. But what of life with consciousness? Surely there are all kinds of creatures without consciousness, such as plants and certain lower-level life forms. And given the way in which evolution works, things could have gone quite differently from how they did. We could have been stuck in a world with single-cell organisms, or a world that consisted primarily of plants and lower-level life forms. How is it that life transitioned from life apart from consciousness to life with consciousness, according to the Darwinian schema?

Philosopher Thomas Nagel, who is himself a non-theist, finds "physico-chemical reductionism" in the field of biology "hard to believe."[29] In his book *Mind and Cosmos*, Nagel sets out to build a case against materialism based on the difficulties of consciousness coming about from within a purely materialist understanding of reality. For physicalists, consciousness reduces to chemical reactions within the brain. Though a bit outdated, philosopher Bertrand Russell paints a portrait of the physicalist conception of the connection between the human body and mind:

Of this physical world, uninteresting in itself, man is a part. His body, like other matter, is composed of electrons and protons, which, so far as we know, obey the same laws as those not forming part of animals or plants. There are some who maintain that physiology can never be reduced to physics, but their arguments are not very convincing and it seems prudent to suppose that they are mistaken. What we call our "thoughts" seem to depend upon the organization of tracks in the brain in the same sort of way in which journeys depend upon roads and railways. The energy used in thinking seems to have a chemical origin, for instance a deficiency of iodine will turn a clever man into an idiot. Mental phenomena seem to be bound up with material structure. If this be so, we cannot suppose that a solitary electron or proton can "think"; we might as well expect a solitary individual to play a football match. We also cannot suppose that an individual's thinking survives bodily death,

---

29. Thomas Nagel, *Mind and Cosmos: Why the Materialist Neo-Darwinian Conception of Nature is Almost Certainly False* (Oxford: Oxford University Press, 2012), 5.

since that destroys the organization of the brain and dissipates the energy which utilized the brain tracks. [30]

It is exactly this type of understanding of physico-chemical reductionism that Nagel questions. For Nagel, any attempt at equating the physical with the mental ultimately fails. One such strategy is conceptual behaviorism, which attempts to identify mental phenomena with "behavior" or "behavioral dispositions" or "forms of behavioral organization."[31] Other attempts, claims Nagel, are primarily verificationist in nature, in that, all that could be said about the content of a mental statement is that which could be confirmed, warranted, or verified about it by some observer. "In one way or another," says Nagel, "they reduce mental attributes to the externally observable conditions on the basis of which we attribute mental states to others."[32] While no doubt a connection obtains between "mental phenomena" and "behavioral manifestations," such theories inadequately and insufficiently analyze the mental, since

> they leave out something essential that lies beyond the externally observable grounds for attributing mental states to others, namely, the aspect of mental phenomena that is evident from the first-person, inner point of view of the conscious subject: for example, the way sugar tastes to you or the way red looks or anger feels, each of which seems to be something more than behavioral responses and discriminatory capacities that these experiences.[33]

In other words, the physical processes cannot adequately explain the subjectivity of our experiences. Yet, Nagel finds untenable even those

---

30. Bertrand Russell, "Why I Am Not a Christian," in *Why I Am Not a Christian*, ed. Paul Edwards (New York: Touchstone, 1957), 49–50.

31. Nagel, *Mind and Cosmos*, 37.

32. Ibid., 38.

33. Ibid. Nagel is not alone in critiquing naturalism's capability for explaining the relationship between physical events and mental events. Philosopher David Bentley Hart argues quite convincingly that naturalists have difficulty explaining the phenomenology of consciousness in six key areas: "The qualitative dimension of experience," "abstract concepts," "reason," "the transcendental conditions of experience," "intentionality," and "the unity of consciousness." For a fuller critique of naturalism's attempt at explaining the phenomenology of consciousness, see Hart, *The Experience of God: Being, Consciousness, and Bliss* (New Haven, CT: Yale University Press, 2013), 152–237, especially 172–203.

nonanalytic attempts that suggest mental phenomena are truly something inside of us, such as J. J. C. Smart's psycho-physical identity theory. Psycho-physical identity theories equate some mental event, such as a pain or taste sensation (Φ), with a corresponding physical event (Ψ). In other words, mental events are identical (theoretically, not analytically) to their corresponding physical events: $\Psi = \Phi$ much like water = H_2O. However, this raises a serious question for the materialist: "What is it about Φ that makes it also Ψ?"[34] In order for the identity to be a scientific truth, rather than a conceptual one, the property that Ψ has must be such that it is conceptually distinct from those "physical properties that define Φ."[35] In an effort to avoid **dualism** (i.e., **mind-body dualism**), says Nagel, materialists must retreat back into some form of analytical behaviorism, whereby "what makes the brain process a mental process … is not an additional intrinsic property but a relational one—a relation to physical behavior."[36] There are problems with this kind of theory, argues Nagel. Just as with the behavioral theories before them, such explanations do little by way of explaining subjective appearances. Furthermore, Nagel suggests that these kinds of solutions proposed by identity theorists suffer from Saul Kripke's critique that whereas "water = H_2O" is a necessary truth, the relation between Ψ/Φ is contingent in nature. When one has H_2O one needs nothing more to have water. The physical components H_2 and O are sufficient for having water. It remains what it is apart from any kind of perceptual experience. But is this the case for the relation between Ψ and Φ?[37] It would seem not, as Nagel explains:

> So if Ψ really is Φ in this sense, and nothing else, then Φ by itself, once its physical properties are understood, should be sufficient for the taste of sugar, the feeling of pain, or whatever it is supposed to be identical with. But it doesn't seem to be. It seems conceivable, for any Φ, that there should be Φ without any experience at all. Experiences of taste seems to be something extra, contingently related to the brain state—something *produced* rather than

---

34. Ibid., 39.
35. Ibid.
36. Ibid.
37. Ibid., 40–41.

constituted by the brain state. So it cannot be identical to the brain state in the way that water is identical to H_2O.[38]

Based on a purely naturalistic understanding of the world, the physical sciences seem to be quite incapable of explaining the connection between mind and body, and thus seem incapable of providing a clear explanation as to how mental events arise out of purely physical processes. Mental events, while no doubt connected to physical experiences, nevertheless seem to be something quite different in nature.[39] Naturalism as a worldview does not give us reason to expect conscious life arising from purely physical processes.

NATURALISM, GOOD, EVIL, AND RESPONSIBILITY

But what of the metaphysics of good and evil? Furthermore, how should we understand human responsibility from a naturalistic perspective? If naturalism is to explain evil, particularly moral evil and certain forms of natural evil, then it must, at least, provide some basis for judging whether some action is evil or not. For a naturalist, what structure is in place to judge some action as being right or wrong, just or unjust?[40]

A naturalist has at least four options available. First, she could opt for some kind of anti-realism, such as emotivism, according to which there is no such thing as moral facts but only human emotional responses. Anti-realism, coupled with naturalism, would lead one to doubt whether

---

38. Ibid., 41.

39. For a similar argument, see Alvin Plantinga, "Is Naturalism Irrational?" in *The Analytic Theist: An Alvin Plantinga Reader*, ed. James F. Sennett (Grand Rapids: Eerdmans, 1998), 72–96. Plantinga argues that evolution and naturalism conflict. At best, naturalism leads to agnosticism and doubt about whether our cognitive faculties lead us to truth about the world, given that the main goal of evolution is to produce adaptive beliefs. Such beliefs need not be true or false about the world; all that they need to do is help us to adapt, survive, or be fit. However, the whole scientific and naturalistic program rests on the ability to understand and know the world in a rational way. Plantinga has sharpened and nuanced this argument in his most recent book on the subject, *Where the Conflict Really Lies: Science, Religion, and Naturalism* (Oxford: Oxford University Press, 2011), especially 307–50.

40. Susan Neiman addresses how discussions on the problem of evil in recent times have focused more on the moral dimension of evil than the natural one. See Susan Neiman, *Evil in Modern Thought: An Alternative History of Philosophy* (Princeton: Princeton University Press, 2002).

naturalism could explain moral evil at all. It would not explain it so much as explain it away. Not wanting to go the way of the anti-realist, the naturalist could, secondly, adopt something along the lines of Platonism, the idea that moral truths exist independently of physical reality, or thirdly **moral supervenience** (moral naturalism), the understanding that moral truths in some sense supervene on conscious intelligent moral creatures. Of these three options, anti-realism may or may not find support from naturalism, but as noted, it does not do much by way of explaining evil, as we are considering evil in this chapter. Platonism and supervenience, on the other hand, in and of themselves, do not seem to be a given from naturalism. We would not expect either given naturalism. Platonism appeals to non-natural properties and objects, and supervenience sounds a bit like a promissory note, an assertion more than an explanation. In addition, both options would be an addition to the naturalistic hypothesis.[41] There is a fourth option for the naturalist, however. Perhaps evolution itself is the key to understanding values?

According to Richard Dawkins, the sense of "right and wrong" can be traced back to our "Darwinian past."[42] If we are to understand the origins of morality, then it must be the by-product of natural selection. While natural selection explains aspects of our species' survival, such as hunger or sexual lust, why do human beings have the powerful urge to contribute to relief efforts or to take care of widows and orphans? Dawkins believes that these powerful urges are founded in our genes. He goes on to explain:

> The logic of Darwinism concludes that the unit in the hierarchy of life which survives and passes through the filter of natural selection will tend to be selfish. The units that survive in the world will be the ones that succeeded in surviving at the expense of their rivals at their own level in the hierarchy .... The whole idea of the selfish gene, with the stress properly applied to the last word, is that the unit of natural selection (i.e. the unit of self-interest) is not

41. Layman, "Natural Evil," 25. David Baggett and Jerry L. Walls, in their book *God and Cosmos: Moral Truth and Human Meaning* (New York: Oxford University Press, 2016), take on both Platonism and ethical naturalism in various formulations, arguing that, with respect to moral facts, moral knowledge, moral transformation, and the convergence of happiness and holiness, classical theism and Christian theology provide the better explanation.

42. Richard Dawkins, *The God Delusion* (New York: Mariner Books, 2006), 245.

the selfish organism, nor the selfish group or selfish species or selfish ecosystem, but the selfish *gene*. It is the gene that, in the form of information, either survives for many generations or does not. Unlike the gene (and arguably the meme), the organism, the group and the species are not the right kind of entity to serve as a unit in this sense, because they do not make exact copies of themselves, and do not compete in a pool of such self-replicating entities. That is precisely what genes do, and that is the—essentially logical— justification for singling the gene out as the unit of 'selfishness' in the special Darwinian sense of selfish.[43]

The way genes insure survival is to program the organism toward selfishness. There are times, says Dawkins, when our genes make sure of their survival by "influencing" the organism "to behave altruistically."[44] Two ways that genes program an organism toward altruism are: 1) "kinship" and 2) "reciprocal altruism."[45] When an organism takes care of its offspring or "genetic kin," it becomes more likely that the genes will survive through several generations. The concept of reciprocal altruism is akin to our notion of "I'll scratch your back if you'll scratch mine." Reciprocal altruism may even occur between species. Nevertheless, this practice is prevalent among human beings and may explain why there are consequences for those who do not fulfill their end of the deal.

Resting on the Darwinian notions of kinship and reciprocation are some "secondary structures." For example, "reputation," explains Dawkins, is important to human society. One individual might have a reputation for kindness while another individual might be known for his conniving. Reputation is a way that an individual might foster reciprocation among one's species, thus preserving one's genes. One other example, argues Dawkins, is "conspicuous generosity." By this, Dawkins means that an individual among a species may participate in "risk-taking" or "ostentatious generosity" in order to "buy mates" or to "buy success."[46] Dawkins believes

---

43. Ibid., 245–46. For a similar view see Victor J. Stenger, *God: The Failed Hypothesis: How Science Shows that God Does Not Exist* (Amherst, NY: Prometheus Books, 2007), 209.

44. Ibid.

45. Ibid.

46. Ibid.

that these four reasons are "good Darwinian reasons" why individuals behave altruistically.[47] Hence our moral behaviors, like other behaviors necessary for survival, are "by-products" from our evolutionary past.[48]

Having dismissed morality grounded in the character of God or divine revelation, Dawkins argues for something like a "consensus" for morality.

> How, then, do we decide what is right and what is wrong? No matter how we answer that question, there is a consensus about what we do as a matter of fact consider right and wrong: a consensus that prevails surprisingly widely. The consensus has no obvious connection with religion. It extends, however, to most religious people whether or not they *think* their morals come from scripture. With notable exceptions ... most people pay lip service to the same broad liberal consensus of ethical principles. The majority of us don't cause needless suffering; we believe in free speech and protect it even if we disagree with what is being said; we pay our taxes; we don't cheat, don't kill, don't commit incest, don't do things to others that we would not wish done to us.[49]

He goes on to propose that humans should adopt something akin to a "New Ten Commandments." "Don't cause harm" or "Do not do to others what you would not want them to do to you" just to name a few of the proposed commandments.[50] He believes that a list, such as the one he duplicates, could be produced by any "decent" individual living today; however, such

---

47. Ibid.

48. Such attempts at explaining why we behave altruistically, however, in no way account for moral obligation. They do nothing by way of giving us reasons as to why we should behave in such-and-such a manner.

49. Ibid., 298.

50. Ibid., 298–99. Interestingly, Dawkins found his proposed (and I should add, only potential) list of "New Ten Commandments" while doing an internet search. He did not, himself, construct the list, but borrowed it from someone's website. Most of the commandments on the list he could agree with, while nuancing some or adding a few of his own. The point, then, argues Dawkins, is not that this particular list should be the complete list, but rather the list exemplifies some of the major moral agreements that exist among people. It would seem that, in order to have a true "consensus," one would have to observe all cultures—something that, from what I can tell, Dawkins has not done. Furthermore, given Dawkins' proclivity toward science, his observations are by no means empirical in and of themselves. One would think that with such a bent toward science, one would provide the appropriate data to support one's conclusions. None is given. Perhaps Dawkins is blind to the significant impact the Judeo-Christian worldview has had upon Western thinking? Even outspoken atheist Jürgen

a list, while not set in stone, exemplifies the spirit of the age (Zeitgeist) in which we live. For instance, the modern world has moved beyond slavery or racial and gender inequality, such offensive and oppressive treatment that is condoned by the Bible.[51] This "shift" of moral conscience is, Dawkins believes, in a positive direction.[52] It is an improvement from times before. What was acceptable, even generations ago, is no longer acceptable by today's standards. Such things as derogatory language or racial slurs, while still going on today, are looked down upon by most of the world. Even regarding the way in which war is approached today, says Dawkins, the aim is to have as few casualties as possible.[53] But what is the cause of this shift? Ultimately, it is not clear what the cause might be, claims Dawkins, but

> for my purposes it is enough that, as a matter of observed fact, it does move, and it is not driven by religion—and certainly not by scripture. It is probably not a single force like gravity, but a complex interplay of disparate forces.... Whatever its cause, the manifest phenomenon of Zeitgeist progression is more than enough to undermine the claim that we need God in order to be good, or to decide what is good.[54]

Habermas recognizes the immense debt recent discussions on human rights owes to the Judeo-Christian worldview:

> Christianity has functioned for the normative self-understanding of modernity as more than just a precursor or a catalyst. Egalitarian universalism, from which sprang the ideas of freedom and a social solidarity, of an autonomous conduct of life and emancipation, the individual morality of conscience, human rights, and democracy, is the direct heir to the Judaic ethic of justice and the Christian ethic of love. This legacy, substantially unchanged, has been the object of continual critical appropriation and reinterpretation. To this day, there is no alternative to it. And in light of current challenges of a postnational constellation, we continue to draw on the substance of this heritage. Everything else is just idle postmodern talk. (Jürgen Habermas, *Time of Transitions*, ed. and trans. Ciaran Cronin and Max Pensky [Cambridge: Polity, 2006], 150–51)

51. Dawkins, in reading the Christian Bible, or any other sacred text for that matter, does so without any hermeneutical sophistication, nor does he provide any interaction with key interpreters of Scripture from the three major Christian traditions. But beyond that, again it seems that Dawkins is oblivious to the key role that the Christian Scriptures and worldview have played in social reform, particularly in the fight over such issues as slavery and inequality.

52. One might ask: "Positive in what sense?" Dawkins is not at all clear on this.

53. Ibid., 300–304.

54. Ibid., 308.

Dawkins has presented, what he takes to be, a clear model that serves as a substitute for any kind of morality based on the character of God or divine revelation. But Dawkins' model is far from clear.

Can natural selection provide for us a proper basis for moral choice? It would seem not. In his twofold theory, Dawkins posits two separate theses:

1. our genes determine our urges, and

2. humans have freedom to reject such urges.

Regarding (2), Dawkins has this to say:

We have the power to defy the selfish genes of our birth and, if necessary, the selfish memes of our indoctrination. We can even discuss ways of deliberately cultivating and nurturing pure, disinterested altruism—something that has no place in nature, something that has never existed before in the whole history of the world. We are built as gene machines and cultured as meme machines, but we have the power to turn against our creators. We, alone on earth, can rebel against the tyranny of the selfish replicators.[55]

But (1) and (2) are contradictory. Given the naturalistic worldview coupled with evolutionary theory, humans are to be understood in strictly physicalist terms. If we are to understand human morality from a naturalistic evolutionary standpoint, is there room left for any kind of **libertarian** or contra-causal "free choice" in how humans are to behave? In the words of David Berlinski: "If evolutionary psychology is true, some form of genetic determinism must be true as well. Genetic determinism is simply the thesis that the human mind is the expression of its human genes. No slippage is rationally possible."[56] Similarly, Stewart Goetz and Charles Taliaferro make the point:

---

55. Richard Dawkins, *The Selfish Gene*, 30th anniversary edition (New York: Oxford University Press, 2006), 200–201.

56. David Berlinski, *The Devil's Delusion: Atheism and Its Scientific Pretensions* (New York: Crown Forum, 2008), 177.

While Dawkins enthusiastically promotes a naturalistic, reductive explanation of the development of morality and values, he believes that we now have morality and values to justify resisting our biological urges and natural impulses. The natural world has, in a sense, produced beings that are in a position to critique the natural world.[57]

On the one hand, Dawkins has gone out of his way to show how altruistic moral choices are the by-product of Darwinian evolution, yet, on the other, he wants to affirm that humans have the ability to accept or reject those altruistic moral choices of our genes.

Furthermore, Dawkins has failed to answer two critical questions: how are human beings to decide right and wrong (i.e., how to come up with this proposed consensus), and why *ought* human beings act morally? Concerning the first question, Dawkins promotes an agnostic approach as to how humans are to decide between right and wrong. All that is important for Dawkins is that a basic consensus exists.[58] By making this move, Dawkins sidesteps the issue and moves from his Darwinian explanation for the origin of morality to his notion of consensus and the moral Zeitgeist. Why should there be a consensus at all? Why should we think that such a consensus corresponds with moral truth? How is it that Dawkins effects the shift from moral epistemology to moral ontology? Furthermore, why is there a progression in moral conscience? Are these progressions of moral behavior the end result of natural selection? It would seem not. According to natural selection, it is not guaranteed that we were supposed to turn out the way that we have, or that the species *Homo sapiens* would have ever existed in the first place. As J. Budziszewski makes clear, "Darwinism is not a predictive theory."[59] Budziszewski goes on to say that "an evolutionary ethicist of this ... sort does not claim that Darwinism itself provides the foundation for ethics. What it does tell us, he thinks, is the general features

---

57. Goetz and Taliaferro, *Naturalism*, 89.

58. Dawkins, *The God Delusion*, 298.

59. J. Budziszewski, "Phillip Johnson Was Right: The Rivalry of Naturalism and Natural Law," in *Darwin's Nemesis: Phillip Johnson and the Intelligent Design Movement*, ed. William A. Dembski (Downers Grove, IL: InterVarsity Press, 2006), 250.

of human nature that ethics must come to terms with."[60] Budziszewski's point is significant. All that evolutionary biology can give us about ethical standards is a description of how humans behave as a result of their genetic predispositions. Furthermore, as Goetz and Taliaferro point out, ultimately, Darwinianism cannot condemn evil:

> If naturalistic determinism is true, then all the evil that has occurred was determined to occur by naturalistic causes. Deterministic naturalists may be deeply committed to fighting injustice—indeed, there is no doubt that many self-described naturalistic determinists are profoundly committed to promoting justice and other virtues .... But while theists maintain that evil is an aberration, an unnecessary violation of the natural goodness of the cosmos and its purpose, deterministic naturalists see evil as an essential part of nature, a necessary feature of reality and not at all in violation of the purposes of the cosmos.[61]

How does Dawkins answer the second question of why we *ought* to act morally? He does not. Dawkins readily admits that *absolute* moral standards need not exist for us to act morally, yet, he has provided no reason why we ought to act morally at all.[62] All he has provided is a description of "positive" behavior. As Arthur Holmes asks, "How can empirical facts (or anything else that 'is,' for that matter) impose duties or obligations on us?"[63] As the Humean dictum goes, one cannot derive an "ought" from an "is." Darwinian determinism ultimately reduces the "ought" to causes rather than to give commands for how we should live.[64] It would seem, then, that naturalism as a metaphysical system is incapable of explaining both the metaphysics of good and evil and human responsibility.

---

60. Ibid., 251.

61. Goetz and Taliaferro, *Naturalism*, 93.

62. Dawkins, *The God Delusion*, 265.

63. Arthur F. Holmes, *Ethics: Approaching Moral Decisions*, 2nd ed. (Downers Grove, IL: InterVarsity Press, 2007), 70.

64. Ibid., 76.

EVALUATING NATURALISM

Given our above discussion, how does naturalism fare overall as a metaphysical system in explaining the phenomena of evil in the world? Let's begin with factual adequacy and logical consistency. Naturalism is a fairly consistent and straightforward system; yet it stumbles in explaining moral facts. Many naturalists try to hold to some kind of objectivist view of morality, but naturalism as a system likely does not provide its best explanations, apart from ad hoc explanations, such as Platonism or moral supervenience—both of which are not a given from naturalistic assumptions.[65] It seems that all the naturalist can do, given her system, is to say that evil (if we can call it that) is a by-product of the way things are. Richard Dawkins has this to say about evil, pain, and suffering in the world:

> The total amount of suffering per year in the natural world is beyond all decent contemplation. During the minute that it takes me to compose this sentence, thousands of animals are being eaten alive; others are running for their lives, whimpering with fear; others are slowly being devoured from within by rasping parasites, thousands of all kinds are dying of starvation, thirst, and disease. It must be so. If there ever is a time of plenty, this very fact will automatically lead to an increase in the population until the natural state of starvation and misery is restored.... In a universe of blind physical forces and genetic replication, some people are going to get hurt, other people are going to get lucky, and you won't find any rhyme or reason in it, nor any justice. The universe that we observe has precisely the properties we should expect if there is, at bottom, no design, no purpose, no evil, no good, nothing but pitiless indifference.[66]

Naturalism, at bottom, is incapable of providing a satisfactory understanding of evil, both moral and natural evil. Regarding natural evil, no doubt that the effects of things like hurricanes or disease are tragic, but those kinds of things cannot be properly called evils, despite how it affects either the human or the animal realm. Where moral evils are considered, it

---

65. This is why many atheists do not consider themselves to be naturalists. They opt for something like Platonism to explain and ground moral facts.

66. Richard Dawkins, *River Out of Eden: A Darwinian View of Life* (New York: Basic Books, 1995), 131–33.

is hard to square human responsibility with naturalism's outlook of deter-minism or near-determinism.

How well does naturalism, as a metaphysical system, fare at explana-tory power and explanatory scope? As mentioned in the introduction, in order to explain the concept of evil, one must explain life, consciousness, the metaphysics of good and evil, and moral responsibility. Naturalism has a difficult time explaining each of these. Regarding the existence of life in the universe, naturalists often posit something like the multiverse to explain the anthropic principle. But positing the multiverse only com-plicates the naturalistic hypothesis. Not only now do they need to explain the anthropic principle, but also an eternal universe generator of sorts. Regarding consciousness, physicalism falls short of adequately providing an explanation. Lastly, how well does naturalism explain the metaphysics of good and evil and human responsibility. Arguably the best that a natural-ist can do for explaining morality, without adding ad hoc hypotheses, is to offer a naturalistic explanation grounded in neo-Darwinian evolution. But such attempts are ultimately insufficient. No matter how deeply committed to and intent on doing the just or virtuous thing that a naturalist might be, it is difficult to see how one can get obligation out of genetic predisposi-tions, imperatives out of indicatives. Furthermore, within the naturalistic system, what we generally call evil is a necessary feature of the cosmos.

There is also a level of ad hoc-ness in naturalism. For naturalists this is mostly seen with respect to positing something like the multiverse—whether such a thing as the multiverse is true or not—in order to explain the anthropic principle. Yet it is also taken to be somewhat of a backdoor way of arguing for certain metaphysical conclusions about the nature of the universe (e.g., that nature is all there is, was, or ever will be). But as we've seen, this only puts the problem one step removed. The multiverse hypothesis comes across as an ad hoc effort to provide explanation for the apparent design of life and to show that the universe is all that there is.

Regarding plausibility, it seems that naturalism is not plausible in and of itself as a metaphysical system. Though simple and straightforward, it fails at adequately explaining each of the four areas needed for explaining the phenomena of evil in the world. Furthermore, while naturalists often see their view as the default position, one will look high and low for any positive reasons or arguments for taking naturalism to be true.

Finally, is naturalism a livable worldview? Naturalism, at bottom, is a thin worldview. Not only does it provide no grounding for objective morality or for human responsibility, it has a bleak outlook on life. There is no afterlife or personal immortality. Moreover, there is no ultimate assurance that the work we do on the earth provides any ultimate significance. Nor is there any final vindication for the evils that we experience in the world. When all is said and done, the naturalistic picture of the world is a world that is unlivable in the face of evil.

CHAPTER 3
PANTHEISM—EVIL IN A WORLD IDENTICAL TO GOD

O Lord, I see within your body all the gods and every kind of living creature. I see Brahma, the Creator, seated on a lotus; I see the ancient sages and the celestial serpents.

I see infinite mouths and arms, stomach and eyes, and you are embodied in every form. I see you everywhere, without beginning, middle, or end. You are Lord of all creation, and the cosmos is your body.

You wear a crown and carry a mace and discus; your radiance is blinding and immeasurable. I see you, who are so difficult to behold, shining like a fiery sun blazing in every direction.

You are supreme, changeless Reality, the one thing to be known. You are the refuge of all creation, the immortal spirit, the eternal guardian of eternal dharma.

You are without beginning, middle, or end; you touch everything with your infinite power. The sun and moon are your eyes, and your mouth is fire; your radiance warms the cosmos.

O Lord, your presence fills the heavens and the earth and reaches in every direction. I see the three worlds trembling before this vision of your wonderful and terrible form.

—*The Bhagavad Gita* 11.15-20[1]

---

1. Eknath Easwaran, trans., *The Bhagavad Gita*, 2nd ed. (Tomales, CA: Nilgiri Press, 2007), 107–8.

H aving considered naturalism and evil in the previous chapter, I now turn to pantheism as an overall worldview response to evil. We begin with defining pantheism and move on to the comparative response. As with naturalism, four areas will be considered: life, consciousness, the metaphysics of good and evil, and human responsibility. Lastly, and quite differently from naturalism, as a theological system, how does the God of pantheism respond to evil in the world? What can the God of pantheism do to defeat evil?[2]

DEFINING PANTHEISM

As with any metaphysical system, it is important, at the risk of reductionism, to recognize that there is more than one variety of pantheism[3] and that pantheism can fit with a variety of ontologies.[4] But this should not keep us from arriving at a basic understanding of pantheistic teaching.

Erick Steinhart suggests that pantheism affirms, minimally, that "(1) all existing things are unified; and (2) the maximally-inclusive unity is divine."[5] Similarly, philosopher Michael P. Levine defines pantheism as the view that there exists an "all-inclusive unity" that is "divine."[6] John W. Grula advocates the following regarding the pantheist conception of God:

The doctrine that God is not a personality or transcendent supernatural being but that all laws, forces, manifestations, and so forth

---

2. Though throughout this chapter I engage various pantheistic thinkers, my primary interlocutor is Michael P. Levine, who has done much in recent years to put forth a systematic work on pantheism. His book *Pantheism: A Non-theistic Concept of Deity* (London: Routledge, 1994) is the definitive work on the pantheistic worldview from a modern philosopher of religion.

3. Norman Geisler and William Watkins identify six varieties: absolute, emanational, developmental, modal, multilevel, and permeational. Geisler and Watkins, *Perspectives: Understanding and Evaluating Today's World Views* (San Bernardino, CA: Here's Life Publishers, 1984), 71.

4. For example, Erick Steinhart suggests that there are at least three live possibilities for ontologies among pantheists: (1) materialism; (2) Platonism; and (3) class-theoretical Pythagoreanism. See Steinhart, "Pantheism and Current Ontology," *Religious Studies* 40 (2004): 63.

5. Ibid.

6. Levine, *Pantheism*, 25.

of the self-existing natural universe constitute an all-inclusive divine Unity.[7]

According to Paul Harrison, pantheists hold that the "Universe" and "Nature"[8] alone should receive the "deepest reverence."[9] For the pantheist "all things are linked in a profound unity."[10] There is a deep interconnection and interdependence among all things, among which, humans are an inseparable part.[11] While pantheists do not always agree on the extent of unity and divinity involved, both factors are, nevertheless, central.

Pantheistic thought can be found in a diverse group of forms, such as scientific pantheism, New Age thought, deep ecology movements, Taoism, Zen Buddhism, Hinduism, ancient Stoicism, and nature-oriented paganism.[12] Some pantheists refuse to use "God" language, so as to not confuse their understanding of the divine with theistic conceptions, while others find no problem saying things like "the Universe is God."[13] Certain Hindu forms of pantheism are multileveled in that they are also polytheistic. The gods are all part of the all-encompassing "Absolute," as demonstrated in the ancient Hindu work, the Bhagavad Gita.[14]

Pantheists give the "Universe" or "Nature" the same primacy that theistic religions give to their conception of God. It is the "Universe" or the "All" or the "One" or the "Ultimate" or the "Unity," rather than a theistic deity, that awakens within people a sense of awe, wonder, love, and acceptance, and hence the Universe should be revered.[15] It is this reverence toward the Universe, which is also divine (in some sense), that separates pantheists from naturalists. Yet, there are at least two ways in which pantheists

7. John W. Grula, "Pantheism Reconsidered: Ecotheology as a Successor to the Judeo-Christian, Enlightenment, and Postmodernist Paradigms," *Zygon* 43, no. 1 (2008): 160.

8. When words like "universe," "nature," "unity," "intelligence," "mind," and so on are capitalized in the ensuing discussions, they are referring to the pantheistic conception of ultimate reality (i.e., God).

9. Paul Harrison, *Elements of Pantheism: A Spirituality of Nature and the Universe*, 3rd ed. (Lexington, KY: CreateSpace Independent Publishing Platform, 2013), 1.

10. Ibid.

11. Ibid.

12. Ibid., 3.

13. Ibid.

14. *The Bhagavad Gita*, 11.1–20.

15. Harrison, *Elements of Pantheism*, 3.

distinguish their views of the divine from those of theists. First, unlike the God of theism, a being that is ontologically transcendent and separate from the universe, God in pantheistic thought is radically immanent (at least ontologically).[16] Second, God for pantheists is non-personal.[17] God does not act or will or want or desire. Such thinking about God is anthropomorphic and is avoided, at least by most pantheists.

One of the more notable Western pantheists is Benedict de Spinoza. Like many other forms, though not all,[18] Spinoza's brand of pantheism is monistic—the view that there is only one Being and that all other parts of reality are in some way identical with this Being, or, at least, modes of it are.[19] For Spinoza, substances are independent existing entities. He agreed with theists that God is an infinite substance and that no contingency exists in God. But if it is the case that God is an infinite substance, he argued, then there could be no such thing as independent substances; rather, all individual things are extensions or "modes" of the attributes of God. If God is infinite—an infinity that includes the world—and if there is no contingency in God, then there would also be no contingency in the world. Spinoza's brand of pantheism is highly deterministic, as are many forms of pantheism.[20]

---

16. Levine argues that transcendence is not completely absent from pantheistic thought, especially as one considers concepts of transcendence and immanence found in certain metaphysical principles of Taoist and Confucianist thought (*Pantheism*, 111-13).

17. Ibid., 95.

18. Levine argues that while many pantheists are monists, it is not the case that all pantheists are. Rather, like most other people, they are pluralists (*Pantheism*, 71-92).

19. H. P. Owen, *Concepts of Deity* (New York: Herder and Herder, 1971), 65. The following passage clearly captures Spinoza's notion of monism:

I do not know why matter should be unworthy of the divine nature, since ... outside God no substance can exist from which the divine nature could suffer. All things, I say, are in God, and everything which takes place takes place by the laws alone of the infinite nature of God, and follows ... from the necessity of His essence. Therefore, in no way whatever can it be asserted that God suffers from anything, or that substance extended, even if it be supposed divisible, is unworthy of the divine nature, provided only it be allowed that it is eternal and infinite. (Benedict de Spinoza, *Ethics: Part I* [Chicago: The Great Books Foundation, 1956], 19)

20. Griffin, *God, Power, and Evil*, 96. Theists would, of course, reject Spinoza's view of God's infinity and his understanding of substances. Moreover, some theists holding to a form of essentialism would no doubt hold that God does have some contingent properties. Such properties are not, however, essential to God's being. See Nash, *The Concept of God*, 16-17; Jay Wesley Richards, *The Untamed God: A Philosophical Exploration of Divine Perfection, Simplicity and Immutability* (Downers Grove, IL: InterVarsity Press, 2003), 82-105.

Robert Corrington, in discussing his version of pantheism, makes a distinction between **natura naturans** ("nature naturing") and **natura naturata** ("nature natured"). Such a distinction is fundamental to his own "Deep Pantheism." Both *natura naturans* and *natura naturata* are "dimensions *of* and *in* nature, not separate orders one in and one out of nature."[21] Of the two, suggests Corrington, *natura naturans* is the more difficult to explain. He describes it as "nature creating itself out of itself alone."[22] There is no "extra-natural creator"; rather "nature is eternal and continually self-renewing." Nature naturing refers to "the dimension of nature churning with potencies, potencies that spawn innumerable orders of the world."[23] *Natura naturata*, on the other hand, is better defined with respect to "the orders of the world," similar to what Christians call "creation."[24] Rather than there being some kind of "order of orders," there are, instead, "innumerable orders" within nature nurtured, some of which are "powerful sacred orders" or "sacred folds" or "numinous orders" "central to human religious experience."[25] These sacred folds, in some way, find their origin in *natura naturans*. Corrington goes on to explain: "nature contains deep unconscious depths from which sacred powers emerge" and such "sacred folds, semiotically dense, have neither internal consciousness nor intentionality."[26] Corrington, however, hesitates to say that all of nature is itself sacred. He reserves the term "sacred" for those "numinous orders" within nature. Yet, human encounter with such sacred folds brings about a religious experience such that it "shakes the self to the core of its being and conveys something of the power of nature."[27] Corrington summarizes his view of Deep Pantheism as follows:

> Deep Pantheism is a form of pantheism in that it affirms that nature is all that there is and that there is no divine agency located somehow outside of nature. It is 'deep' in the sense that it recognizes

---

21. Robert S. Corrington, "Deep Pantheism," *Journal for the Study of Religion* 1, no. 4 (2007): 505.

22. Ibid.

23. Ibid.

24. Ibid.

25. Ibid., 505–6.

26. Ibid., 506.

27. Ibid.

a churning unconscious depth of nature from whence all orders, sacred or otherwise, come. The gods and goddesses we encounter in sacred folds are all ejects from the primal potencies of nature naturing. They combine power and meaning, as Tillich would say, but in ambiguous ways that do not have a teleological cumulative force. So I would say that the sacred is in and of nature and that nature per se is neither sacred nor non-sacred.[28]

Corrington's view of pantheism diverges from the Hindu and Spinozistic variants on one central point. Unlike the Hindu and Spinozistic versions, there is no one overarching divine to which all things ultimately belong; rather, there are various divine touching points or, as Corrington calls them, "sacred folds" throughout nature. There is not one thing which orders all the other orders; rather, in some sense, the various orders work together to "combine power and meaning" without some ultimate direction or *telos* in view. So, for Corrington, the divine or sacred is found within nature, but it is not all-encompassing. Such encounters with various sacred folds ("gods and goddesses") bring about awe and wonder. In this sense, Deep Pantheism is considerably religious.

Given the diversity of pantheistic thought, how ought one to define pantheism? There seems to be at least seven major strands that make up pantheistic thought:

1. All things are interconnected and deeply unified

2. This all-inclusive unity is divine (in some sense)

3. The all-inclusive divine unity is the self-creating and self-organizing cause of all things

4. The all-inclusive divine unity is either eternal or necessary or both

5. The divine is non-personal

6. The divine neither transcends the world nor is it ontologically distinct from the world

---

28. Ibid.

7. The divine unity (or divine within the unity) is the object of one's ultimate concern, worship, and pleasure

I take pantheism to mean *the view that there is a reality such that all things are unified and that this all-inclusive unity is divine (in some sense); that the non-theistic concept of the divine is neither personal nor ontologically distinct from the world (as compared with theistic conceptions of God); and that the all-inclusive divine unity is the self-creating and self-organizing cause of all things, eternal and/or necessary, and the object of one's ultimate concern.*

PANTHEISM AND LIFE

How does pantheism as an overall metaphysical system explain the phenomenon of evil? To account for evil, pantheists, like naturalists, must be able to explain life, but in order to explain life they must be able to explain the existence of the universe as it is. Pantheists of all stripes recognize that something like the "Universe," "Nature," "God," "All," "One" or "All-Inclusive Divine Unity" (AIDU) is either eternal or necessary. As noted already, pantheists reject anything like a transcendent God of theism, who exists apart from the space-time universe, creating the heavens and the earth. Pantheists, such as Paul Harrison, also postulate that there is no need for a transcendent, first cause to the universe. He finds no reason, given our having "no problem imagining an infinite future," as to why there cannot also be a chain of causes that extend infinitely into the past.[29] If there is no external creator or transcendent first cause, one is left pondering where it all came from. Harrison suggests two options: (1) the universe is self-created; or (2) the universe has existed eternally.

Another pantheist, Michael Levine, suggests that the creation of the universe is something of a mystery. Most pantheists reject creation *ex nihilo* (creation out of nothing). Though the teaching itself would not violate the main claim of pantheism, claims Levine, the pantheist has other options available to him when it comes to creation, particularly **emanationism**.[30]

---

29. Harrison, *Elements of Pantheism*, 37.

30. Levine, *Pantheism*, 195. Others, however, are doubtful that emanation is a viable option for the pantheists. Douglas Hedley argues that Levine makes a serious mistake in conflating "subtle theism" with pantheism simply because each is concerned about unity. A subtle theist, such as Plotinus or Hegel—both of whom Levine claims as pantheists—is one who holds to

Emanationism is the view that creation is a flowing forth from God, rather than God, in some sense, making, forming, or fashioning the world. Such a view recognizes that, in some sense, God is *in* the world and the world is *in* God.

In addition to being eternal and self-existent, the all-inclusive divine unity is self-organizing. Most pantheistic systems are compatible with something like neo-Darwinian evolution, especially those pantheistic systems which place a high view on science and nature.[31] Even those that do not emphasize evolution, they nevertheless understand life existing as a series of cycles of birth and rebirth. All life is intricately connected and interdependent.

Let us begin by considering the claim that AIDU is self-created and self-organizing. In order to suggest that the something is self-created and self-organizing, it implies that it must also be necessary. For something to be necessary, it must be the case that it exists in such a way in all possible worlds. There is no possible world in which it exists differently—in its essential nature—from the way it does. Theists generally claim that God is a necessary being, that is to say, that which makes God what God is (God's essential nature) must be the case in all possible worlds. It could not be otherwise. But can a pantheist claim that the divine is necessary? The idea of **necessity** raises a significant problem for pantheists. Many pantheists hold that the world is either in some sense identical to the divine or, at least, an expression of the divine, that is, creation flows forth out from the divine. Yet, in any case, this would prove to be incompatible with the idea that the divine is necessary and self-existent, particularly if we think that there is any kind of contingency in the world. For the "All" or the "Ultimate" or "God" to share being with the world would result in its being limited by the

---

"a transcendent creative unity who may or may not be deemed personal." Plotinus and other Neo-Platonists held to the "One" as radically transcendent, which stands in contradistinction to the pantheistic view of the divine and reality. Emanation has to do primarily with the production of lower things from the higher. See Douglas Hedley, "Pantheism, Trinitarian Theism and the Idea of Unity: Reflections on the Christian Concept of God," *Religious Studies* 32, no. 1 (1996): 62–65, 70, http://www.jstor.org/stable/20019794. See also Keith Ward, *God: A Guide for the Perplexed* (London: Oneworld, 2002), 158–62, who suggests that those who are often labeled as "pantheists" are panentheists instead. Anytime that God transcends nature, then one is faced with a panentheistic conception of God. It seems to me that something like this would be the case with respect to emanationistic accounts of creation.

31. Harrison, *Elements of Pantheism*, 38–39.

world.[32] Further, as H. P. Owen put it, "Alternatively, if the world is (as it manifestly is and must be) contingent, and if it is part of God, he cannot be necessary."[33] To say that some being is both necessary and contingent results in a contradiction, which Owens likens to saying that some "figure is both a circle and a square."[34] Especially if one were to take Spinoza's brand of pantheism, one in which there is no contingency in the universe, then one would have a highly deterministic universe. For some forms of pantheism, creation flows by necessity from God. This stands in stark contrast to theistic views that recognize that God creates *ex nihilo* out of his free decision. But as David Clark and Norman Geisler suggest: "Now there is nothing inherently incoherent with viewing creation as necessary.... If God creates necessarily, then God *must* create. If creation is necessary, then God cannot not create."[35] Whether the universe is an extension of God, as in Spinoza, or the universe flows from God by necessity, as with some other pantheists, such a universe would have significant implications for human responsibility and evil in the world (which we will consider below).

We shall now consider the claim that AIDU is eternal. What does it mean to say that something is eternal? At minimum, this must mean that it has no beginning or ending. In theism, this is known as the *everlasting* view of eternity, in which God exists without a beginning or end.[36] This everlasting eternal view of the world seems to be the view that most Hindus and Buddhists hold,[37] and it is the view that Harrison and Corrington favor. Though, like most pantheistic views on nature and the universe, it is difficult to pin down just exactly what it is that a pantheist believes. Harrison finds as a live possibility something like the multiverse hypothesis or Stephen Hawking's suggestion that space-time curves back on itself

---

32. Owen, *Concepts of Deity*, 70.

33. Ibid.

34. Ibid.

35. David K. Clark and Norman L. Geisler, *Apologetics in the New Age: A Christian Critique of Pantheism* (1990; repr., Eugene, OR: Wipf & Stock, 2004), 149.

36. See Nicholas Wolterstorff, "God Everlasting," in *Contemporary Philosophy of Religion*, eds. Steven M. Cahn and David Shatz (Oxford: Oxford University Press, 1982), 78. The majority of Christians have held to God's temporal mode of existence as timeless, that is, God exists apart from any kind of temporal or spatial extension. I will consider the idea of divine eternity a bit further in chapter 4.

37. Ninian Smart, *Worldviews: Crosscultural Explorations of Human Beliefs*, 3rd edition (Upper Saddle River, NJ: Prentice Hall, 2000), 52.

much as a sphere curves back on itself.[38] For some Hindus, the cosmos has expanded and retracted many times (which sounds similar to the oscillating Big Bang model). Buddhists, too, hold that there is no ultimate beginning to the world.[39] Whichever is the case, there would be no true beginning or end. As considered in our discussion on naturalism, there are some significant problems with the idea of the multiverse, particularly in view of the **anthropic principle**. I will not rehearse those here. Rather, I will consider some difficulties with the notion of an infinite past.

As noted earlier, Harrison sees no problem with the idea of an infinite past. After all, we can imagine a limitless future (though, this too, has some issues of its own, as we will see), so why cannot the same be true of the past? When critiquing the **Thomistic Cosmological Argument** (TCA), Harrison suggests that there must be another cause—something that caused God. Otherwise, theists are being inconsistent. If God is the final stop for them, then why could the universe itself not also be the final stop for pantheists? He argues:

> The argument for a creator God also has a very serious logical flaw. It is based on the premise that everything requires a cause—and yet theists accept that one thing does exist without a cause: God

---

38. Harrison, *Elements of Pantheism*, 38. Hawking's proposal employs the use of imaginary time, which requires the use of imaginary numbers. This results in an understanding of space-time that is Euclidean in nature, meaning that space-time has four dimensions. According to a classical understanding of gravity, grounded in "real space-time," says Hawking, only two options can explain the behavior of the universe. Either the universe is infinite and has always existed, or the universe began to exist at a singularity, a finite time in the past. By postulating Euclidean space-time, using imaginary time and numbers, the requirement for a singularity forming the boundary or edge to space-time is eliminated. Space-time in the Euclidean sense, then, is rounded, much like the surface of the sphere, such as the earth. Though the earth's surface is "finite in extent," it has neither a boundary nor an edge to it. In a similar way, this may apply to our understanding of the universe. On such a view, the universe would be self-contained. If there is no edge to space- time, then there is no need to postulate God or some law that sets the conditions for space-time's boundaries. However, Hawking recognizes that his suggestion is a proposal that, like many other scientific proposals, is based originally in aesthetics or ontology. He recognizes the implications for "the role of God" in a universe with no boundaries. Such a universe, he believes, would indicate there is no need for a Creator. But, as will be discussed below and in chapter 7, even if the universe had no finite beginning in the past, that doesn't mean there's no need for such a being as God. For fuller discussion on Hawking's use of imaginary time, see Stephen Hawking, *A Brief History of Time*, Updated and Expanded Tenth Anniversary Edition (New York: Bantam Books, 1996), 138–46.

39. Smart, *Worldviews*, 52.

himself. This tends to undermine the basic premise of the argument. God is thought to exist without a cause. But if one thing can be self-existing, why can this one thing not be the Universe itself?[40]

Part of the problem with Harrison's argument, like many others who misunderstand TCA, is that Thomas Aquinas is not primarily concerned with arguing for a temporal cause—he actually held to the possibility of infinitely long temporal regress of causes and effects within the space-time universe—rather, the ultimate cause exists as a prior cause logically, which would not need a cause for its existence—such a cause would be necessary. Here we might follow Stephen Davis and make a distinction between "linear causation" and "hierarchical causation," where linear causation has to do with causation in a temporal or linear fashion and hierarchical causation is concerned with causes that are logically related to some object.[41] Let us suppose that some object *x* is the temporal or linear cause of some object *y*. We can imagine *y* remaining in existence even if *x* were to cease to exist. For example, a shoe depends on its being formed by a shoemaker. The shoemaker could cease to exist while the shoe remains. In this case, the shoe is dependent only temporally or linearly on its formation from the shoemaker; however, the shoe can remain in existence despite what happens with respect to the shoemaker.

But how might we understand the notion of hierarchical causation and logical dependency? Perhaps Greek mythology can lend us an example—a character known as Atlas who eternally holds the world on his shoulders. If Atlas were to cease to exist, then the world would no longer be sustained. In this case, the world is dependent on Atlas for its continually being sustained in existence.[42] The dependency is not in any way temporal or linear (or, at least, not merely so); rather, it is a logical kind of dependency. For Aquinas, God not only created the world, but God sustains the world in existence. If God were to cease to exist (which is impossible), then so, too, would the world. If God were to remove his sustaining power, then the

---

40. Harrison, *Elements of Pantheism*, 37.

41. Stephen T. Davis, *God, Reason and Theistic Proofs* (Grand Rapids: Eerdmans, 1997), 62.

42. I am indebted to Alan Padgett for this analogy in his fine work on God's relationship to time. See Alan G. Padgett, *God, Eternity and the Nature of Time* (1992; repr. Eugene, OR: Wipf & Stock, 2000), 59.

world would cease to exist. It is this kind of dependency—logical dependency—that Aquinas had in mind with respect to causation in the second of his famous **Five Ways**.

But how is it that we can have something like a linear regress but not a hierarchical one? Unfortunately, Aquinas does not tell us. Stephen Davis suggests two possibilities. Aquinas, says Davis, was opposed to the idea of an *actual infinite*. In the world, there cannot be an infinite number of members of any one thing. For example, it would be impossible to have an infinite number of, say, dogs, cats, people, or atoms in existence all at once or at the same time.[43] Davis goes on to say,

> Now if there were an infinite number of *linear* causal ancestors of some presently existing thing—some human being, say—those ancestors would not all have to be existing right now.... Most of them would presumably be dead and gone. No actual infinite would be required to exist all at once.[44]

Rather, what we have in the world is a *potential infinite*—the idea that the world is ever increasing toward an infinite without ever reaching it. But why couldn't this be the case with respect to hierarchical causation, in which the effect depends on the continued existence of its cause? Here Davis responds: "the effect cannot exist unless all its hierarchical causes simultaneously exist."[45] In other words, "if there were an existing human being who had an infinite number of hierarchical causes, that would require the existence all at once, here and now, of every one of them—an actual infinite,"[46] which for Aquinas, would be impossible.

The objector might obviously retort back by asking: "Why couldn't there be something like an infinite temporal regress in the world?" or, at least, "Why couldn't the past extend backwards infinitely?" In response to such questions, theistic philosophers, *pace* Aquinas, have argued that it is impossible for infinite temporal regress to exist in the world since such would in reality be an actual infinite. In their formation of the **kalam cosmological**

---

43. The idea of an actual infinite existing in the world would lead to all kinds of absurdities, which I will consider below.

44. Davis, *God, Reason and Theistic Proofs*, 62.

45. Ibid.

46. Ibid.

argument, William Lane Craig and James D. Sinclair have put the argument against the actuality of an infinite temporal regress in the following way:

2.11 An actual infinite cannot exist.

2.12 An infinite temporal regress of events is an actual infinite.

2.13 Therefore, an infinite temporal regress of events cannot exist.[47]

But why think that an actual infinite could not exist in the world? Craig and Sinclair provide a variety of thought experiments illustrating the kinds of absurdities that result from the instantiation of an actual infinite in the world. The primary example is that of Hilbert's Hotel, which goes as follows. Suppose we have a hotel with a finite number of rooms, and none of those rooms has a vacancy. If a guest were to show up, the doorman would have to kindly turn the guest away since all the rooms are currently occupied. Now let's suppose that, rather than the hotel having a finite number of rooms, it contains an infinite number of rooms, with each of the rooms currently occupied by a guest. But in this scenario, if a guest was to show up, the doorman could easily accommodate him. "Sure," says the doorman, "we can make room." The doorman proceeds to move each guest over one room. The guest in room #1 he moves to room #2, the guest in room #2 to room #3, and so on *ad infinitum*. Having moved all the guests over one space, room #1 now becomes vacant. The doorman checks the guest in, and all rooms are now once again occupied. Things get stranger, suggest Craig and Sinclair. Suppose an infinite number of guests show up at the desk. Just as what happened with the one guest, the doorman now shifts each person over. But rather than moving all of the guests only one room over, he places each person in a room twice his own, such that the person in room #1 goes into room #2, the person in room #2 goes into room #4, the person in room #3 goes into room #6, so on *ad infinitum* until all of the even rooms are now occupied, leaving vacancies in all of the odd numbered rooms for the guests, and thus all of the guests would be accommodated.[48]

---

47. William Lane Craig and James D. Sinclair, "The Kalam Cosmological Argument," in *The Blackwell Companion to Natural Theology*, ed. William Lane Craig and J. P. Moreland (Oxford: Wiley-Blackwell, 2009), 103.

48. Ibid., 108–9.

These are just two examples of the kinds of bizarre occurrences that would take place if an actual infinite existed in reality.

Per 2.12, then, an infinite temporal regress of events would constitute an actual infinite. Such would also mean that a beginningless set of past events or moments would constitute an actual infinite. But do Craig and Sinclair's thought experiments automatically rule out the notion of an infinite set of past events? Stephen Davis suggests that these kinds of thought experiments argue only against the notion that an infinite series of a set can exist *at any given time.* In order to demonstrate this, Davis gives the example of a library. Rather than an infinitely large library containing an infinite set of books all at once, suppose that the library was a smaller one with an emphasis on the longevity of it rather than its size. Suppose further that this particular library only contains one book in its collection at a time, and each year the librarian destroys the book and then replaces it with a new one. While a book's life is only a year in the library's collection, the library itself has existed an infinite number of years.[49] Davis goes on to argue:

> Here then truly would be a library with an infinitely large collection of books, but it would seem that Craig's paradoxes no longer apply. Taking away one book at any given time *would* reduce the collection in size (to zero); adding ten books *would* increase the size of the collection (to eleven), etc. If I am right, the critic ... can argue that there is no incoherence in the idea of an infinite number of past events. As long as past time is infinite, the infinite number of past events can occur in serial order, one at a time (or any finite number at a time); at no one time do an infinite number of events occur.[50]

If this kind of objection is correct, then, perhaps, the pantheist has good grounds for thinking the universe is infinitely old. It is important to note that the kind of argument Davis puts forth assumes time is dynamic and in process (an "A Theory" of time) and assumes something like presentism— the ontological view that the only temporal objects, items, or things that

---

49. Davis, *God, Reason and Theistic Proofs,* 153.
50. Ibid.

exist are those that exist in the present.[51] According to presentism, the past no longer exists and the future has not yet occurred. Whether presentism is true or not is not something that I can consider here, but for our purposes we will assume that something like presentism is true.

If something like presentism were true, would it allow for an infinite set of past events, as Davis' presumed critic might argue? It does not seem so. Craig and Sinclair provide an independent argument based on the notion of successive addition. The argument goes as follows:

2.21 A collection formed by successive addition cannot be an actual infinite.

2.22 The temporal series of events is a collection formed by successive addition.

2.23 Therefore, the temporal series of events cannot be an actual infinite.[52]

This argument does not so much argue against the possibility of an actual infinite, as did the previous one, but only against the notion that an actual infinite can be formed through successive addition. By "successive addition," Craig and Sinclair mean "the accrual of one new element at a (later) time."[53] The crucial element in the process is the temporality of it. What they are concerned with is the "temporal process of successive addition of one element after another."[54] No one would doubt the impossibility

51. Craig and Sinclair, "The Kalam Cosmological Argument," 115. Philosophers of time make a distinction between an "A Theory" and a "B Theory" of time. A Theorists hold that time is dynamic and that there is a real progress to it—a real moving from the past to the present to the future. Most A Theorists are presentists in some sense and hold that the past no longer exists while the future has not yet occurred. B Theorists reject that time is dynamic. Rather than thinking of time as moving in a direction, we should think of all events somehow existing simultaneously within the entire four-dimensional space-time universe. We speak of time in "earlier than" and "later than" relations. For a fuller discussion on the A Theory and B Theory of time, see J. M. McTaggart, "Time: An Excerpt from *The Nature of Existence*," in *Metaphysics: The Big Questions*, eds. Peter van Inwagen and Dean W. Zimmerman (Malden, MA: Blackwell, 2004), 67–74; Garrett J. DeWeese, *God and the Nature of Time* (Burlington, VT: Ashgate Publishing Company, 2004), 4, 15–16; William Lane Craig, *Time and Eternity: Exploring God's Relationship to Time* (Wheaton, IL: Crossway, 2001), 115–216; Padgett, *God, Eternity and the Nature of Time*, 82–121.

52. Craig and Sinclair, "The Kalam Cosmological Argument," 115.

53. Ibid.

54. Ibid.

of an actual infinite by successive addition in the case that there is a beginning point that is moving toward infinity. Suppose we have a finite number *n*. If one were to make an addition to it, say, *n* + 1, then what we are left with is a finite number. But the problem is more complicated than that. Craig and Sinclair put the problem in the following way:

> The question then arises whether, as a result of time's asymmetry, an actually infinite collection, although incapable of being formed by successive addition by beginning at a point and adding members, nevertheless could be formed by successive addition by never beginning but ending at a point, that is to say, ending at a point after having added one member after another from eternity. In this case, one is not engaged in the impossible task of trying to convert a potential into an actual infinite by successive addition. Rather at every point the series already is actually infinite, although allegedly successively formed.[55]

But this, too, is problematic. If one cannot expect to count to an infinite, how can one expect to count down from an infinite? Moreover, if one cannot traverse the infinite by moving in one direction, then how can one expect to traverse an infinite going the other. Craig and Sinclair continue:

> In order for us to have "arrived" at today, temporal existence has, so to speak, traversed an infinite number of prior events. But before the present event could occur, the event immediately prior to it would have to occur; and before that event could occur, the event immediately prior to it would have to occur; and so on *ad infinitum*. One gets driven back and back into the infinite past, making it impossible for any event to occur. Thus, if the series of past events were beginningless, the present event could not have occurred, which is absurd.[56]

They further support this claim by providing a thought experiment. Suppose we have a person named Tristram Shandy, who has set out to write his autobiography. It takes Shandy a full year to write about one day's worth

---

55. Ibid., 118.
56. Ibid.

of events. Shandy opines that at such a rate he will never finish his autobiography. Sadly, since Shandy is mortal, surely he would die before finishing a year's worth of his life. But let us suppose that Shandy somehow stumbles upon immortality. Would not this change the game and allow him to complete his task? The great atheist philosopher Bertrand Russell seemed to think so. Given an average of one day per year, all that one would need in order to write about an infinite number of days is an infinite number of years. Such would be plenty of time for Shandy to accomplish his autobiography, provided that he is diligent in his task. But Russell's solution will not do. Despite Shandy's best efforts, the opposite would seem to be true. Rather than finishing the book, provided he lived forever and had an infinite amount of time to complete it, Shandy would only get further and further behind. Each day that he writes would only lead to another year of laborious work. But that is not the only difficulty. If Russell's argument was correct, why is it, then, that Shandy did not finish his autobiography sooner, say, yesterday, the day before, or last month? After all, could he not have finished it at any time in the past? But such would be absurd since he has been writing an infinitely long time.[57] Thus one can conclude that a temporal series of events cannot become an actual infinite through successive addition.

Given such arguments as the ones presented here by Craig and Sinclair, it would seem that the pantheist does not stand on good ground for thinking that the universe is eternal; rather, it would seem more likely that the universe began to exist at a finite time in the past, which would align with standard Big Bang cosmology. If that is the case, then the universe cannot, itself, be necessary; rather, it must be contingent and dependent on something else for its existence. But that would raise a significant problem for the pantheist, since in some sense or another, the universe is identical with God. But as H. P. Owens argued, "if God to any extent transcends the world—if there is any element of his being that is not contained in the world—pantheism, in the strict sense, is false."[58] This would seem to hold for those pantheists who argue that the universe is in some sense a self-expression of or emanation out of God. Owen further argues, "Merely

---

57. Ibid., 120; Davis, *God, Reason and Theistic Proofs*, 153–54.

58. Owen, *Concepts of Deity*, 70.

to speak of the world as a self-expression of the One is to imply that the One has a separate nature to express."[59]

Despite those immense difficulties that come with expressing how AIDU can be either eternal or necessary, it does seem that, depending on the kind in consideration, pantheism has one up on explaining the complexity of life in the universe. Unlike the turn in recent forms of naturalism, which posit something like an eternal universe generator that perpetually or eternally produces universes, the pantheist can chalk it up to the divine. Though not personal, the pantheistic concept of deity functions as an eternal organizer of sorts. The various laws or forces at work in nature are all encompassed in the divine Unity.

Assuming something like neo-Darwinian evolution, pantheists have a mechanism for how life emerges on earth. Harrison believes that evolution is a "successful scientific explanation of how design emerges in the most complex things" and that it is "a wonderful mechanism for perfecting design, and like any great designer, it has both creativity and rigorous discipline."[60] Evolution is creative in the sense that it brings about new variations through random mutations and sexual reproduction.[61] The environment weeds out poor design, allowing those organisms that are best adapted to thrive and those that are not to die off. Harrison further describes evolution in pantheistic terms in the following way:

> For pantheists, evolution is a universal force that works even on non-living things. From the very instant of our universe, every individual thing has existed in the midst of other things, and has had to adapt to the community of beings in which it finds itself. Evolution is at work even in the realms of mind and society. Ideas, scientific theories, technologies and products are tested against each other and the most effective survive.[62]

---

59. Ibid.

60. Harrison, *Elements of Pantheism*, 39.

61. Though, given the impersonal nature of the divine in pantheism, one may question Harrison's enthusiastic use of terms like "design," "designer," "create," and "rigorous discipline."

62. Harrison, *Elements of Pantheism*, 39.

When Harrison speaks of evolution as a "force," he does not go into detail about what he means by that. Is such a force eternal? Is it necessary? Has it always been a part of the nature of the universe? Is evolution one of many of the forces that are part of AIDU or is it the driving force behind everything? All this needs fleshing out. But what is clear for Harrison, and for most pantheists, is that the force cannot be personal in nature. It should be noted, however, that some pantheists such as Plotinus and Spinoza do see something like a Mind at work in creation. It is, as Norman Geisler describes it, an *"immanent* providence" at work.[63] In his assessment, Geisler recognizes that the providence takes place from within creation rather than over or beyond it, as it does in theism, and it is the immanent nature of God that leads him to suggest that it is pantheistic. If one accepts emanationist accounts of God,[64] then the pantheistic view can accommodate for a kind of Intelligence at work in the world, which is an improvement over a purely atheistic or naturalistic understanding that all things came about through mindless or purposeless chance.[65]

PANTHEISM AND CONSCIOUSNESS

Despite the limitations of explaining either the eternality or the necessity of AIDU, and assuming something like neo-Darwinian evolution, pantheism fares much better at explaining life than does naturalism, but how well does it fare at explaining consciousness? As noted, an explanation of consciousness is required for providing an adequate explanation of evil in the world, particularly any kind of suffering. Again, pantheism fares better than naturalism when it comes to the notion of consciousness. Pantheism has available to it a wide variety of resources regarding consciousness. There are some pantheists who are also physicalists. This tends to be a Westernized pantheism influenced by naturalism.[66] Such

---

63. Norman Geisler, *Systematic Theology, Volume 2: God, Creation* (Minneapolis: Bethany House, 2003), 567. Not everyone is in agreement that Plotinus and other emanationists can be called pantheists. Moreover, if one were to suggest that the Divine is in some sense intelligent, then would that not stand in contrast to the pantheistic view that God is impersonal?

64. I am inclined to think that such thinking is confusing pantheism with panentheism.

65. Ibid.

66. Harrison, *Elements of Pantheism*, 84. On this point, it does not seem that pantheism as a system differs much from naturalism. Harrison admits that while for physicalist pantheists the universe has no mind, it does feature various minds in humans and in other sentient life.

pantheists will run up against the same kinds of issues we saw that naturalists face regarding the nature of consciousness. Thus, I will not consider physicalist pantheism here.

Non-physicalist pantheists, however, may ascribe to something like *panpsychism, animism,* idealism, or a general dualism in order to explain consciousness in the world. While not a pantheist himself, philosopher Thomas Nagel has recently gravitated toward panpsychism—the view that all things in the physical world are also mental—as a means to explain not only consciousness, but also cognition and values, which, he argues, is something that psycho-physical reductionist theories cannot do.[67] Animism is the view that a living soul or life spirit is behind the organization and animation of various phenomena of the world, including plants, trees, and certain inanimate objects (e.g., stones). Idealist pantheists are monists, recognizing that the material world is *maya* (illusion) and does not really exist. Mind or spirit is ultimate.[68] Lastly, some pantheists are also dualists.[69] It is a misconception that all pantheists are monists. For pantheistic dualists, the key is not in understanding whether just one kind of substance exists or not; rather, emphasis is placed on the Unity. Though pantheism does not entail any one of these options, all seem to fit well within a pantheistic

---

Moreover, the Universe has no ultimate purpose or meaning. Of course, Harrison suggests, this does not mean that the universe is utterly absurd. Perhaps the decisive factor which separates physicalist pantheists from naturalists is that of worship. But why then call oneself a pantheist at all? Why not hold to something like religious naturalism? For an example of a recent work advocating religious naturalism, see Loyal Rue, *Nature is Enough: Religious Naturalism and the Meaning of Life* (Albany, NY: State University of New York Press, 2011). See also Sam Harris, *Waking Up: A Guide to Spirituality without Religion* (New York: Simon & Schuster, 2014).

67. Nagel, *Mind and Cosmos*, 56–57. While I do not deal with it in this chapter, it seems that panpsychism has some major difficulties, particularly the combination problem. I discuss these difficulties more fully when I consider the process pantheistic view of panexperientialism in the next chapter.

68. An idealist understanding would raise many questions of its own. Would all suffering be an illusion? Or would all suffering primarily be a matter of mental pain? Furthermore, would such a view align with the salient facts of pain and suffering that we see taking place in the world, especially how we think of physical pain? For a modern idealist pantheistic perspective see T. L. S. Sprigge, *The God of Metaphysics* (Oxford: Oxford University Press, 2008).

69. Levine, *Pantheism*, 114–15; Harrison, *Elements of Pantheism*, 85–87.

scheme, and each provide a possible explanation for consciousness in the world, though some fit better than others.[70]

PANTHEISM, GOOD, EVIL, AND RESPONSIBILITY

But what of moral responsibility and the metaphysics of good and evil? Before discussing human responsibility, it may be helpful to consider whether pantheism has any basis for values. A central tenet of theism is that God is perfectly good. When theists speak of God as "good," they mean that God is good both ontologically and morally.[71] Within the very nature of God, there is no evil or badness, nor any sort of metaphysical deficiency. Furthermore, not only is God himself good, from the theistic perspective, but God cannot perform any action that is rightly deemed irremediably immoral or unjust or wrong or bad. By this is not meant that God's goodness is to be understood Ockhamistically,[72] but rather, substantively; God, in the ultimate sense, is constitutive of goodness itself. God is *the* Good, essentially, by which all other goods find their source; and God always does that which is right. Theists generally draw a distinction, here, between the Creator, who is infinite, and the creature, who is finite. Since the world is ontologically distinct from and dependent on God ontologically, though originally created as good, it can be corrupted and flawed. Creation's original goodness, or any other good for that matter, is derivative from God and not so essentially. Such good things possess potentiality. Pantheists, however, do not see things quite the same way. Rather than seeing AIDU as supremely good or perfectly good as theists do, some strands of pantheism see God as neither good nor evil; rather, the divine transcends such qualities. Consider the following passage from the *Bhagavad Gita:*

One man believes he is the slayer, another believes he is the slain. Both are ignorant; there is neither slayer nor slain. You were never

---

70. Though, it seems to me that the only viable option, other than dualism, is something like panpsychism, which I will consider extensively in chapter 3, when discussing process panentheistic views.

71. Edward R. Wierenga, *The Nature of God: An Inquiry into Divine Attributes* (Ithaca, NY: Cornell University Press, 1989).

72. Here I am alluding to a form of **divine command theory**, often attributed to William of Ockham, whereby some action (e.g., theft or murder) becomes obligatory if God commands it.

born; you will never die. You have never changed; you can never change. Unborn, eternal, immutable, immemorial, you do not die when the body dies. Realizing that which is indestructible, eternal, unborn, and unchanging, how can you slay or cause another to slay.[73]

This passage affirms that "good" and "evil" are false categories and ultimately an illusion. But even for those Western pantheists who are more naturalistic in orientation, the categories of good and evil seem to be nothing more than human invention. Regarding good and evil, Harrison claims:

The focus of pantheist reverence is not a good God. The Universe is neither good nor evil. The human categories of good and evil do not apply. It simply is. Again, this conception is easier to square with reality than the idea of an omnipotent and perfectly good God who allows or even causes devastating hurricanes, floods, epidemics claiming millions of lives—actions that in human terms would usually be seen as monstrously evil. The question why God would allow pain and evil to exist is one of the most difficult of all for theists to answer. Pantheists do not have to answer it. The Universe is what it is. ...

[Furthermore,] the Universe has provided us all with an indescribably beautiful home and a consciousness with which to appreciate it. True, it could wipe us out tomorrow in a hurricane or a meteor strike—as could the "loving" God of theist religion. But natural disasters are easier to accept if you do not imagine there is a personal God sending them to destroy the innocent and the guilty alike, or creating a world in which such things happen. Nature does not plan or act out of anger or retribution: if a natural catastrophe strikes, it is simply the working out of the laws of nature on the social and physical structures of humankind.[74]

For Harrison, like many pantheistic Hindus, the categories of good and evil are not the kinds of categories that one can ascribe to reality in any objective sense—they are merely "human categories." Yet, it is interesting

---

73. *The Bhagavad Gita*, 2.19-21 (Easwaran).
74. Harrison, *Elements of Pantheism*, 44.

that Harrison criticizes the actions of the God of theism on what seems to be objective standards that hold true in all circumstances. If they are not objective in nature, then why the big fuss? It seems that Harrison feels the existential pull and weight of the injustice of such actions that he attributes to the theistic God. If there were such a God, he should not act in such a way. But why think that some set of actions are "monstrously evil" unless there is such a standard by which one can judge them? To claim that good and evil are only human categories takes the bite out of Harrison's objection. Why think these human categories ought to apply toward God at all? Harrison does not say. But what of Harrison's argument that natural disasters are easier to accept for pantheists over against theism? We cannot, here, deal with Harrison's criticism of theism.[75] For Harrison's type of pantheism, the same God whom the pantheist worships is the same God that can wipe them out in an instant. Because AIDU is non-personal, it is indifferent to such tragedies. Furthermore, if one takes Harrison's line of thought, could we truly call such tragedies "evil" in an objective sense? That is just the way things happen. If we are to accept the pantheistic God of Harrison and the Bhagavad Gita, then the criticism of Michael Peterson et al. is fitting of such an understanding of the pantheistic God and evil:

> Perhaps the most striking point to be made, however, is that *the God of pantheism cannot distinguish between good and evil.* All actions performed in the universe are *equally* manifestations of the power of God; the notion that some of these actions are in an ultimate sense "good" and others "evil" must in the end be dismissed as an illusion. Pantheists may be, and often are, extremely upright and scrupulous

---

75. The theistic response to evils that occur through nature will be considered more fully in later chapters. For now, theists no doubt would reject Harrison's caricature and oversimplification of God's dealings with humanity through natural disasters. It is not at all clear that the majority of theists think that something like "God's dealing with people through nature" is God's primary modus operandi for bringing about judgment on people. Most Jewish and Christian theists recognize that the Old Testament Scriptures portray certain instances of God using natural disaster to punish wickedness, but such instances are the exception and not the norm. Sadly, some theists, in light of recent tragedies, have suggested that certain natural disasters were the result of God's judgment on a nation or group of peoples or because of a certain sin. Such statements are unwarranted and are a matter of conjecture. There is no reason to think that God's use of nature to judge is a central part of theism. One cannot but help get the impression that Harrison is throwing out a straw man argument in order to make the pantheistic view more palatable for his readers.

in their personal ethics, but in the ultimate perspective good and evil—or, what *we call* good and evil—are transcended.[76]

The pantheistic God, though the power of being in all things, cannot and does not really do anything about evil. Pantheists consider the divine Unity as the source of value in the world, yet pantheism can make no real distinction between "good" and "evil."[77]

Not all pantheists, however, wish to deny that good and evil are objective categories in the world. But what counts as "good" and "evil" for such pantheists? How do they handle the concept of evil within their systems? According to Levine, the traditional "problem of evil" does not apply to pantheists, since pantheists reject those aspects of theism that generate the problem (e.g., that God is all-good and all-powerful and yet evil exists in the world; that such things as gratuitous evils exist and that an all-good and all-loving God does nothing about them; and so on); rather, the problem from evil is "peculiar" to theism alone. For theists, says Levine, "'evil' is essentially metaphysical rather than a moral concept; or it is a moral concept with a particular theistic metaphysical commitment."[78] Nevertheless, pantheists have their own formulation of the problem. Levine continues,

> The pantheist may prefer, as most contemporary ethical theorists do, to talk of what is morally or ethically right and wrong. The term "evil" could be retained and applied to particular (usually extreme) instances of moral wrongness, but it would be understood in a sense that divorces it from its original theological and metaphysical context.[79]

---

76. Michael Peterson, William Hasker, Bruce Reichenbach, and David Basinger, *Reason and Religious Belief: An Introduction to the Philosophy of Religion* (Oxford: Oxford University Press, 2009), 82–83.

77. William Hasker, *Metaphysics: Constructing a World View* (Downers Grove, IL; InterVarsity Press, 1983), 110.

78. Levine, *Pantheism*, 197.

79. Ibid. Though, it seems, here, that Levine is confusing categories. He is blurring the lines between the "good" and the "right." Issues of moral goodness have to do with axiological matters, while issues of moral rightness are deontological in nature. For a helpful discussion, see David Baggett and Jerry Walls, *Good God: The Theistic Foundations of Morality* (Oxford: Oxford University Press, 2011), 44.

With respect to the divine Unity, pantheists do not claim that the divine Unity is all-good or omnibenevolent, nor is the divine Unity a "perfect being" (or a being at all, for that matter). "In theism," claims Levine, "it is assumed that what is divine cannot also be (in part) evil. But why assume this is the case with pantheism?"[80] He states,

> There seems to be little reason to suppose that what is divine cannot also, in part, be evil. To say that everything that exists constitutes divine Unity (i.e. pantheism's essential claim) need not be interpreted in such a way that it entails that all parts and every aspect of the Unity is divine or good. There can be a Unity and it can be divine without everything about it always, or even sometimes, being divine.[81]

Evil seems to be, then, for the pantheist, primarily a moral issue, fundamentally connected to the pantheist's conception of the AIDU. To claim that some action is "evil," it must be seen (in some sense) as a disruption of the divine Unity. But what exactly is "evil" for the pantheist? What exactly is the "good"? Are we to understand good and evil primarily in moral terms? Levine does not say. It is clear, however, that he rejects the theistic understanding of evil as privation.[82] It may be that "privation" applies to pantheists in the sense that evil reflects a "disunity or the absence of whatever it is the pantheistic Unity is predicated upon."[83] It is not at all clear what Levine means by this. But what of the good? In his discussion on evil, Levine gives little attention to it. Should the notion of good, then, be predicated on whatever brings about pantheistic Unity?[84]

Levine does, however, hold to a form of moral realism, which, as he claims, is generally the case for pantheists (or at least the brand of pantheism that he is promoting). There are objectively real moral facts in the world. Some things are ethically right or wrong independent of human

---

80. Ibid., 208.

81. Ibid.

82. Ibid., 212–14.

83. Ibid., 213.

84. But that is the rub—in pantheism, everything contributes to the divine Unity. It seems that Levine is picking and choosing what does and does not contribute to AIDU, perhaps to make the pantheistic conception of God more palatable to his readers.

beliefs about them. According to Levine, pantheists do not equate moral properties with natural properties, as some naturalists are wont to do. Such properties are not empirically verifiable. Rather, the pantheist, like the theist, will find such moral facts as "X is wrong" in something other than the natural; such facts are grounded in the non-natural.[85] For theists, "X is wrong" finds explanation and partial analysis in God's will and nature. Pantheists, on the other hand, find such facts explained and partially analyzed in "terms of (even if not reducible to) non-natural facts about the divine Unity."[86] Like Spinoza, Levine finds a strong connection between metaphysics and ethics. Regarding this point, Levine elaborates:

> The belief in a divine Unity, and some kind of identification with that Unity, is seen as the basis for an ethical framework (and "way of life") that extends beyond the human to nonhuman and non-living things. The divine Unity is, after all, "all-inclusive."[87]

The close connection and intricate interrelatedness between the human, nonhuman, earth, and divine Unity often leads to strong emphasis on environmental ethics. Pantheists often find such interrelatedness as advantageous over other systems. On this point Levine explains:

> The pantheist's ethic, her environmental ethic and her ethics more generally, will be metaphysically based in terms of the divine Unity. It will be based on the Unifying principle which accounts for an important commonality, and it will be the grounds for extending one's notion of the moral community to other living and non-living things. Everything that is part of the divine Unity (as everything is) is also part of the moral community.[88]

---

85. Ibid., 221. A "non-natural fact," says Adams, "is one which does not consist simply in any fact or complex of facts which can be stated entirely in the languages of physics, chemistry, biology, and human psychology." See Robert M. Adams, "A Modified Divine Command Theory of Ethical Wrongness," in *The Virtue of Faith and Other Essays in Philosophical Theology* (Oxford: Oxford University Press, 1987), 105, quoted in Levine, *Pantheism*, 221.

86. Ibid. It should be noted that Levine leaves open the possibility of a pantheist holding to something like ethical naturalism, if the pantheist were to make a case much in the same way that Richard Swinburne does for naturalistic theistic ethics.

87. Ibid., 222.

88. Ibid., 233.

Here, Levine cites Taoism as an example of how this may work. For Taoists, the Tao (the way) is the unifying principle. What it means for one to act correctly is for one to act in accordance with the Tao. Levine explains:

> In the context of the *Tao Tê Ching* (Taoism's primary "scripture") what the Tao is and how to act in accordance with it are explained in terms of one another. The *Tao Tê Ching*, like most other primary sacred sources, is at one and the same time an ethical treatise on how to live and a metaphysical treatise analyzing reality. One does not understand the Tao unless one understands what it means to live in accordance with it. Ethics are intrinsically related to the Tao, and "value" is associated with it at the most basic level.[89]

Another example available to the pantheist is the Hindu notion of **karma**, which can also be interpreted pantheistically. One can act either in accordance with or in defiance of the "all-pervasive principle" found within the karmic system.[90] The principle by its very nature is "associated with value," promoting the good.[91]

In working out his pantheistic understanding of ethics, Levine opts for something similar to the **divine command theory** found in theism. He does not mean by "command" that AIDU gives commands as such and that such commands are to be followed; rather, the notion of commands has more to do with living in accordance to the Unity. For the pantheist, then, living in accordance with AIDU is the "ethically good" thing to do, while living defiantly toward or violating the Unity is "ethically wrong."[92] Levine says,

> What is right and wrong is to be explained by reference, essential reference in some cases, to the divine Unity, just as what is right and wrong for the theist is, in some cases, to be explained by reference to the nature of God.[93]

---

89. Ibid., 238.

90. Levine distinguishes between the divine Unity and monism. For Levine, divine Unity neither entails nor requires monism, which many have falsely misunderstood. It is for this reason that Levine believes that one can act in accordance to or against the Unity.

91. Ibid., 238.

92. This sounds more like natural law than it does a form of divine command theory.

93. Ibid.

It seems, here, that Levine has provided a step up over naturalists and other pantheists, such as Harrison, in providing a way of thinking objectively about the metaphysics of good and evil and moral responsibility. Nevertheless, there are some difficulties with Levine's system. First, while Levine finds the notions of "good" and "evil" and "moral rightness" and "moral wrongness" in relation to that which promotes or deviates from the pantheistic Unity, there is ambiguity regarding just what it is that makes up that Unity. Levine spends quite a bit of space discussing what the divine Unity is not, but he never nails down just exactly what the divine Unity is.[94] This is a common pattern among pantheists. If the pantheist expects his understanding of the God-world relation to be taken seriously, then he would need to bring greater clarity to just what he means by the divine Unity. Philosophically speaking, the way in which pantheists describe the divine Unity leaves one to question whether it really makes much difference if pantheism is true rather than if no God existed at all? As William Hasker says about the divine Unity,

> Considering what is known of the universe, it is hard to see how it is a unity in any stronger sense than that it is a single space-time continuum in which things are interrelated according to a single set of natural laws.[95]

Second, while Levine is quick to argue that pantheism avoids the theistic problems of evil and that pantheism has a problem of evil unique to its own system, he does not say just what such a problem is. Levine defines evil ambiguously as that which disrupts the divine Unity. However, to say that evil disrupts the divine Unity does not really tell us anything much about evil itself. Moreover, Levine acknowledges that such a view of evil may count as a kind of "privation," yet he is adamant that the pantheistic system avoids the theistic notion of evil based on a theistic metaphysic.[96] But given that Levine holds to an objectivist view of moral rightness and

---

94. For an extensive discussion on this issue, see Michael P. Levine, "Pantheism, Substance and Unity," *International Journal of Philosophy of Religion* 32, no. 1 (1992): 1–23.

95. Hasker, *Metaphysics*, 110.

96. One wonders if pantheists like Levine, Harrison, and Corrington take the problem of evil seriously. The inability to articulate what is intuitively an extremely difficult problem is a deficiency in any worldview.

wrongness, he is acknowledging that there is a way that something *ought* to be—a moral order of sorts (e.g., the Tao). But to suggest that something ought to be a certain way indicates that something is just not quite right—a kind of privation of the good. If this line of thinking is correct, then it is questionable whether Levine, and other pantheists, have fully escaped the problem of evil claimed to be "unique" to theism. But of course, the God of pantheism escapes the charge of the problem from evil in the sense that the pantheistic conception of God is neither all-loving nor all-powerful. Furthermore, the God of the pantheist is not the perfect being of the God of theism. But it should be noted that the God of pantheism is also non-responsive to evil in the world. Supposing that something like the Tao is true, what can such a unifying principle do about evil or the disruption of the divine Unity other than to suggest (if we can speak of a principle suggesting) a way that one ought to follow? Moreover, what can the divine Unity itself do? It would seem nothing more, at most, than to promote the good, and even that much is suspect. In Levine's form of pantheism, humans are *the only moral agents* in the world; yet, humans are expected to do what the divine Unity itself cannot do—administer justice. What if humans reject the good? What then? Such a view of the God-world relation leaves us to question whether final justice will ever come about. Will the world's wrongs ever be put to rights? We might think that some eternal principle, such as karma, may bring about final justice for atrocities performed by people. But how can a principle or force bring about justice? A force or principle has no intentions, nor does it have any intelligence.[97] But moreover,

---

97. Take, for example, the following argument from Layman regarding such impersonal laws:

> Given that reincarnation and karma hold in the absence of any deity, the universe is governed not only by physical laws (such as the law of gravity) but by impersonal moral laws. These moral laws must be quite complex, for they have to regulate the connection between each soul's moral record in one life and that soul's total circumstances in the next life, including which body it has, its environment, and the degree of happiness (or misery) it experiences. Thus these impersonal moral laws must somehow take into account every act, every intention, and every choice of every moral agent and ensure that the agent receives nothing less than his or her just desserts in the next life. Now, the degree of complexity involved here is obviously very high, and it serves a moral end, namely, justice. But a highly complex structure that promotes justice can hardly be accepted as brute fact. Such a moral order cries out for explanation in terms of an intelligent cause. And if the moral order is on a scale far surpassing what can be attributed to human intelligence, an appeal to divine intelligence is justified. Hence, the moral order postulated by

the notion of final justice could only be the case if there is such a thing as an afterlife. Levine, however, rejects both personal immortality and the hope for an afterlife. It is hard to see, then, how final justice can ever be fully brought about in such world.

EVALUATING PANTHEISM

As with naturalism, shall we now evaluate pantheism on how well it explains the phenomena of evil in the world? Regarding factual adequacy, to what extent can the pantheist make sense of the salient facts of evil—the types and kinds of evil in the world (moral and natural), along with the quantity and intensity of such evils? If one were to take a position such as Levine's, a pantheist may have a better time of making sense of moral evil in the world than those forms of pantheism which deny the reality of good and evil altogether, or at least see evil as nothing more than an illusion. One would have to adopt a principle that always promotes the good. But making sense of how a principle enforces or promotes the good is difficult and needs further explication on the part of the pantheist. Given something like the karmic system, how can such a law or principle judge whether a person has done the right or enough good, especially since laws, principles, and forces are not the kinds of things that can judge? Regarding natural evil, pantheism has much of the same difficulty as naturalism, being incapable as a system of calling the effects of natural disasters, disease, and the like as "evil." These are tragedies, to be sure, but on what basis might one call them evil?

As for logical consistency, pantheism is much less straightforward as a system than naturalism. It is difficult to nail down just what a pantheist means by things like "the divine," "all-inclusive Unity," or "Absolute." Minimally, pantheists agree that there is a Unity and this Unity is in some sense divine. But with respect to the Unity, how much better off is the pantheist than the naturalist? How is the pantheistic Unity any stronger of a unity than the naturalistic understanding of the four-dimensional space-time universe? Furthermore, pantheists are not agreed over whether all

---

nontheistic reincarnation paradoxically provides evidence for the existence of a personal God. (C. Stephen Layman, "A Moral Argument for the Existence of God," in *Is Goodness without God Good Enough*, ed. Robert K. Garcia and Nathan L. King [Lanham, MD: Rowman and Littlefield, 2009], 58–59)

reality is one substance (monism) or if a plurality of substances (pluralism) exists (or exist) in the world. Pantheists like Levine seek to eschew, or at least put on hold, a conclusion about the notion of substance, opting for some minimal kind of explanation like a force or organizing principle that brings order to the various parts of the universe. But it is hard to see how this solves the problem of ambiguity within the pantheistic system. Epistemically, what reasons do we have for thinking something like Levine's notion of the organizing principle or force is the case? Perhaps the pantheist can employ the anthropic principle and something like neo-Darwinian evolution as supporting evidence that something is behind the events in the universe. But as shown earlier, the pantheist will run up against the difficulties that such a system face with the notions of eternity and necessity. With respect to the metaphysics of good and evil, it does seem that a pantheist can, at least, provide some categories for thinking about morality and evil that are consistent within its system. If one were to take a view such as Levine's, then one might say good is that which promotes the divine Unity, while evil is that which goes against it. But even here, such an understanding of good and evil is vague.

How does pantheism fare regarding explanatory power and scope? As we saw in the previous chapter, when explaining life, naturalists posit something like the multiverse and neo-Darwinian evolution. They believe that something like the multiverse accommodates for the findings of the anthropic principle. But as was shown, positing the multiverse only complicates the naturalistic hypothesis. Not only now do they need to explain the anthropic principle, but an eternal universe generator of sorts. Pantheists, too, have their own troubles. While a pantheist may hold to something like the anthropic principle and neo-Darwinian evolution in their systems, given that the pantheistic understanding of a force or unifying principle is at work at organizing the universe, it runs up against the problem of necessity and the eternality of the universe. If the universe at any time began to exist, as confirmed by standard Big Bang cosmology, then it would seem difficult to explain how the universe is identical to God in any meaningful way. For if God transcends the universe, would we, then, truly have a pantheistic system? But on the other hand, if all things exploded forth through the Big Bang, this leaves the problem of where it all came from—something would have truly come from nothing. Yet, as noted, actual infinites are impossible in the world and would lead to all kinds of absurdities.

Regarding consciousness, the metaphysics of good and evil, and moral responsibility, pantheism provides both greater explanatory power and scope than does naturalism. Pantheistic views that adhere to physicalism face many of the same difficulties as naturalists. However, pantheists have a variety options open to them for explaining consciousness (e.g., animism, dualism, or panpsychism), and in this sense, pantheism fares much better as a system than naturalism. Moreover, pantheists can better accommodate the notions of good, evil, and morality in their metaphysical system than can a naturalist, provided that one hold to something like Levine's modified command theory, whereby one does what promotes the Unity and avoids those things which defy it. The ground for the "good" is the Unity itself, which always promotes the good and moral rightness. Evil and moral wrongness, then, is that which goes against the Unity. But what exactly is it that promotes the Unity? How are we to make sense of this? The pantheists will need to flesh this out more if they expect their system to provide greater explanatory power. The strength of the pantheistic system—that such a system can provide some explanation for morality—is counteracted by the lack of clarity in the metaphysics behind key parts of the system. Regarding human responsibility, for pantheistic systems that are deterministic in nature, it is hard to make sense of human responsibility. But as Levine has argued, pantheism need not entail determinism. If we are to understand human freedom as libertarian freedom, it must be seen in connection to the divine Unity and in some sense found within the basic structures of the universe.

What level of ad hoc-ness does the pantheistic system promote? For pantheists like Harrison, who run closer to naturalism than theism, positing something like the multiverse comes across as ad hoc, especially when confronted with the conclusions of the anthropic principle.[98] Moreover, both Harrison and Levine have as their modus operandi of argumentation to show why the various other systems do not work (namely theism), and then make assertions regarding their own systems about how things either are or could be. Such methods of argumentation come across as ad

---

98. I will not rehearse those arguments here. See chapter 2 for fuller discussion.

hoc, especially since assertions are not arguments, nor do they sufficiently ground metaphysical positions.

How plausible is pantheism, first in itself, and secondly, in comparison to naturalism? It seems the pantheistic hypothesis is implausible in and of itself given evil, or at least given how we generally think of evil in the world. Perhaps, the pantheist might think this judgment unfair, especially since their system provides reasons for believing that evil exists as something that disrupts or goes against the divine Unity. But the critic of pantheism may well argue that it would increase the plausibility of pantheism if it could explain just what it is that such a disruption consists of, or, more importantly, just what the divine Unity is. Despite this significant weakness, the critic of pantheism might agree that, in comparing the two hypotheses, evil is more plausible given pantheism than naturalism. Though naturalism as a metaphysical system is more consistent than pantheism (if we grant something like neo-Darwinian evolution), it lacks in both explanatory power and scope when it comes to our general understanding of the concepts of evil. It fails to adequately explain life, consciousness, the metaphysics of good and evil, and human responsibility. Pantheism, though it lacks overall coherence and consistency, fares much better at explaining each of these, particularly the latter three. Yet, its overall explanatory adequacy depends on whether pantheism can give us good reason for thinking that the universe has always existed. From the above analysis, it does not seem that it can. Furthermore, pantheism runs up against many of the same pitfalls found in the naturalistic hypothesis. We must, therefore, deem pantheism as implausible as a metaphysical system when it comes to explaining the phenomena of evil in the world, though it is a step up from naturalism, in making sense of the salient facts of evil, as well as in providing greater explanatory scope and power with respect to each of the four areas of life, consciousness, the metaphysics of good and evil, and human responsibility.

Finally, to what extent is pantheism a livable system? In my own estimation, I find pantheism a better system than naturalism, despite its limitations and difficulties. Certain forms of pantheism hold to laws or principles within the Unity, such as karma or **dharma**, which suggestively promote justice within the universe. But the critic will want to know just how such laws or principles of cause and effect bring about justice. Do they function

like the laws of nature? It is hard to see how the effects of morally significant actions can be equated with the effects brought about by the laws
of physics, unless, of course, all things are determined. After all, many
theists would agree with something like natural law theories of ethics,
that such laws are in some sense built-in, but they also recognize that the
universe itself cannot explain such theories. Furthermore, another issue
is the administration of justice. How can such laws administer justice if
broken? It is not at all clear that a law or principle can. A yet further issue
is this: Are the laws themselves eternally existing, or were such laws put in
place by God? Pantheists are in basic disagreement about this. Regarding
immortality, some pantheists teach that there is such a thing as an afterlife. Some hold to the existence of individual souls living on after death,
while others hold that eventually all things will be absorbed back into the
Absolute or the Unity. While there is some hope in the former, the latter
leads to a bleak outlook on life.

CHAPTER 4

PANENTHEISM—EVIL IN A WORLD EXPERIENCED BY GOD

Suppose, for a moment, that each cell in your body possesses a consciousness, a center of awareness of its own. Each cell, then, would be aware of the organic processes in its immediate environment and would have, through this, a very limited and obscure apprehension of what is happening to the body as a whole. In addition to all these individual cellular awarenesses, there is also *your mind*, the awareness which "draws together" all the "cellular minds" and expresses them in a unified awareness of your entire body. Your mind *includes* the various cellular minds, but it also *transcends* them in a "unity of the whole." It is in some such way as this that panentheism conceives of the relationship between our minds and the mind of God.[1]

H aving considered pantheism and evil in the previous chapter, I now turn to panentheism, and especially process panentheism, as an overall worldview response to evil. We begin with defining panentheism and providing an overview of process philosophy before moving on to the comparative response. Following the format in the previous chapters, we will consider how process panentheism fares in four areas: life, consciousness, the metaphysics of good and evil, and human responsibility.

---

1. William Hasker, *Metaphysics: Constructing a World View* (Downers Grove, IL: InterVarsity Press, 1984), 111.

DEFINING PANENTHEISM

In its basic sense, the word "panentheism" means something like "all-is-God-ism"[2] or that the world is in God. Panentheism is somewhere in between pantheism and theism, expressing both God's transcendence and immanence (though, panentheists often place stronger emphasis on God immanence, and that is especially true of process panentheists). Like pantheism, the entirety of the world is (in some sense) in God, but God has an identity and unity all of God's own. Yet, unlike pantheism, this unity is not identical with all of God's finite parts.[3] In this way, panentheism is more like theism in that God (in some sense) transcends the world.

There are a variety of panentheistic systems; for economy's sake, we cannot consider each of them here.[4] This chapter is focused primarily on process panentheism. But before turning to the process panentheistic response to evil, we must first sort out the nuances of process philosophy by summarizing the work of its key thinker, Alfred North Whitehead.

ALFRED NORTH WHITEHEAD'S
PROCESS PHILOSOPHY

Perhaps no twentieth-century thinker has done more to bring back metaphysics as a respectable enterprise within theological circles than Alfred North Whitehead (1861–1947). Stephen Davis deems Whitehead's philosophical system as "one of the most brilliant intellectual accomplishments of the twentieth century."[5] Whitehead is one of the first thinkers to formulate

---

2. John W. Cooper, *Panentheism—The Other God of the Philosophers: From Plato to the Present* (Grand Rapids: Baker Academic, 2006), 26.

3. Hasker, *Metaphysics*, 111; Niels Henrik Gregersen, "Three Varieties of Panentheism," in *In Whom We Live and Move and Have Our Being*, ed. Philip Clayton and Arthur Peacocke (Grand Rapids: Eerdmans, 2004), 22.

4. For a detailed discussion, see Cooper, *Panentheism*; Gregersen, "Three Varieties of Panentheism," 19–35.

5. Stephen T. Davis, "Is the God of Process Theology a Valid Option?" in *Disputed Issues: Contending for Christian Faith in Today's Academic Setting* (Waco, TX: Baylor University Press, 2009), 121.

a systematic process philosophy,[6] which is most fully represented in his magnum opus, *Process and Reality*.[7]

PRIMARY CATEGORIES

As with all process thought, central is the notion that everything that is "actual" is in process. Whitehead calls his own system a "philosophy of organism,"[8] and Victor Lowe expresses it in the following way:

> Whitehead's amazing philosophical achievement is the construction of a system of the world according to which the basic fact of existence is everywhere some process of self-realization, growing out of previous processes and itself adding a new pulse of individuality and a new value to the world.[9]

Lowe further describes Whitehead's system as "pluralistic."[10] The reason for this has to do with Whitehead's rejection of the view that there is only one individual who is "ultimate."[11] Fundamental to Whitehead's "philosophy of organism" is the postulation that "creativity," the "many," and the "one" make up the "Ultimate."[12] This stands in stark contrast to classical theism, which understands God as ultimate and all other entities that exist as contingent, owing their existence to God. Moreover, classical theists believe God is eternal, immutable, and impassible. God is not affected by anything outside of himself. This is not the case with Whitehead's view, however.

In working out his speculative philosophy, Whitehead employed a variety of new terms and concepts to articulate the contours of his overall system, but most important are **actual entities**, **prehension**, and

---

6. Norman Geisler and William D. Watkins, "Process Theology: A Survey and an Appraisal," *Themelios* 11, no. 1 (1986): 16.

7. Alfred North Whitehead, *Process and Reality*, corrected ed., ed. David Ray Griffin and Donald W. Sherburne (New York: The Free Press, 1978).

8. Ibid., 21.

9. Victor Lowe, "Whitehead's Metaphysical System," in *Process Philosophy and Christian Thought*, ed. Delwin Brown, Ralph E. James Jr., and Gene Reeves (Indianapolis, IN: Bobbs-Merrill Educational Publishing, 1971), 3.

10. Ibid.

11. Ibid.

12. Whitehead, *Process and Reality*, 21.

creativity.[13] Actual entities, or "*actual occasions*" as they are sometimes called, refer to "the final real things of which the world is made up."[14] For Whitehead, one cannot go behind actual entities. All are uniquely different and are considered to be "drops of experience"; nevertheless, they are "interdependent."[15] He viewed actual entities as the "'cells' of the universe."[16] Lowe describes Whitehead's notion of actual entities in the following way:

> Each pulse of existence—Whitehead calls them "actual entities"—requires the antecedent others as its constituents, yet achieves individuality as a unique, finite synthesis; and when its growth is completed, stays in the universe as one of the infinite number of settled facts from which the individuals of the future will arise.[17]

Thus, unlike philosophical systems that stress "being" over "becoming," actual entities do not have sustained permanence over time. Each actual entity is, in the words of Charles Hartshorne, "a momentary state or single instance of process or becoming."[18] But becoming does not have to do so much with change, for actual entities are unchanging. Rather, becoming has more to do with "addition" and not "subtraction."[19]

For Whitehead, each experience is interrelated, dependent, and inseparable. In other words, each momentary experience (actual occasion) is related to previous experiences, which he calls a "prehension."[20] In the words of John Cobb and David Griffin,

> The present occasion "prehends" or "feels" the previous occasions. The present occasion is nothing but its process of unifying the particular prehensions with which it begins.[21]

---

13. Charles Hartshorne and W. Creighton Peden, *Whitehead's View of Reality* (New York: The Pilgrim Press, 1981), 7.

14. Whitehead, *Process and Reality*, 18.

15. Ibid.

16. Lowe, "Whitehead's Metaphysical System," 13.

17. Ibid., 4.

18. Hartshorne and Peden, *Whitehead's View*, 7.

19. Ibid.

20. John B. Cobb and David Ray Griffin, *Process Theology: An Introductory Exposition* (Louisville, KY: Westminster John Knox, 1976), 19; Whitehead, *Process and Reality*, 19.

21. Ibid., 19–20.

The entire process of the unification of experience is known as "concrescence."[22] There are two aspects to every prehension, the first is the "objective datum," which has to do primarily with the "content" of the prehension, whereas the second, the "subjective form," refers to the thing that has been felt, and how it has been felt.[23] Griffin gives an analogy of how the two might occur. Say, for example, that a person sees a big dog walking down the street; the "objective datum" is found in the content of the prehension. In this case, it refers to the big dog as appearing to the person (the experience). The "subjective form," however, refers to the kind of emotion that is produced by the datum.[24]

Another important feature of Whitehead's thought is creativity. It is for Whitehead the central metaphysical principle of the universe—"the universal of universals."[25] Whitehead goes on to say that "it is the ultimate principle by which the many, which are the universe disjunctively, become the one actual occasion, which is the universe conjunctively."[26] According to Charles Hartshorne, creativity is Whitehead's

> "intuition" ... of the act of existing. That this is not a single substance or a mere attribute seems clear. It is not God, because each creature exists by its *own* act of existing, dependent to be sure upon antecedent acts, including the antecedent actions of deity. But finally each actuality exists by its own self-activity: it is creative, however trivially, of new determinateness, thereby enriching reality as previously there, including divine reality as previously there.[27]

Thus, in some sense, because all that is actual is in process, including God, and because all that is actual is interrelated and interdependent, creatures "enrich" or "enhance" and "contribute" to the "divine life."[28] Moreover, because each actual entity is in the process of becoming, and because such

---

22. Griffin, *God, Power, and Evil*, 277.

23. David Ray Griffin, *A Process Christology* (Philadelphia: Westminster Press, 1973), 168.

24. Griffin, *God, Power, and Evil*, 277.

25. Whitehead, *Process and Reality*, 21.

26. Ibid.

27. Charles E. Hartshorne, *Aquinas to Whitehead: Seven Centuries of Metaphysics of Religion: The Aquinas Lecture, 1976* (Milwaukee, WI: Marquette University Publications, 1976), 42.

28. Ibid., 43.

self-creation is necessary and not contingent—a fundamental aspect of reality—this raises several implications about God and the God-world relation. If all actual entities possess the ability of self-creation, necessarily, then such is, as Griffin says, "beyond all volition, even God's."[29]

GOD AND THE WORLD

Whitehead rejects the Aristotelian view of God simply as the "unmoved mover" that has pervaded classical Christian thought. God does not stand over and against the world. Moreover, he did not create the world out of nothing, nor is God "before all creation"; rather, God is "*with* all creation."[30] In Whitehead's view, God is no exception to metaphysical principles; "he is their chief exemplification."[31] Thus God and the world are intricately connected. Not only does God affect the world, but the world affects God.

Whitehead thinks of God's essential nature as having two poles. In other words, God's nature is "dipolar."[32] The first pole he calls the "primordial" pole. The primordial pole of God is infinite and unlimited regarding potentiality. Moreover, it is impersonal and "conceptual."[33] In regard to the primordial side of God's nature, Whitehead makes the following comment:

> One side of God's nature is constituted by his conceptual experience. This experience is the primordial fact in the world, limited by no actuality which it presupposes. It is therefore infinite, devoid of all negative prehensions. This side of his nature is free, complete, primordial, eternal, actually deficient, and unconscious.[34]

God's second pole, the "consequent" pole, is "personal," "conscious," and concrete. It "is the realization of the actual world in the unity of his nature, and through the transformation of his wisdom."[35] This side of God's nature, says Whitehead, "originates with physical experience derived from the temporal world, and then requires integration with the primordial side.

---

29. Griffin, *God, Power, and Evil*, 278.

30. Whitehead, *Process and Reality*, 343.

31. Ibid.

32. Ibid., 345.

33. Ibid.

34. Ibid.

35. Ibid.

It is determined, incomplete, consequent, 'everlasting,' fully actual, and conscious."[36]

For Whitehead, God is not the all-powerful sovereign who reigns over creation. God's power is not unlimited controlling omnipotence; rather, it is persuasive. The reason for this has to do not so much with a moral issue or whether or not God limits his power, but because it is impossible for God. On this point Griffin explains: "God does not refrain from controlling the creatures simply because it is better for God to use persuasion, but because it is necessarily the case that God cannot completely control the creatures."[37]

Whitehead rejected Aristotle's God, who is unaware of the world. Instead God knows and loves his creatures intimately. God's being moved by his creatures demonstrates God's ability to sympathize with and to love them. Love is God's chief attribute. Whitehead criticized Thomas Aquinas (and classical theists) on this point. In the Thomistic view, any relation that takes place between God and his creatures is only a real relation for the creature, not for God.[38] God is not affected by the creature. For Whitehead, only a God that can sympathize with his creatures is a God worthy of worship.[39]

Because God's primary means of interacting with the world is through persuasion, God provides each actual entity with an "**initial aim**."[40] In providing the initial aim, God's purpose is that the subject will choose through the occasion the best option. However, whatever actualizes is up to the subject. That which the subject chooses becomes the "**subjective aim**,"[41] as Cobb and Griffin explain:

> The subject may choose to actualize the initial aim; but it may also choose from among the other real possibilities open to it, given its context. In other words, God seeks to persuade each occasion toward the possibility for its own existence which would be best

---

36. Ibid.

37. Griffin, *God, Power, and Evil*, 246.

38. Thomas Aquinas, *Summa Theologica*, vol. 1, part 1, trans. Fathers of the English Dominican Province (1912; repr., New York: Cosimo Books, 2007), I, Q. 28, Art. 1.

39. Hartshorne and Peden, *Whitehead's View*, 12.

40. Cobb and Griffin, *Process Theology*, 52.

41. Ibid., 52–53.

for it; but God cannot control the finite occasion's self-actualization. Accordingly, the divine creative activity involves risk. The obvious point is that, since God is not in complete control of the events of the world, the occurrence of genuine evil is not incompatible with God's beneficence toward all his creatures.[42]

Thus, the ultimate outcome for the shape of the world is not up to God alone, but up to God and the world, since each actual entity has within it the capability of self-creation and self-actualization.

Having examined the process thought of Whitehead, how are we to think of evil in light of process panentheistic thought? In the following sections, we will consider how process panentheism fares as a response to the problem of evil in these four areas: life, consciousness, the metaphysics of good and evil, and human responsibility.

PROCESS PANENTHEISM AND LIFE

If *process panentheistic thought* (abbreviated PPT for the rest of this chapter) is to explain evil, it must also explain life—given that evil has to do with the existence of sentient creatures who experience pain and suffering in the world. But, in order to explain life, a metaphysical system must also be able to explain the existence and nature of the universe.

When it comes to the nature of the universe, process theologians reject **creation ex nihilo**, opting for something more like the Platonic view that God created the world out of already pre-existing matter (**creation ex materia**).[43] In a helpful passage, David Ray Griffin provides a look at God's relationship to the world and the process view of creation:

---

42. Ibid., 53.

43. Not all panentheists opt for this view, which is one of the reasons that I focus on process panentheism in this chapter and not other forms of panentheism. Some panentheists, like Jürgen Moltmann, hold to a more Christian understanding of creation, opting for creation *ex nihilo*. Yet, Moltmann is a panentheist in the sense that, following the ancient Jewish kabbalah tradition of God's "self-limitation" (*zimsum*), God makes room or space within God's self. In that sense, creation is *in* God, yet God is distinct from the rest of creation. There is another sense in which Moltmann is panentheistic. For Moltmann, the relationship between the world and God is a "reciprocal" one. If God is love, then there is a real sense in which God not only gives love, but also that God needs love. Creation itself is a necessity in that God created in order to bring about an "Other" that is unlike the "Other" within God. See Jürgen Moltmann, *God in Creation*, trans. Margaret Kohl (Minneapolis: Fortress, 1993), 86–93;

According to process panentheism, God is essentially soul of the universe. Although God is distinct from the universe, God's relation to it belongs to the divine essence. This does not mean, however, that our particular universe—with its electrons, inverse square law, and Planck's constant—exists necessarily. This universe was divinely created, evidently about 15 billion years ago. It was even created out of "no-thing" in the sense that, prior to the creation, there were no enduring individuals sustaining a character through time (such as quarks and photons), which is what is usually meant by "things." With Berdyaev, therefore, we can say that it was created out of *relative* nothingness. This relative nothingness was a chaos of events, each of which embodied some modicum of "creativity," which is the twofold power to exert self-determination and then efficient causation on subsequent events. Each event in this chaos, therefore, influenced future events after being influenced by prior events, so that the creation of our universe was not the beginning of temporal relations and hence of time. It was, however, the beginning of the particular contingent form of order that physicists have been progressively discovering. Our universe began when God got this order instantiated in what had previously been a chaotic situation consisting of extremely brief, trivial, random happenings in which no significant values could be realized.[44]

It would seem, here, that Griffin has quite a few things going on that need unpacking. First, like Whitehead, Griffin recognizes that God has a significant role in the formation of the universe, much like the Platonic demiurge. For Plato, the demiurge infuses chaotic matter with form.[45] In that light *only* can he be called "Creator." In much the same way, God, for process thinkers, gets the whole process of our current universe going. God is not primary. God is neither the source of the universe's being nor

Moltmann, *The Trinity and the Kingdom of God*, trans. Margaret Kohl (Minneapolis: Fortress, 1993), 19, 98–99, 105.

44. David Ray Griffin, "Panentheism: A Postmodern Revelation," in *In Whom We Live and Move and Have Our Being*, ed. Philip Clayton and Arthur Peacocke (Grand Rapids: Eerdmans, 2004), 42–43.

45. W. Norris Clarke, *The Philosophical Approach to God: A New Thomistic Perspective*, 2nd rev. ed. (New York: Fordham University Press, 2007), 94.

is God the source of the built-in self-creativity that makes up the under-lying structure of the universe. But what is this self-creativity and why is it the primary metaphysical principle (or, at least, one of the primary metaphysical principles)? Furthermore, why think that the PPT view of the universe, along with its metaphysical underpinnings, is the correct one?

As noted earlier, self-creativity is a central feature of Whitehead's metaphysics. Unlike theism, PPT recognizes that God's modus operandi of activity in the world is, indeed, one of persuasive activity rather than controlling activity. Some theists also embrace the notion of persuasive over controlling activity; however, the theistic view is different in that God does this out of God's self-limitation. The reason is moral in nature. For defenders of PPT, on the other hand, the reason for God's persuasive activity in the world is metaphysical. In other words, God has no power to control—only the power to persuade. It is a matter of necessity that God cannot control anything outside of God's self.[46]

The metaphysical category behind this necessity is, as discussed ear-lier, what Whitehead calls the "ultimate," which involves three elements: "creativity," "many," and "one." According to Griffin,

> "Creativity" (by which the many become one and are increased by one) is a universal feature of actuality. It is inherent in actuality .... This does not mean that creatures derive their creative power from themselves, or that they are not dependent upon God for their exis-tence. But it does mean that to be an actuality is to exercise creativ-ity and that there is necessarily a realm of finite actualities with creativity of their own.[47]

But this notion of the ultimate is precisely one of the peculiarities of this view. I would agree with Stephen Davis that process ontology raises some troubling difficulties. For Whitehead and other process thinkers, there are no enduring substances; rather, what we have is something more like enduring events. Events consist of real changes in a thing, or, at least, relational changes between things. As Davis notes, this stands in contrast to the Aristotelian view, adopted by classical Christian theists (we will

---

46. Griffin, *God, Power, and Evil*, 276.
47. Ibid.

follow Davis in calling this Aristotelian ontology), whereby a thing is said to be "an enduring object with properties, relations, and an identity apart from other things."[48]

Defenders of PPT reject any hint of Aristotelian ontology by denying that entities have substances altogether. But denying substances is difficult to do, even if something like actual occasions are true. Davis suggests that there are at least two reasons to think that process thinkers do not escape Aristotelian ontology. First, if these events endure for any finite amount of time, then such are, indeed, substances by virtue of being enduring property bearers. To say that these events do not endure would lead us to think that they are nothing more than mere limits or boundaries, much like Euclidian points. But why think boundaries can do things like create or consist within reality? Second, if Aristotle was correct in thinking that a substance persists through time, one can explain what a thing is without an event. However, the opposite is not true. We cannot explain events without reference to or presupposing things. In other words, things are individuated by their properties and relations; whereas events are individuated by things. A thing can exist without an event. After all, we can imagine a possible world whereby only immutable objects exist. Yet, it is difficult for us to imagine some event taking place apart from some entity. Substances, then, are ontologically superior to events.[49] If Davis's arguments are correct (and I believe that they are), then we cannot do without substances. But moreover, this would cripple Whitehead's view that creativity lies behind the basic structure of reality, since events are not ontologically prior.

There is yet another difficulty facing process metaphysics—a difficulty that, as we saw in the previous chapter, pantheists, too, run up against. If God is not the primary organizing source in the universe, as important as God is to the process system of thought, then what is? How can we explain the unity? In the Whiteheadian view of things, we have God and the multiplicity of others, all of which work together to make a tight unified overarching system. But how is this the case? Whitehead falls prey to the same difficulty Plato faced, as W. Norris Clark explains:

---

48. Davis, "God of Process Theology," 127.
49. Ibid., 127–28.

If there is to be any ultimate source of unity in the universe at all—which is dubious, just as it was for Plato—it seems to be pushed back beyond even God to an inscrutable, faceless, amorphous force of creativity, which is just *there*, everywhere in the universe, as a primal fact with no further explanation possible—a kind of generalized necessity of nature, with striking similarities to the ancient Greek *Ananke*.[50]

But the problem is further complicated. Creativity is not an actuality in and of itself, says Clarke; rather, it is "a generalized abstract description of what is a matter of fact instantiated in every actual occasion of the universe. Creativity seems to be an ultimate primordial *many*, with no unifying source."[51] Clarke describes this as an "irreparable deficiency" that any "dualism" or "multiplicity" faces when not grounded in the "prior unity of creative mind."[52] Further, if such creativity does not find its source ultimately in God, from whence does it come? "Why," asks Clarke, "does this creativity continue to spring forth endlessly and inexhaustibly, all over the universe, in each new actual occasion, from no actually existing source?"[53] It would seem as though such bursts of individual self-creativity, which bring about each and every actual occasion, emerge *ex nihilo*, since there is no prior source. Some friends of PPT bite the bullet and recognize the difficulty, suggesting that if one were to grant this first step all else follows. Clarke (and most other theists) finds such an enigma too high a price to pay and metaphysically untenable.[54]

Lastly, regarding panentheism and life, it seems that process panentheists run up against the same problem of infinite regress that both naturalists and pantheists face. I will not rehearse those issues here but will only stress that one must face the complications implicit in positing an infinite universe (or multiverse).[55] Furthermore, in positing something like evolution behind the PPT portrait of the emergence of sentient life

---

50. Clarke, *The Philosophical Approach to God*, 102.
51. Ibid.
52. Ibid.
53. Ibid., 103.
54. Ibid., 104.
55. For further discussion, see chapter 3.

(or biological life in general), it would seem that process panentheists have, as considered below, a better theory behind the process of evolution than, say, naturalists do (since there is, at least, something—God—giving each actual occasion an initial direction or aim); however, as specified earlier, defenders of PPT will need to sort out just what lies behind Whitehead's notion of creativity. Until they are capable of doing so, defenders of PPT are at a metaphysical disadvantage for explaining life within the universe.

In what follows, I will consider in more detail how evolutionary theory dovetails with the process theory of consciousness. This will also setup a discussion on the process view of the metaphysics of good and evil.

PROCESS PANENTHEISM
AND CONSCIOUSNESS

Keeping in line with our approach, any metaphysical system that attempts to explain evil must also explain consciousness. How does PPT fare with respect to consciousness?

Consciousness is grounded in experience; yet while consciousness presupposes experience, experience itself is not consciousness.[56] For defenders of PPT, then, there is no separation between an entity and experience, nor is there any dualism between entities that experience and entities that do not experience. There are, nevertheless, different levels of experiences among entities. In order to see this, one must grasp the central role evolution plays in PPT ontology, along with the key process concepts of *"concrescence"* and *"transition,"* which are central to the process view of creativity. Griffin explains these important concepts:

> An occasion comes into being as an experiencing subject. The data of its experience are provided by previous actual occasions. Its reception of these data is called its "feelings" or "positive prehensions" of those previous occasions. (There are also "negative prehensions," which are said to "exclude from feeling.") It becomes a unified subject by integrating these feelings [concresence]. ... When the process of concrescence is complete, so that the actual occasion has achieved a unified experience of all its data and its subjective reactions to

---

56. Cobb and Griffin, *Process Theology*, 17.

them (each feeling has its "objective datum" and its "subjective form" of response to the datum), the occasion becomes an objective experience, i.e., an object from other subjects. Its subjectivity perishes, and it thereby acquires objectivity. It transmits some of its feelings to subsequent actual occasions [transition]. ... These two processes, concrescence and transition, embody the two forms of creativity, the two types of power, inherent in each actual occasion. The process of concrescence embodies the occasion's power of self-determination, its power of final causation. Although the present occasion is largely determined by the power of the past upon it, it is never thus completely determined.[57]

The evolutionary development of our world is a manifestation of God's work and creative purposes in the world.[58] Whitehead called each stage of the evolutionary process of the universe "cosmic epochs." Central to each epoch is a particular form of order. God's purpose in bringing order out of the chaos is to evoke certain intensities among the occasions by means of persuasion. God sends each actual occasion an *initial aim*. It is up to the occasion to accept or reject the aim. Order is needed to maintain the intensity among the various occasions, thus God seeks to bring about and maintain order through each initial aim, which occurs through God's persuasive power. Each stage of the evolutionary process is gradual, bringing more and more order out of chaos.

Actual occasions, retaining the datum from prior prehensions, begin to form into societies, beginning with the most primitive of forms, such as the proton, neutron, or electron, on to the atom and molecule, and finally up to more complex enduring entities such as the cell. With each advancement, enduring entities increase in intrinsic value. It should also be noted that each actual occasion has its own "mental pole." This does not mean that every occasion has some form of thought or consciousness; rather, "mentality" refers to the occasion's ability to receive and respond to data

---

57. Griffin, *God, Power and Evil*, 277–78.

58. Note that in the initial chaos, there were no "enduring objects"—not even the most primitive kinds (e.g., electrons, neutrons, or protons). These occasions would happen at random. Nevertheless, such a state would retain value because of the occasions themselves (Griffin, *God, Power and Evil*, 285–86).

from other actualities.[59] In this case, then, PPT is a form of *panpsychism* or, more specifically, *"panexperientialism,"* as Griffin calls it.[60] As actual occasions become more complex structured societies, they increase in intensity and beauty, and hence in intrinsic value. The soul or psyche is not, however, something ontologically different from other things; rather, "it is simply a higher-level series of occasions of experience."[61] Given the process notion of panexperientialism, consciousness, then, is not so much a function of the brain; rather, it is a function of experience.[62] It is, in the words of Griffin, a "very *high-level form of experience*, enjoyed by relatively few individuals."[63]

The process understanding of consciousness, compared with, say, materialism, is quite impressive and novel, to say the least. Yet, the pan-experientialism of PPT is not without its difficulties. It suffers from many of the same difficulties as its older cousin, panpsychism.[64] We shall now turn to some objections to panexperientialism.

---

59. Griffin, *God, Power, and Evil*, 285–90; for fuller discussion, see David Ray Griffin, *Unsnarling the World-Knot: Consciousness, Freedom, and the Mind-body Problem* (Berkeley, CA: University of California Press, 1998), chapters 9 and 10, especially.

60. Griffin, *God, Power, and Evil*, 248. See also David Ray Griffin, *Whitehead's Radically Different Postmodern Philosophy: An Argument for Its Contemporary Relevance* (Albany, NY: State University of New York Press, 2007), 58–61.

61. Ibid., 290.

62. Griffin, *Whitehead's Radically Different*, 62.

63. Ibid., 59.

64. To be fair to process thinkers, panpsychism and panexperientialism are not exactly the same thing, however. According to Griffin, panpsychism refers to the view that all things have a "psyche" or a "high-grade, conscious mentality." Panexperientialism, on the other hand, recognizes that certain aggregates, such as sticks and stones, do not have a "unified" or "high-grade" experience. Rather, only "genuine individuals" have such an experience. There are two basic kinds of genuine individuals: "simple individuals" and "compound individuals." Simple individuals are the "most elementary units of nature," such as quarks; whereas compound individuals are comprised of simpler individuals, such "as when atoms are compounded out of subatomic particles, molecules out of atoms, living cells out of macromolecules, and animals out of cells." Compound individuals are true individuals because each of the parts contributes to a higher level of experience. It is this higher level of experience that becomes the "dominant" member, which provides unity of both experience and action. A further difference between the two is that panexperientialism does not consider each genuine individual to have con-sciousness, though they have a unified experience. As already noted, Whitehead's notion of the "mental" is not the same thing as consciousness but has more to do with a minimal ability within an entity to have some basic level of experience. Despite these distinctions, there are enough similarities that panexperientialism could warrant some of the same critiques as panpsychism. See Griffin, *Whitehead's Radically Different*, 59.

One of the central issues of the process view of panexperientialism is, as we have already discussed, the problem with Whitehead's metaphysics and ontology. It is not at all clear that experience stands as the fundamental ontological structure of reality, and it is hard to think that process thinkers believe that it is experienced all the way down, either. To underscore this, let us consider a passage from Griffin:

> Each event ... is *experiential* from beginning to end, which means that, in distinction from usage reflecting dualism, the physical aspect of the event is not devoid of experience, hence the mental aspect is not uniquely associated with experience. An event's mentality is simply its experience insofar as it is self-determining. Whitehead emphasizes the experiential nature of unit-events by calling them "occasions of experience."[65]

Griffin is considered to be one of the ablest process thinkers alive today, and I believe that he has explained the above concept as clearly as is possible. *Yet, even with such clarity it seems that he cannot but help fall into what sounds like substance language.* In order to speak of both "experience" and "event," he must employ words like "physical aspect" or "mental aspect," even if it seems that he is equating the mental with experience itself. Nevertheless, he cannot but help speak of the event or experience apart from that to which it is happening. Now, it would seem absurd to think that the experience is experiencing itself. But perhaps that is what Griffin and other process thinkers have in mind. Either way, I find such a view difficult to accept on metaphysical grounds.[66] Even more, it seems that much of Whitehead's rejection of substance had to do with a Cartesian understanding of substance, and not the classical notion, which understood substance, in the words of W. Norris Clark, "as active nature imbedded in a network

---

65. Ibid., 61.

66. A recent article from *Process Studies* has made an interesting case that both process and substance are required. One cannot have the one without the other. See Richard Mattessich, "No Substance without Process, No Process without Substance, and Neither without Energy: Some Thoughts and Extensions on Whitehead and the Endurants (Continuants) v. Perdurants (Occurrents) Controversy," *Process Studies Supplement* 19 (2014): 1–36, http://www.ctr4process .org/publications/ProcessStudies/PSS/PSS_19_2014-Mattessich.pdf.

of relations resulting from its acting and being acted on."[67] Lastly, there are problems, as we have seen, with thinking that creativity is the primary metaphysical principle behind the four-dimensional space-time universe.

Even if one were to grant the process metaphysical and ontological understanding of reality (which I am unwilling to do), there is a further problem with panpsychism/ panexperientialism—a problem philosopher J. P. Moreland calls "the Combination Problem" (CP).[68] Moreland states CP in the following way:

> There are different ways of stating the problem. For example, if each particle of matter has its own unified point of view, how do they combine to form the same sort of unity when they interact to form larger wholes, a unity that appears to be unanalyzable and primitive? How do low-order experiences of ultimate atomic simples combine to form a single, unified field of consciousness or a unified self in larger wholes? Some panpsychists hold that all composed objects above the level of atomic simples have their own unified consciousness while others distinguish mere mereological aggregates without such a unity from "true individuals" that have it. Those who make such a distinction face two additional problems: How does one characterize the difference between the two? How could "true individuals" arise from processes that are combinatorial?[69]

Moreland's understanding of CP is largely set against the backdrop of panpsychism, but it seems that he has something like PPT's panexperientialism in mind, especially with respect to the process distinction between aggregates and "true" or "genuine" individuals. How might we formulate CP specifically to PPT? Following Moreland here, it seems that there are three unique questions that the defender of PPT will need to face regarding what we will call the "panexperientialist combination problem" (abbreviated PECP).

---

67. W. Norris Clarke, *Explorations in Metaphysics: Being, God, and Person* (Notre Dame, IN: University of Notre Dame Press, 2008), 102. See also 109-10.

68. J. P. Moreland, *Consciousness and the Existence of God: A Theistic Argument* (New York: Routledge, 2008), 128.

69. Ibid.

1. How is it that actual occasions combine to form into larger societies?

2. How do we draw the line between "aggregates" and "genuine individuals"?

3. How could "genuine individuals" arise from such combinatorial processes?

Having stated PECP, I will begin with (2) and then take (1) and (3) together, since the answer to (3) anticipates both (1) and (2).

Regarding (2), Griffin makes a distinction between mere "aggregates" and "genuine individuals."[70] There are two kinds of genuine individuals—"simple" and "compound." What is it, however, that qualifies some entity as a genuine individual? We have such things as animals, human beings, single-celled organisms, viruses, molecules, and atoms, which all qualify as genuine individuals. There are, however, certain qualities, that if an entity lacks them, then it would not be counted as a genuine individual. For example, some items, such as ceramic cups, safety pins, and pencils all lack "natural bodies" and an "evolutionary history," and these would not be counted as genuine individuals. Rocks would be disqualified by the fact that, as an aggregate, they have no overarching "organizing structure." Trees, too, would not be considered as genuine individuals, since they have structures that serve to merely "transport nutrients to their constituent cells."[71] A central feature, then, that distinguishes genuine individuals from aggregate individuals is in how those individuals can be organized. A rock, says Griffin, has no experience of its own, and hence no power for response to its surrounding community; rather, the highest level of experience is found in the billions of molecules that are found within it. The organization into "aggregational societies" and "compound individuals" leads Griffin to call his own position "panexperientialism with organizational duality."[72]

---

70. Griffin, *Unsnarling the World Knot*, 186.

71. D. S. Clarke, "Panpsychism and the Philosophy of Charles Hartshorne," *Journal of Speculative Philosophy* 16.3, no. 2 (2002): 151.

72. David Ray Griffin, *Religion and Scientific Naturalism: Overcoming the Conflicts* (Albany, NY: State University of New York Press, 2000), 167; Griffin, *Unsnarling the World Knot*, 186.

Given this, certain criteria distinguish between aggregates and genuine compound individuals. Whether this is adequate or not must be left up to the reader. But what of (1) and (3)? In order to get at (3) we will need to consider (1), which is the central question of PECP, and to which we now turn.

In *Unsnarling the World Knot*, Griffin makes an attempt at answering CP. He begins by considering William James's version of CP in his *Principles of Psychology.* James' argument goes as follows:

> Where the elemental units are supposed to be feelings, the case is in no wise altered. Take a hundred of them, shuffle them and pack them as close together as you can (whatever that may mean); still each remains the same feeling it always was, shut in its own skin, windowless, ignorant of what the other feelings are and mean. There would be a hundred-and-first feeling there, if, when a group or series of such feelings were set up, a consciousness *belonging to the group as such* should emerge. And the 101st feeling would be a totally new fact; the 100 original feelings might by curious physical law, be a signal for its *creation*, when they came together; but they would have no substantial identity with it, nor it with them, and one could never deduce the one from the others, or (in any intelligible sense) say that they *evolved* it.[73]

Here, Griffin suggests that James' argument was pointed at a particular type of compounding, one that does not touch his own Whiteheadian-Hartshornean view of compound individuals. The intended target was a form of "pantheistic idealism," which suggests that the emergence of the collective experience is in some way logically identical to the individuated experiences of the group. "James's point," suggests Griffin, "was that the more inclusive experience is a *new* experience, numerically distinct from the more limited experiences it includes."[74] Griffin continues, "James's argument, then, counts only against the identist form of panpsychism, according to which our unified conscious experience is supposed to be strictly (numerically) identical with the much more restricted experiences of the

---

73. William James, *Principles of Psychology*, Vol. 1 (New York: Henry Holt and Co., 1890), 160.

74. Griffin, *Unsnarling the World Knot*, 178.

billions of neurons in the brain."[75] Griffin would agree that such a view is unwarranted and "logically self-contradictory."[76] On the Whiteheadian/ Hartshornean view, rather than saying that the many *are one*, it would be more accurate to say that the many *become one*, while also *increasing by one*. It is through his acceptance of the subjective and objective modes of the existence of each occasion that, Griffin believes, Whitehead avoids the self-contradiction. Take, for example, neuronic experiences. When such occasions occur simultaneously, in their subjective mode they are many, but in their objective mode, they are the "many becoming one."[77]

Despite Griffin's response, it seems that the fundamental difficulty of the process notion of consciousness still runs up against CP, though the problem is not quite how Griffin has spelled it out; rather, the problem is one of the continual subsistence of such combinatorial states. Let us call this the "panexperientialist continuation combination problem" (abbreviated PECCP). To see this, it is important to briefly rehearse how process thinkers understand God's role in the whole ordeal.

God seeks to woo the various occasions into some directed aim, which I would take it to be how PPT would explain (3). Given that each occasion has its own level of freedom to accept or to reject God's initial aim, then, metaphysically speaking, neither God nor anyone else can cause them to do otherwise. This, it would seem, requires quite a bit of cooperation between the various occasions as they form into societies, especially as this process has been going on since the original chaotic state. But why do these various occasions move toward societies? Why cooperate in the first place (in whatever capacity they can)? What keeps them together? Furthermore, what keeps the whole ordeal from stopping and going back on itself? Perhaps the defender of PPT will want to say that it is God who keeps the whole thing going by repeatedly sending out initial aims. Given the sheer amount of occasions within the cosmos (and, perhaps, beyond), how is it, one wonders, that God keeps up with it all (especially since God is part of the mix)? Despite God's intimate awareness of each genuine entity (whether simple or compound) and God's ability to send initial aims,

---

75. Ibid.
76. Ibid.
77. Ibid., 180.

seemingly, at instantaneous speed—all the while providing the direction of the world through each initial aim—God can do nothing about whether occasions will follow suit. There is, however, another issue. These occasions are to make less than split-second decisions. The decision making of occasions is meant to simulate something similar to how people make decisions. But the ways occasions make decisions are not always how people do. When humans make decisions, it often takes time and much thought. There are instances where a person will have to make a split-second decision, but that is not always the case. Yet, that is how it is for these occasions *in every instance*. There seems to be something of a paradox involved, as William Hasker explains:

> Now even the simplest actions take more than a tenth of a second or so during which the "actual occasions" are supposed to endure; furthermore, humans are capable of forming and carrying out plans over periods lasting weeks, months, or years. Clearly, the process of "concrescence," in which the occasions selects its "subjective aim" and is guided thereby in the way it incorporates past experiences into the present, is modeled on the process of decision making by actual persons as it is empirically observed. Yet the frame for an actual occasion (which is never actually specified but can hardly be more than a small fraction of a second) is far too brief for any meaningful decision making to occur.[78]

The novelty of the PPT view on consciousness does not seem to outweigh the difficulties that the defender of such a view must take with respect to God's role in sending out such initial aims and the even bigger difficulty that the occasions must make such split-second decisions, while maintaining unity within the various genuine societies, especially those which are of greater complexity, such as the human soul. This, I take, to be the first leg of PECCP. The second leg has to do with the nature of consciousness itself as an emergent property, to which I now turn.

"Consciousness" or "mind" or "soul" for process thinkers remains, nevertheless, an emergent feature, or, at least, a "true individual," especially since it is grounded in prehensions of a multiplicity of prior occasions. If

---

78. William Hasker, *The Emergent Self* (Ithaca, NY: Cornell University Press, 1999), 145.

consciousness is a society in and of itself, then the defender of PPT runs up against another problem. Moreland argues:

> If an emergent property is depicted as contingently linked to the base properties causing it to emerge, then apart from an appeal to God's contingent choice that things be so and to God's stable intention that they continue to be so, there will be no explanation for the link or its constancy.[79]

But this applies equally to CP, as Moreland further explains:

> If a *sui generis* emergent property or a new "true individual" is acknowledged and its appearance is correlated with a certain set of circumstances formed by combinatorial processes acting on myriads and myriads of subvenient entities, then apart from an appeal to God's contingent choice that things be so and to God's stable intention that they continue to be so, there will be no explanation—naturalistic, panpsychist, or otherwise—for its appearance or constancy.[80]

Here, I think, is the key weakness of the panpsychist/panexperientialist view of consciousness, which is the second leg of PECCP. But it is also a key weakness of process ontology in general. There is nothing that requires or causes the various societies—aggregational or genuine—to persist. As we saw, God, according to PPT, does not do this, nor could God ever do this. It is metaphysically impossible for God to do so. It is doubtful that something else lies behind the structure. Creativity is a central feature of PPT, but it is more of a description of what is taking place in the universe at all times rather than functioning as some kind of force (as one might see in pantheism) that controls, causes, or even sustains all things within existence.

PPT, by postulating panexperientialism is, it would seem, one-up on reductionistic materialism for explaining consciousness, since the notion of "mental" is already a metaphysical fact of the universe. It avoids the complications of naturalistic viewpoints that posit that mental properties are in some way a new and novel part of the universe. Nevertheless, such

---

79. Moreland, *Consciousness*, 131.
80. Ibid.

a view fails to fully explain consciousness, in part due to CP, but more specifically PECCP, the version argued for, here.

PROCESS PANENTHEISM, GOOD, EVIL, AND RESPONSIBILITY

Having explored life and consciousness, we now turn to the PPT view on good, evil, and human responsibility. Griffin suggests that there are two dimensions to something that is intrinsically evil. These two dimensions are the opposite of the two criteria for intrinsic goods. For Whitehead, claims Griffin, goodness is related to beauty, and hence the two criteria for intrinsic goodness are aesthetic in nature. The first is "harmony" and the second is "intensity." To say that some experience is good is to say that it is both harmonious and intense. The opposite of harmony is "disharmony" or "discord." Disharmony occurs through the clashing of elements within an experience, bringing about a "feeling of mutual destructiveness."[81] The opposite of intensity is "triviality," which includes things such as boredom or lack of excitement.

At times there is tension between harmony and intensity, which may endanger one or the other. For example, when there is an increase in intensity there is also an increase in complexity. The more complex that an experience may become, the more it may upset the harmony that has already been achieved. In order to maintain harmony, it (harmony), too, must become more complex. According to Griffin, there are two ways that an experience may be considered as "complex," both of which contribute to its intensity. The first has to do with the amount and variety of elements belonging to the experience in question.[82] Griffin explains it as follows:

> Each experience begins by appropriating data from previous experiences. For example, an occasion of human experience receives influences from its own past experiences, from its body, and from God. The act by which an occasion of experience absorbs data from other experiences is called a "feeling" or a "positive prehension."

---

81. Griffin, *God, Power, and Evil*, 282.
82. Ibid., 283.

What is excluded are some of the feelings that were combined in the previous experience.[83]

An occasion has the ability to combine the received data either positively or negatively. A positive prehension of the data leads to the occasion accepting and accommodating it; whereas a negative prehension leads to its exclusion.[84] Griffin continues:

> To be able to appropriate the data means to be able to bring it together into effective contrasts. Some data which a more complex occasion would integrate into *contrasts* will constitute *incompatibilities* for a less complex occasion. Hence, the less complex occasion will negatively prehend feelings which a more complex occasion could have integrated into a more complex and thereby more intense harmony. Hence, the growth of complexity in his first sense means the growth in the intensity of experience.[85]

The second kind of complexity has to do with the occasion's ability to simplify. Once the complex occasion has sifted through the variety of data, it can then rid itself of unwanted or unnecessary data in order to integrate "a greater intensity of experience."[86] As we will see, complexity as a condition for intensity is a central feature of the process view of evolution.

Griffin further distinguishes between discord and triviality. Discord differs from triviality in the sense that it is "absolute" or "noncomparative," that is to say, "it is evil in itself, apart from any comparison with that which might have been."[87] Triviality, on the other hand, is comparative in the sense that some experience is more trivial than it need have been. Whitehead (and Griffin, too, for that matter) rejects a metaphysical view of evil, one whereby something is considered evil simply by nature of it being finite.[88] That is not exactly what the adherent of PPT means when

---

83. Ibid.
84. Ibid.
85. Ibid.
86. Ibid., 284.
87. Ibid.
88. It is not at all clear, here, whether Griffin has in mind the Augustinian view of evil as *privatio boni*. If so, it should be noticed that the view given by Griffin was not Augustine's view.

he speaks of triviality, either. It is evil not because it is trivial; rather, it is evil only relative to what it could have been.[89] Griffin thinks that having forms of experience emerge that are more intense and more discordant is not "necessarily inconsistent with moral goodness."[90] Hence, the two kinds of evil—discord and triviality—cover the full range of intrinsic evil. Discord refers to the main kinds of evil that is often considered in these types of discussions: physical and mental suffering. Triviality, on the other hand, covers a kind of evil that is often overlooked—the loss of a higher experience for a lower one.[91]

Discord and triviality are the two forms of evil that prevent maximum enjoyment. Thus, to speak of a morally responsible person is to speak of a person who seeks those things that are intrinsically good. Stated negatively, such a person would avoid or prevent any unnecessary triviality or discord that she could. This requires a certain amount of freedom. Incompatibilist freedom is a central feature of Whiteheadian/Hartshornean metaphysics. Whitehead's entire notion of creativity requires that every actual occasion have a certain amount of freedom. The higher the complexity the greater the freedom. Besides God, the pinnacle of freedom is displayed in those creatures with a "soul," "mind," or "consciousness," namely humans.[92]

For process thinkers, in a real sense God is responsible for all the evil in the world, yet God is not indictable or blameworthy of such evil. In God's effort to lead the world to perfection out of triviality and chaos through persuasive activity, discord has appeared. Though, it should be made clear that God is not totally responsible for the horrors that appear in the world

---

Something was not considered evil because it was finite; rather, something was considered an evil if it was a lack in something that should have been present in the thing, such as the absence of sight in a human, which should be present but was not. For Augustine and those Christians who followed his thinking, here, it was never an evil for a thing to lack something that it was not supposed to have. For example, it would not be an evil for a pig to walk on all fours instead of walking upright or for a canine to be unable to fly.

89. Ibid.

90. Ibid., 285.

91. Ibid. Interestingly, it seems that Griffin and other process thinkers are on to something important here with respect to triviality. Though somewhat different, it goes along similar lines as our discussion in chapter 1 on the notion of suffering brought on by a lack of flourishing, though, there are some distinctions.

92. Cobb and Griffin, *Process Theology*, 70.

since creatures have a certain level of freedom for self-determination and other-determination.[93]

Critics have raised questions about God's moral goodness on three levels, says Griffin. First, the God of PPT is morally deficient for primarily seeking goodness that is essentially aesthetic in nature. Second, the God of PPT is morally deficient since evil is overcome through God's experience. Third, the God of PPT is morally deficient for leading the world out of chaos and yet does not have the power to prevent discord or horrendous evils. Let us take each of these in order.[94]

Regarding the first level of criticism, Griffin believes that the critics of PPT have misunderstood what Whitehead meant by speaking of good and evil in primarily aesthetic terms. They assume that aesthetic goodness somehow excludes notions of physical and moral qualities. But if one were to take physical pain, for instance, there is sense in which pain represents a kind of disharmony or discord. With respect to moral goodness, such things as "rightness of conduct" are a kind of beauty in and of themselves. The kind of beauty that God seeks, say Griffin, is one that includes moral goodness, not one that is indifferent to it.[95]

As for the second line of attack, critics have again misunderstood Whitehead. Whitehead did hold that events that are intrinsically evil "are transformed or transmuted as they are received into the divine experience," says Griffin, but "evil never loses its character of evil so that the divine experience would be ... 'pure bliss'" for God.[96] Rather, Whitehead thought ascribing pure happiness to God was a "profanation" and, instead, believed God's happiness always to coincide with "sympathy and tragedy."[97] When speaking of God overcoming evil through good, Whitehead meant "that God, in responding to the evil facts in the world, provides ideal aims for the next state of the world designed to overcome the evil in the world."[98]

How do defenders of PPT address the third line of attack from critics? Here, Griffin believes, critics have failed to see that discord is not the only

---

93. Griffin, God, Power, and Evil, 300.
94. Ibid.
95. Ibid., 300–301.
96. Ibid., 303.
97. Ibid.
98. Ibid.

kind of evil in the world. One must also come to terms with unnecessary triviality, which is also a kind of genuine evil. If God is a morally perfect being, then such a being would want to stop all genuine evil so far that it can be done. Since unnecessary triviality is a genuine evil, God could not leave things as they were in the original chaotic state. Another important consideration is that God is sympathetic toward the world. According to PPT, God is not the God of classical theism, impassive and unconcerned with the world; rather, in bringing creation up out of the initial chaos, God is the great sympathizer sharing with creation in all its suffering, pain, and sorrows. God suffers with us.[99] "Since the world always contains a mixture of good and evil, beauty and ugliness," says Griffin, "the divine beauty is always tragic beauty."[100] Risks for creation are also risks for God. As God stimulates the world toward greater intensity, God too risks the potential for a greater intensity of suffering.[101]

So, how are we to think of the PPT view on the metaphysics of good and evil and on moral responsibility? One of the advantages of the PPT view is that it is far reaching. If PPT's metaphysical and ontological perspectives on creativity and process are correct, then there is an explanation for why evil (understood in process terms) affects all of reality, including not only human creatures, but also other areas of creation. God is at work moving all of creation out of the chaos of triviality toward greater enjoyment. Granting such metaphysical and ontological commitments, PPT provides both explanatory power and explanatory scope for the reality of evil in the world. Though, as we have seen, there are reasons to call into question the very notions of creativity and process as the underlining principles of all reality. Besides this, there seem to be three other problems with the PPT view on good, evil, and moral responsibility:

1. The problem of redefining good and evil

2. The problem of a limited God

3. The problem of eschatological pay off

---

99. Ibid., 308–9.
100. Ibid., 309.
101. Ibid.

Let us take each one of these in order. Regarding (1), process thinkers have redefined good and evil. As shown earlier, criteria for intrinsic goodness includes harmony and intensity. God's perfect goodness is seen in the attempt to bring about the world out of triviality and chaos, through discord, into greater harmony and intensity. The PPT view stands in stark contrast to the traditional theistic view and how most everyone understands good and evil, which is in moral categories. For theists, the criteria for moral goodness is found in God's moral nature. But as Michael Peterson suggests, the problem is that now "good" and "evil" are understood in primarily aesthetic terms, instead of moral ones. Peterson objects to the process view that divine goodness would seek to bring about greater intensity and harmony in the world. By doing so, God may break a number of moral principles along the way. As we saw, Griffin addresses such a criticism. He argues that Whitehead's view on aesthetics includes both physical and moral aspects. In other words, aesthetic aims include moral aims. Peterson thinks that this will not do since moral values should be seen in their own right and not as subordinate to aesthetic values. If the process view were correct, then it would seem to make our ordinary moral principles illusory, and it would make it difficult to see God's goodness in any kind of way as recognizably good.[102] But the problem is even more difficult, as Peterson suggests:

> Process thinkers hold that God's efforts to evoke beauty in temporal experience are not simply for the finite actualities involved, but ultimately to provide appropriate data for His own unified and comprehensive experience. In the Whiteheadian scheme, then, the suffering and difficulties, as well as the pleasures and achievements, of finite beings become material for God's aesthetic composition, i.e., for fitting inclusion in His consequent nature. But the previous question simply recurs at another level: Is it morally permissible for deity to risk evil in order to enrich its own experience?[103]

---

102. Michael L. Peterson, "God and Evil in Process Theology," in *Process Theology*, ed. Ronald Nash (Grand Rapids: Baker, 1987), 130–31.

103. Ibid., 131.

That God uses the experiences of creatures to maximize the divine experience calls into question whether God is worthy of all worship.[104]

How are we to understand (2)? Process thinkers recognize that their understanding is of a limited God. That God does not control all things, nor could God ever control all things, is a central feature of process thought. Metaphysically it is impossible for God to coerce or control creatures. Furthermore, for PPT, it is impossible for God to exist apart from a world. God in this sense is not necessary, that is to say, though God may be, in some sense, everlasting, the nature of God's existence and God's becoming are contingent features of the world, depending on the existence of a world. It may not be this world, but there must be *a world* nevertheless. This, again, stands in contrast to the theistic understanding whereby God is unlimited in nature. The theistic understanding is such that God has the power to bring about a world or to refrain from creating a world. God in no way depends on a world for his existence. Moreover, theists have understood God to have the power to control all things both actually and potentially.[105] But it is at this point of God having the power to control all things (whether actually or potentially) that process thinkers have issues. In his critique of the classical view of omnipotence, Griffin makes the following claim:

> If the world is understood as *actual*, the traditional idea of what is entailed by "omnipotence" involves a fallacy, and hence cannot be used as a standard by which to consider imperfect the power of God as conceived in a non-traditional way.[106]

It is not exactly clear here what Griffin means by "actual," but it seems that he means something like this: if the world is actual, then it is actual in the sense that it *consists of entities that have self-determining freedom that is over against God.* Griffin takes this as a metaphysical principle, which would require that such a state of affairs be what it is by necessity.[107] Griffin

---

104. Ibid.

105. Griffin, *God, Power, and Evil*, 251; Stephen T. Davis, "God the Mad Scientist: Process Theology on God and Evil," *Themelios* 5, no. 1 (1979): 18.

106. Griffin, *God, Power, and Evil*, 251.

107. Davis, "God the Mad Scientist," 21.

brings up the principle on multiple occasions. Take, for example, the following passage.

> If there is an actual world, and an actual world by metaphysical necessity contains a multiplicity of beings with power, then it is impossible for any one being to have a monopoly on power. Hence, the greatest conceivable power a being can have cannot be equated with all the power.[108]

But, as Stephen Davis rightly suggests, Griffin and other process thinkers never give us any reason for thinking that such a metaphysical principle is true.[109] Rather, it is simply assumed and asserted without argument throughout. Why should the theist (or anyone else for that matter) accept this principle as true? Why think that the world containing "a multiplicity of beings with power" is a metaphysical necessity? Griffin's objection turns on the assumption of process metaphysical and ontological commitments, which traditional theists would no doubt reject. Traditional theists would want to argue that the world is contingent, even if the world were in some sense everlasting. It would still depend, logically, on God for its existence. Since the world is *ipso facto* contingent, per the classical theistic view, then any power that the world has depends on God. But this does not mean that God gives no creatures power of their own to do otherwise in certain circumstances, especially if one holds to something like human libertarian freedom.[110]

Griffin recognizes that Plantinga and others, in putting forth their responses to the logical problem from evil, have argued for such a view that God gives creatures a certain amount of power and freedom, but he thinks that such views simply will not do. The free-will defense has some difficulties. First, such a view opens the possibility that God could, on occasion, violate human creaturely freedom, if he so chooses to do so in order to thwart some horrible evil. Griffin argues, "Of course, in those moments,

---

108. Griffin, *God, Power, and Evil*, 268, see also page 12.

109. Davis, "God the Mad Scientist," 21.

110. Sourcehood theorists like Kevin Timpe argue that libertarian freedom is best explicated in terms of our being the source of our own actions, rather than the source being a causal chain that was underway before we were born. Even if this is right, though, it typically entails the requisite ability to do otherwise.

the apparent human beings would not really be humans, if 'humans' are by definition free."[111] This is a non sequitur, however. One instance of a violation of a creature's freedom does not mean that the creature would no longer have freedom in other instances. If my child was playing in the back yard and I stopped him just before stepping into a bee's nest, it does not follow that by violating his freedom to step in that one place at that one particular time that he no longer has the freedom to step into a bee's nest any other time. After all, our criminal systems are often designed to do exactly what Griffin thinks that God could not do by thwarting some evil action without also changing that person's metaphysical stature. When a criminal has broken the law, depending on the crime, she might be thrown into prison. This type of punishment may be given as a consequence of the use of her freedom and, perhaps, in order to thwart other such crimes that the criminal may perform later on. But the impingement of such freedoms does not mean that she can no longer exercise her ability to choose. She still remains, ontologically speaking, who she is, but now with just certain limitations. In the same vein, God's interaction does not change who or what a person is ontologically.

Griffin gives a second objection. Could not the atheist suggest that it would be more preferable to bring about a world with "happy beings who are just like us, except that they are predetermined always to do right" than a "world such as ours with genuine free will but also with all its correlative evils"?[112] There are some problems with such an objection. First, the theist may respond that to have creatures who are predetermined to always do the right would entail a world in which the creatures would not be "just like us." There would be a significant ontological difference between those creatures and us, namely that they do not have libertarian freedom and, hence, are not free in any kind of morally significant way. But even more, a theist might respond that happiness itself may require some kind of freedom in the libertarian sense. Some naturalists have described a human person as a meat-machine. Like a computer or some other processor, the brain downloads information that is input into it. Computers and the like are programmed to do certain things by the person who programs

---

111. Griffin, *God, Power, and Evil*, 271.
112. Ibid., 271–72.

them. They are, in a sense, predetermined to perform and operate a certain way. If the human being is similar to some computational system or the like, programmed to respond in such-and-such a fashion, then it is hard to see how she can be described as happy. After all, when I think of my computer, I might consider it to be running efficiently or that the programs are uncluttered and operating in some kind of optimal capacity. But I doubt that I would call my computer happy. I take it, and perhaps many other theists would as well, that without libertarian freedom, or something in this vicinity, we might think of our general overall stature as human beings as running efficiently or optimally, but it is unclear that we can call it happiness. Happiness, as understood by Aristotle, and many of a religious persuasion, does not mean pain-free living or that no suffering is involved. Quite the contrary. Some of the greatest joys of life come from or in the midst of great trials and struggles. Such an understanding of happiness that Griffin provides here is a deflationary, hedonistic understanding of happiness, which may be nothing more than pleasure. However, there are many pleasure seekers who are not happy. Happiness for finite creatures, however, requires something of risk (though not evil itself) and moral significance that can only come about if there is such a thing as genuine agency.

Griffin provides a third argument that if one limits creaturely freedom to humans, then some other principle must explain all the evil in the subhuman world. He believes that all such attempts are unsatisfactory. One might extend the free-will defense and posit something like Satan and his cohorts as behind much of the evil in the natural world not directly related to human moral agency,[113] but he finds such a view somewhat implausible in our day and age. Though I myself find such a view limited in explanatory power, it should be noted that just because something is unfashionable

---

113. For defenders of such a view, see John C. Peckham, *Theodicy of Love: Cosmic Conflict and the Problem of Evil* (Grand Rapids: Baker Academic, 2018). Gregory A. Boyd, *Satan and the Problem of Evil: Constructing a Trinitarian Warfare Theodicy* (Downers Grove, IL: InterVarsity Press, 2001); Plantinga, *God, Freedom and Evil*, 57–59. It should be pointed out, however, that Plantinga, in giving the Free-will defense, is not saying that such is the case that Satan and his minions are in fact behind natural evil in the world, but only that there is no logical contradiction between the existence of an omnipotent, omniscient, perfectly good God and the existence of evil. Boyd, on the other hand, advocates *that such is the case*. Plantinga's is a defense; Boyd's a theodicy.

by today's standards does not make it false. Several theists have provided alternate responses to natural evil in the world,[114] some of whom Griffin considers in his work, *Evil Revisited*.[115] Many of these theists appeal to, what has come to be called, "natural order theodicies." Natural order theodicies suggest that the various conditions that often bring about certain goods in this world, also have the potential for bringing about certain evils. Take, for example, the rain cycle. That the earth continually has a rain cycle is a great good for the earth. Yet, there are times when humans and other creatures are affected negatively by such things as floods caused by an overabundance of rain. Griffin doesn't deny that such natural evils are by-products of a good-working natural order, since such a point is central to his own theodicy. Nevertheless, he finds it utterly inadequate for traditional theism.[116] Much of Griffin's critique rests on his interpretation of the theistic understanding of divine omnipotence, which is a much larger issue than I can get into in this chapter. For now, I will defer my discussion on natural order theodicies and pick up the discussion in the next chapter.

There are other reasons, however, for rejecting the notion of a limited God. Such a God as that of PPT would not be worship-worthy. Though God may be the greatest conceivable being (in Hartshorne's understanding of Anselm), such a God would be quite impotent—and God according to PPT, says Stephen Davis, must be "sufficiently impotent" in order for God not to be blameworthy for the horrendous evils in the world.[117] "God," continues Davis, "must be weak enough to be incapable of unilaterally preventing evil from existing."[118] The God of PPT can seek to persuade actual entities to do this or that, but there is no guarantee that it will ever happen. Furthermore, the kind of persuasive power that the God of PPT has is partial and in need of supplementation. Michael Peterson suggests

---

114. For other responses to the problem of natural evil, see Bruce R. Reichenbach, *Evil and a Good God* (New York: Fordham University Press, 1982), 87–118; Diogenes Allen, "Natural Evil and the Love of God," in *The Problem of Evil*, ed. Marilyn McCord Adams and Robert Merrihew Adams (Oxford: Oxford University Press, 1990), 189–208; Richard Swinburne, "Some Major Strands of Theodicy," in *Evidential Argument from Evil*, ed. Daniel Howard-Snyder (Bloomington, IN: Indiana University Press, 1996), 30–48.

115. David Ray Griffin, *Evil Revisited: Responses and Reconsiderations* (Albany, NY: State University Press of New York, 1991), 89–94.

116. Ibid., 92.

117. Davis, "God of Process Theology," 123.

118. Ibid.

that "presenting to creatures purely ideal logical possibilities is a rather sterile kind of persuasive effort."[119] He continues,

> It is not clear that any notion which locates persuasive power in the subliminal, almost subconscious experience of creatures is fully adequate. The standard concept of moral persuasion denotes much more conscious and rational activity than the process concept of subconscious urges, experiential nudges, or lures for feeling. Persuasion is characteristically understood as a process of argumentation in which each party attempts to find premises which the other accepts and which leads to the desired conclusion. Traditionally, the morality of persuasion has been mutual respect for the other's rational dignity and thus not seeking consent on less than reasonable grounds. Ironically, process thinkers, who loudly decry the immorality of coercion, typically describes their rendition of persuasion in terms which do not even sound remotely similar to those of classical moral persuasion.[120]

Peterson's argument is on point. It is doubtful that actual entities, given the Whiteheadian notion of "mentality," especially in lower forms, can discern anything like a rational understanding of what is and is not the best through the initial aims sent by God. What makes up the content of such nudges that God gives to his creatures? Davis is surely correct in saying that we may admire such a being for the hard work of bringing the world to the point where it is. Nevertheless, evil runs rampant within the world and there is no guarantee that it will ever get better. Griffin and other PPT defenders have responded that traditional theists have fallen into the worship of omnipotence. But as Davis rightly points out, it is not that omnipotence is to be worshiped. We might think, here, of an evil omnipotent demon, powerful as it might be, but not worthy of worship. Rather, omnipotence/power is only one of the criteria for saying that some being is worship-worthy.[121] There are many other qualities, as well, such as being morally perfect or eternal, just to name a few.

---

119. Peterson, "God and Evil," 128.

120. Ibid., 128–29.

121. Davis, "God of Process Theology," 124.

Besides not being worship-worthy, it would seem that such a God would also be religiously inadequate. By "religiously inadequate," we mean that the God of PPT is incapable of answering certain kinds of petitions, such as petitions of prayer or deliverance from certain instances of evil. Any God that cannot answer such petitions is religiously inadequate. But I would agree with Davis that there is another way to think of some being as religiously inadequate, namely, that such a being cannot accomplish its own purposes. In other words, if God is to be religiously adequate, then God must be able to bring about God's own purposes and desires. It may be, in the end, that the God of PPT will pull through, but there is no guarantee, which leads us to (3).

On the PPT hypothesis, God has gotten this whole process started, but there is no ultimate assurance that God will bring about his purposes in the end. Despite all of God's efforts to persuade, struggle for, and suffer with the creatures in this world, we are left wondering whether God has the power to ultimately succeed. If God took a great risk in creating the world and in the end does not accomplish his aims, then God would be indictable for the horrendous evils in the world.[122] But even more damaging is that all hope of ultimate resolution is lost.

EVALUATING PROCESS PANENTHEISM

So far, we have considered naturalism and pantheism. How well does process panentheistic thought (PPT) meet each of the criteria?

Let's begin with factual adequacy, logical consistency, and ad hoc-ness. Regarding factual adequacy and logical consistency, I take it that PPT fares better than either naturalism or pantheism in explaining the salient facts of evil. Given something like libertarian freedom, moral evil does not at all seem surprising for PPT. As for logical consistency, process panentheism is less straightforward than naturalism, yet it is generally consistent. Yet, the factual adequacy and logical consistency of PPT depends quite a bit on Whitehead's complex process metaphysics. For PPT, the "many," the "one," and "creativity" are central features of reality, although, as we have suggested throughout, serious difficulties saddle Whitehead's metaphysics. First, the whole of process metaphysics centers on creativity, but, even,

---

122. Ibid., 130–31.

here, there is nothing that underlies or grounds the creativity necessary for the various occasions to take place. If God is not the primary organizing source, then what is? Process thinkers believe that it is creativity, but just what is "creativity"? It is not its own entity, nor does anything ground it; nevertheless, it is behind all the goings-on in reality. This leaves us wondering: From whence does the energy that fuels the universe come? What perpetuates this endless supply of creativity? Many defenders of PPT bite the bullet and accept the principle of creativity as brute fact. If one were to grant it, suggests the process theist, then all else would follow. But this is something that theists will be unwilling to do. Furthermore, much rides on the notion that the fundamental basic unit of reality is the actual occasion or event, instead of substance. Here, too, as I have argued throughout this chapter, there is reason to doubt this particular tenet of process metaphysics.

A second difficulty is that process thinkers must couch good and evil primarily in aesthetic terms rather than moral ones. This goes against how good and evil are usually understood, despite the fact that there may well be all manner of organic connections between the good and the beautiful. But even more so, if aesthetic principles take priority, then a number of moral principles may be violated in order to achieve the aims of those aesthetic principles. Even more damaging, however, is the fact that it seems the sufferings and pains of creatures become a means to an end in order for God to achieve certain aesthetic purposes. Despite these difficulties, taken on its own terms, PPT is logically consistent and better explains some of the features of the universe—more so than either pantheism or naturalism; however, certain features, such as the brute-fact nature of creativity, come across as ad hoc.

When it comes to explanatory power and scope, despite the above difficulties related to process metaphysics, PPT falls prey to some of the same difficulties the other two metaphysical systems face. Defenders of PPT fail to adequately explain the existence of the universe. Like naturalists, process panentheists take it that something has always existed—though the universe, as we know it, has not. More so than pantheism or naturalism, PPT as a metaphysical system provides some explanation for the anthropic principle. God is the motivation behind the universe getting its start and direction, but how the universe has turned out is not entirely up to God.

Yet, why is there a God or nature in the first place? Here, the theist can press the defender of PPT. While there is a sense that in the "primordial pole" God is both "eternal" and "infinite," we cannot, nevertheless, properly call God "necessary" or "eternal" in the same sense that theists can. God, for defenders of PPT, is dependent on a universe for his actualization. It does not have to be this universe; rather, all that is needed is a universe. But not only is God's actualization dependent on a universe, so too is God's existence. God and the world are co-dependent and intricately connected. If there were no world (pre-existing matter and the like before the Big Bang), then we can presume that there would be no God, either. Moreover, when it comes to consciousness, there are some major difficulties with panexperientialism, such as the combination problem. Finally, what of the metaphysics of good and evil and moral responsibility? Defenders of PPT can accommodate quite well for human freedom, given their emphasis on libertarian freedom. While good and evil can be explained within process thought, both are at risk of being redefined to fit within primarily aesthetic categories. This is problematic, however. While doing so does not completely wipe out good and evil in moral terms, the moral categories become subordinate to aesthetic ones, which, as discussed earlier, allows for certain moral principles to be violated, perhaps even vitiated. There are, however, two other problems with PPT, as we saw. God, for process panentheists, is limited, and there is no eschatological payoff. There is no guarantee that evil will ever be thwarted in the end. The problem of evil defeats any hope of ultimate resolution.

Before turning to the criterion of plausibility, there are two additional problems with PPT related to explanatory scope and power. First, the concept of a limited God raises several difficulties. Can such a God really do anything about evil in the world? Perhaps the process panentheist will argue that the God of panentheism can suffer along with his creatures and provide them with the initial aims to direct them toward a more harmonious and intense reality. As discussed, we might commend such a God for the work in thwarting evil and choose to fight along in the good fight, but in the end, would such a God be worship-worthy? It seems not. Furthermore, it is not at all clear how the God of PPT directs the affairs of all the world in sending the initial aims, given that the actual entities are responding to such aims immediately. How does such a God send these aims instantaneously without the kind of omniscience ascribed to the God of theism, particularly some kind of knowledge of the future free acts of the actual entities? This would be required for the creatures to make the right decisions necessary to follow God's aims and purposes. Second, there does not seem to be much of an eschatological payoff for God's creatures if they choose to follow the God of PPT. At most, all of God's creatures' lives are in some sense absorbed into God's experience, remaining a part of God's self-actualization. Some process thinkers are open to the idea of an after-life, but do not press it as a significant part of the PPT view. Thus, while PPT is more plausible of a system for explaining evil than either natural-ism or panentheism, this is necessary but not sufficient to argue that it is plausible in and of itself. It is quite an ingenious system, but quite a few unexplainable features undermine its *ultima facie* plausibility.

Lastly, how livable is process panentheism? Defenders of PPT recog-nize that there is a moral order. The God of PPT sends initial aims to its creatures in hopes that the actual entities will choose the right path which will ultimately lead to higher levels of harmony and greater intensity. But why should any of God's creatures follow suit? Why should these actual entities heed God's initial aim? But even more damaging is that many of these actual entities are incapable of making any kind of rational decision. Such capacities are found only in the higher forms of genuine societies. If these entities rebel against God (if we can even call it that), there is no ultimate justice for their rebellion, despite their response to God's initial aims. Even more troubling is PPT's theodicy. The process theodicy is not strongly eschatological. I would agree with Stephen T. Davis that any the-odical solution to the problem of evil must maintain some kind of refer-ence to the future. In response to the theodicy put forth by Griffin, Davis asks, "Does God have the power, influence, or persuasive ability to make the divine intentions succeed?"[123] If the process understanding of God is correct, then all that we can say is that God's desires might come out in the end. There is, however, no ultimate assurance or guarantee that they will. At best, Davis says, we might say that God is a good being who works hard. We might even sympathize with such a God, joining in the fight to thwart evil. But such a God would not be worthy of worship. Unless God

---

123. Davis, "God of Process Theology," 130.

is able to bring about more good in the world than evil, such a God would be fully indictable.[124] Davis puts it as follows: "God will be something like a mad scientist who creates a monster he hopes will behave but whom he cannot control; if the monster does more evil than good the scientist's decision to create the monster will turn out to have been terribly wrong. The scientist will be indictable."[125]

---

124. Ibid., 130–31.
125. Davis, "God the Mad Scientist," 23.

CHAPTER 5
THEISM—EVIL IN A WORLD CREATED BY GOD

P erhaps the most influential worldview in the history of Western
thought has been theism. Philosophers generally speak of theists in
a "broad sense" and in a "narrow sense." A theist in the broad sense of the
word refers to someone who holds to the belief that some sort of divine
being or reality exists; whereas, a theist in the narrow sense is someone
who places emphasis on certain attributes of a divine being, such as a
being who is an "omnipotent, omniscient, eternal, supremely good being
who created the world."[1] Paul Tillich would be an example of a theist in the
broad sense and Thomas Aquinas would be an example of a theist in the
narrower sense. When speaking of theism in this chapter, we are going to
focus more on the narrower sense of the word.[2]

Here, I take theism to mean that *exactly one God exists who is non-physical,
possesses perfect moral goodness, is omnipotent, omniscient, eternal, and necessary, and is the creator of all things.*[3] Christian theists have often held to a
variety of other attributes, such as, pure actuality, immutability, impassibility, timelessness, simplicity, and omniscience.[4] I will not pursue these
attributes here, unless our discussion requires it, but I will give further

---

1. Rowe, "The Problem of Evil," 1–2.

2. For a fuller discussion on classifying theism, see John S. Feinberg, "Theism," in *The
Evangelical Dictionary of Theology*, 2nd Edition, ed. Walter A. Elwell (Grand Rapids: Baker
Academic, 2001), 1182–83.

3. Layman, "Moral Evil," 5. Here, I follow Layman's understanding of theism closely,
though I will differ in certain respects.

4. Nash, *The Concept of God*, 20.

consideration to some of these in chapter 7. In this chapter I want to stick with as bare a variant of theism (in the narrow sense) as possible since I am not at this point arguing for one specific stripe of theism.

Let's consider each of these definitional points in order. By saying that only one entity exists, I mean that only one God exists, excluding anything like a cosmic dualism of beings or the polytheism of ancient Greek, Roman, Egyptian, or Norse religions. This God does not have a body, nor is the world God's body, as some pantheists and panentheists hold. Further, being a non-physical being, God is in no way constrained by the laws of physics that govern the universe.[5]

When theists say that God is good, they mean that God is perfectly good. God's perfect goodness might be taken in two ways. First, we might understand God's goodness as *wholly* good. By this, theists mean that goodness is such that there are no defects in God's character or God's actions. Taken negatively, God never does any action that could be considered as evil. That God is *necessarily* good is a second way that theists have understood God's perfect goodness. This claim is stronger than the first, in that, it entails that goodness is such a part of God's nature that it would be impossible for God to have any kind of flaw or blemish.[6] In the words of Thomas Morris, "to claim that God is necessarily good is to claim that he is utterly invulnerable to evil."[7]

To say that God is omnipotent is to say that he has maximal power. This does not mean, however, that God can do just anything that he so chooses. Omnipotence is limited by certain logical restrictions. For example, God could not create a square circle or make a married bachelor. Furthermore, when considering the problem from evil, I take it that, if God grants his human creatures something like libertarian freedom, then it is not possible

---

5. Layman, "Moral Evil," 6.

6. Morris, *Our Idea of God*, 48.

7. Ibid. In addition to such predications, some would further suggest that God is the good, in the sense of "is of identity." Robert Adams provides an example of this analysis in his *Finite and Infinite Goods: A Framework for Ethics* (Oxford: Oxford University Press, 1999). On the assumption of divine simplicity, this could be taken to mean either that God himself is the good, or that God's nature is, as these would amount to the same affirmation, despite their conceptual distinctness. A denial of divine simplicity might render these two formulations as more than conceptually distinct.

for God to actualize just any world that he so chooses. Alvin Plantinga defines libertarian freedom as follows:

> If a person is free with respect to a given action, then he is free to perform that action and free to refrain from performing it; no antecedent conditions and/or causal laws determine that he will perform the action, or that he won't. It is within his power, at the time in question, to take or perform the action and within his power to refrain from it.[8]

If something like libertarian freedom is true, then it is solely up to the individual to perform or refrain from some action. If God were to cause some person to do or refrain from an action, then the person would not be free in the libertarian sense. This does not mean that God is incapable of causing someone to do some action—God has the power to do so—but God, in his choosing to create free creatures, has given them certain powers of their own. Now, what God can do, with respect to power, is to create a world, but how that world turns out, if creatures are free in the libertarian sense, is partly up to the creatures. Such a world would be a *weakly* actualized world, as opposed to one that is *strongly* actualized. While it might be logically possible for God *to create* a world in which creatures always did that which is right, it would be logically impossible for God *to cause* such a world to exist, since how the world turns out is partly up to the creature. Furthermore, along the lines of God's power, theists have held that God has maximal knowledge. There are differences of opinion among theists as to whether or not God could know the future free actions of his creatures. I take it that he can, but some theists, particularly openness theists, argue that it is logically impossible for God to know the future free acts of his creatures. For those theists who believe that God knows the future free actions of his creatures, they hold to something like simple foreknowledge or middle knowledge (Molinism).

When theists speak of God as eternal, they mean, minimally, that God has always existed. Some theists have taken God's eternality to mean that God's temporal mode of existence is timelessness, that is to say, God's temporal mode of existence is such that God has no temporal location or

---

8. Plantinga, *God, Freedom, and Evil*, 29.

extension. Generally, the timelessness view goes along with a number of other theses, namely that God is immutable, impassible, and simple. The total combination of such a view is known as eternalism.[9] Other theists have held that God is omnitemporal or everlastingly eternal, that is to say, God is temporal in some sense. Such a view does not mean that God is bound by the four-dimensional space-time universe. Nor does it require God to be in some way limited by the laws of nature.[10] These thinkers believe that God transcends all created time, but is, perhaps, temporal by virtue of being in a causal relationship to the universe.[11] In some ways, this is an in house debate, which I will not take space to discuss here, but will consider further in chapter 7.[12]

As Thomas Morris points out, theists understand necessity in two important ways: necessity *de dicto* and necessity *de re*.[13] Take, for example, the following propositions:

1. Necessarily, God is good.

2. Necessarily, God is omnipotent.

3. Necessarily, God is omniscient.[14]

Each of these propositions are expressions of necessity *de dicto*. There can be no being that counts as God who does not also have such properties as omnipotence, omniscience, and perfect goodness in every world in

---

9. For modern defenders of this view, see Paul Helm, *Eternal God: A Study of God without Time* (New York: Oxford University Press, 1988); Eleonore Stump and Norman Kretzmann, "Eternity," *Journal of Philosophy* 78, no. 8 (1981), 429–58; Brian Leftow, *Time and Eternity* (Ithaca, NY: Cornell University Press, 1991).

10. Some modern representatives of this view include William Lane Craig, *Time and Eternity: Exploring God's Relationship to Time* (Wheaton, IL: Crossway, 2001); Padgett, *God, Eternity, and the Nature of Time*; John Feinberg, *No One Like Him: The Doctrine of God* (Wheaton, IL: Crossway, 2001); Richard Swinburne, *The Coherence of Theism* (Oxford: Oxford University Press, 1986), 210–29.

11. For an excellent discussion on omnitemporality and divine causation, see Garrett J. DeWeese, *God and the Nature of Time* (Burlington, VT: Ashgate Publishing Company, 2004), 239–76.

12. For discussion on the theological costs, see Ronnie P. Campbell, Jr., "The Eternality of the Immutable God in the Thought of Paul Helm" (master's thesis, Liberty University, 2008), 59–83.

13. Morris, *Our Idea of God*, 106.

14. Ibid.

which such a being exists. Each property (i.e., perfect goodness, omnipotence, and omniscience) is a conceptual requirement for deity.[15] We may understand necessity *de re*, on the other hand, by considering the following propositions:

4. God is necessarily good.

5. God is necessarily omnipotent.

6. God is necessarily omniscient.[16]

The above propositions tell us something that is essential about the individual involved. In this case, God is essentially omnipotent, essentially omniscient, and essentially good. The being who in fact is God has such properties in this and all possible worlds.[17] Hence, when we say that some entity *E* has property *P* essentially, we mean that that *E* has *P* in every possible world that *E* exists. In other words, there is no possible world in which *E* exists that *E* does not also have the property *P*. Furthermore, if *E* has *P* essentially, then there are no worlds in which *E* has the complement ~*P*.[18] Here, we must also distinguish essential properties from contingent properties. A contingent property is a property *P* such that an entity might have it in one world but have its complement ~*P* in another. Contingent properties are such that they do not alter the essence of the person in question. There are some possible worlds where I became a barista or a rock star instead of an academic. But becoming a rock star or a barista does not change who I am essentially. There is, however, one additional claim that theists make when speaking of God as necessary. Theists believe that any individual who is God exists in every possible world. There are no possible

15. Ibid.

16. Ibid., 107.

17. Ibid., 106–7.

18. Alvin Plantinga, *The Nature of Necessity* (Oxford: Oxford University Press, 1982), 56. When philosophers speak of "possible worlds," they mean the sum total or compossible collection of states of affairs. There is the actual world—the world as it has turned out—but some worlds are merely possible, that is to say, the states of affairs that make up the actual world could have turned out otherwise than they did. We can imagine some world in which my mother and father never married. The result of such a state of affairs would have consisted of Ronnie Campbell, the person who is now typing this sentence, never existing. Some of the circumstances surrounding such a world would have been completely different from those found in the actual world.

worlds in which God does not or could not exist. It is impossible for God not to exist. This is known as *necessary existence*.[19]

Lastly, theists believe that God is the creator of all things. Unlike process theists, who hold to creation out of pre-existing materials, theists believe that God created all things out of nothing (*ex nihilo*), including the entirety of the four-dimensional space-time universe. By "nothing," theists mean that no prior thing existed other than God. All created entities are contingent and dependent on God for their existence. Furthermore, theists believe that there is a clear ontological distinction between God and creation, which theists call the *Creator/creature* distinction. God is infinite and unlimited whereas creatures are finite and limited. Theists recognize that any being or power that creatures have is given to them by God, who continually upholds and sustains them in their existence. Yet, unlike deists, who hold to a radical transcendence, theists argue that God is both transcendent and immanent. God is transcendent in the sense that God, as the creator of all things, exists apart from and is not in any way dependent on his creatures for his own existence. God is immanent in the sense that he cares for the world, intervenes through miraculous interaction, sustains it in its existence, and is religiously available to his creatures in a variety of capacities.

As with the other three metaphysical systems, there are four areas that test the theistic hypothesis's ability to explain evil: life, consciousness, the metaphysics of good and evil, and human responsibility. To each of these we now turn.

THEISM AND LIFE

If theism is to explain evil in the world, then it must be able to explain life. In order to explain life, theists must explain the existence of the universe. According to the theistic hypothesis, God created the entire space-time universe a finite time ago in the past. In postulating a created universe, theists avoid certain dangers seen in the three other worldviews considered thus far, namely, the brute fact that the universe has always existed. Theists do not run up against the problem of infinite regress, since the universe has a first cause for its existence, who is also a necessary being. Furthermore,

---

19. Morris, *Our Idea of God*, 108; Nash, *The Concept of God*, 107.

the finite existence of the past seems to be confirmed scientifically by Big Bang cosmology, which suggests that the universe exploded into existence a finite time in the past from infinite density. As we saw in chapter 2, in order to counter the conclusions from the Big Bang, some naturalists have postulated something like a multiverse, according to which the universe is just one of an infinite number of universes. I will not rehearse the complications of such a view here. Suffice to say, even if something like the multiverse hypothesis was true, there is still the difficulty of infinite regress that a defender of such a position must consider. But even if we were to find out that, indeed, something like the multiverse is true, there are still resources within the theistic worldview that would allow for such an option without damaging the theistic hypothesis.[20]

But what of the development of life in the universe? Theists have long held that God is the originator of life in the universe. Recently theists have put forth powerful arguments demonstrating the fine-tuning of the universe. Philosopher Robin Collins has suggested evidence for fine-tuning comes from three areas: laws of nature, constants of nature, and initial conditions of the universe. Regarding the laws of nature, Collins argues that if certain laws or governing principles, such as that of gravity, the strong nuclear force, or the electromagnetic force, did not exist, or, at least, if they were not replaced with a similar principle that serves the same function, "complex self-reproducing material systems could not evolve."[21] The same goes with certain constants of physics, such as the constant of gravity, which I considered in chapter 2, and the initial conditions of the universe. If these constants and conditions were slightly different, then the basic structure of the universe would be quite different and life as we know it would not exist. Collins provides the following helpful analogy:

> Imaginatively, one could think of each instance of fine-tuning as a radio dial; unless all the dials are set exactly right, life would be impossible. Or, one could think of the initial conditions of the universe and the fundamental parameters of physics as a dart board

---

20. For a recent defense, see W. David Beck and Max Andrews, "God and the Multiverse: A Thomistic Modal Realism," *Philosophia Christi* 16, no. 1 (2014): 101–15.

21. Robin Collins, "The Teleological Argument," in *The Blackwell Companion to Natural Theology*, ed. William Lane Craig and J. P. Moreland (Oxford: Wiley-Blackwell, 2009), 211.

that fills the whole galaxy, and the conditions necessary for life to exist as a small one-foot wide target: unless the dart hits the target, life would be impossible. The fact that the dials are perfectly set, or that the dart has hit the target, strongly suggests that someone set the dials or aimed the dart, for it seems enormously improbable that such a coincidence could have happened by chance.[22]

The fine-tuning argument, taken with other theistic arguments, such as certain versions of the *cosmological argument*, provide the theist with the resources needed for thinking that the universe is caused and that an intelligent mind is behind the existence of life in it. If other naturalistic hypotheses fail, as I have argued so far, then the theist is on good epistemic grounds for thinking that God designed the universe.

Granted, not everyone will accept this line of reasoning. Perhaps one objection to the theistic hypothesis from naturalists is the "Who designed God?" argument. Such an argument, popularized by Richard Dawkins in *The God Delusion*,[23] is also found among some philosophically astute thinkers, such as J. J. C. Smart. Smart reasons:

> If we postulate God in addition to the created universe we increase the complexity of our hypothesis. We have all the complexity of the universe itself, and we have in addition the at least equal complexity of God. (The designer of an artefact must be at least as complex as the designed artefact.)[24]

According to this line of thinking, postulating a designer does not really solve the issue; rather it moves the apparent design of the universe back one more level. There are, at least, three lines of response the theist can give to this argument.

First, the theists might respond that postulating the designer to be more complex than the design is not, necessarily, obvious. Nevertheless, as Collins suggests, there is something intuitive about the critic's belief, namely that when we see such organized complexity in the world, it

---

22. Collins, "A Scientific Argument," 49–50.

23. Dawkins, *The God Delusion*, 147, 151.

24. J. J. C. Smart, "Laws of Nature and Cosmic Coincidences," *Philosophical Quarterly* 35, no. 140 (1985): 272–80.

generally is produced from systems that also demonstrate such complexity. Collins believes there is a better, second response to the critic's objection. The critic's argument stands only if the design argument in question claims that every instance of organized complexity in the world needs explanation and that the theist suggests that God is the ultimate explanation for such complexity in the world. But not all design arguments require this; rather, all that the design argument needs to show is that the fine-tuning of the universe be more probable given theism than naturalism. In this way, the requirements have been met, says Collins, even if it turns out that God "exhibits tremendous internal complexity."[25] Hence, even if the theist were to grant the critic's point that God is as least as complex as the artifact, the fine-tuning argument would still provide reason to prefer the theistic hypothesis over the naturalistic one.

Third, the critic's challenge based on the complexity of God assumes that God is like the universe, or, at least, the individual things found within the universe, that is to say, that God at some time came into existence. But that is precisely where the critic misunderstands the theistic hypothesis. According to the variety of theism understood here, God is both eternal and necessary. Regarding God's eternality, there was never a point when God came into existence. God was never created nor could God ever be destroyed. Furthermore, as a necessary being, there are no possible worlds in which God does not exist. God instantiates those properties that are essential to him in every possible world. On what basis do theists believe that God is a necessary being in the sense described above?

First, theists arrive at this conclusion based on "perfect being theology" (PBT). According to the medieval philosopher and theologian St. Anselm of Canterbury, God is by definition "that-than-which-a-greater-cannot-be-thought."[26] Most theists take something like Anselm's notion of perfect being as a proper method for thinking about God. Based, then, on PBT, theists recognize that there are many things within the universe that are contingent—things that are fragile, vulnerable, and tenuous in their existence; things that move in and out of existence; and things that could

---

25. Collins, "A Scientific Argument," 59.

26. Anselm, *Proslogium*, 3, in *Anselm of Canterbury: The Major Works*, ed. Brian Davies and G. R. Evans (Oxford: Oxford University Press, 1998), 88.

have been, but never exist. But there is a greater mode of existence imaginable than what we see in contingent things. We can conceive of a being whose existence is such that it never ceases to exist or that it never came into being "from nothing."[27] As Thomas Morris contends, such a being's "anchorage in reality is so great that it is not even possible for the being to have failed to exit."[28] Morris continues, "surely it is only this necessary existence, this firmest possible foothold in reality, which is appropriate for a maximally perfect being."[29]

Second, theists arrive at God's necessary existence through their understanding of creation. If God is conceived of as the creator of and ultimate cause for the existence of all things that are distinct from himself, then it follows that God must be conceived to exist in all possible worlds. If God does have necessary existence, as theists believe, then God is not in any sense cobbled together from various parts.

Some critics have argued against the theistic hypothesis by suggesting that evolution removes the need for a creator. Such an objection is faulty from the start. While I myself am sympathetic to something more akin to Intelligent Design and find evolutionary theory problematic, I do not find such an objection to hold for two reasons.

First, if it turns out that evolution is true, as most naturalists and a growing number of theists hold, there is no contradiction between evolutionary theory and the existence of God. Some theists may argue that while there is a good amount of support for evolution, it is doubtful that one can understand it in any mechanistic manner. It would be more plausible to see it as guided. Further, as we saw in chapter 2, critics of physicalism, such as Thomas Nagel, find it implausible that something such as consciousness could come about through evolutionary processes alone. Other theists may concur with all the scientific conclusions of evolution and yet question whether it could provide any ultimate explanation. Mechanical explanations and design are not, necessarily, at odds. It may be the case,

---

27. Morris, *Our Idea of God*, 108.
28. Ibid.
29. Ibid., 109.

argue such theists, that evolution is the process or mechanism by which God brings about his ultimate purposes for human life.[30]

Second, the theist may respond based on the incompatibility of evolution and naturalism. Both Thomas Nagel and Alvin Plantinga have advanced such arguments. Plantinga, in *Where the Conflict Really Lies*, has argued that there is deep conflict between naturalism and science, and particularly between naturalism and evolution. Plantinga's argument centers on our cognitive faculties—faculties such as memory, perception, *a priori* intuition, and sympathy—and their reliability. Theists believe that our cognitive faculties are reliable since God has made humans in his image and likeness (or something of the like). Naturalists, on the other hand, understand our cognitive faculties as a direct result of coming together by the processes of evolution and natural selection. Given the reliability of our cognitive faculties, which, asks Plantinga, seems more plausible? Evolution, it would seem, at best guarantees that we humans behave a certain way. Evolution, understood by naturalists, promotes such things as survival or reproductive success. Our cognitive faculties, however, are not geared toward producing true beliefs; rather, they are geared toward contributing to the species' survival.[31] On this point, following non-theist Patricia Churchland, Plantinga says,

> What evolution underwrites is only (at most) that our behavior is reasonably adaptive to the circumstances in which our ancestors found themselves; hence it does not guarantee mostly true or verisimilitudinous beliefs. Our beliefs *might* be mostly true or verisimilitudinous... but there is no particular reason to think they *would* be: natural selection is interested, not in truth, but in appropriate behavior.[32]

Naturalistic evolution gives us reason to doubt that: (a) the purpose of our cognitive faculties is to supply humans with true beliefs and (b) that such faculties, do, indeed, supply us on most occasions with true belief. Plantinga continues by arguing that when they are not malfunctioning,

---

30. C. Stephen Evans and R. Zachary Manis, *Philosophy of Religion*, 2nd ed. (Downers Grove, IL: InterVarsity Press, 2009), 82–83.

31. Plantinga, *Where the Conflict Really Lies*, 308–16.

32. Ibid., 316.

we all tend to rely on our cognitive faculties. We all, naturalists and theists alike, tend to go through life assuming that such faculties are reliable and that they produce true beliefs. But why should the naturalist think this? Plantinga believes that the naturalist is "rationally obliged" to give up such an assumption if the naturalist holds to something along the lines of our underlying neurology as being products of adaptive behavior.[33] Plantinga explains:

> And here's the question: what reason is there for supposing that this belief content is *true*? There isn't any. The neurology causes adaptive behavior and also causes or determines belief content: but there is no reason to suppose that the belief content thus determined is true. All that's required for survival and fitness is that the neurology cause adaptive behavior; this neurology also determines belief content, but whether or not that content is *true* makes no difference to fitness.[34]

The whole scientific and naturalistic program rests on the ability to know and understand the world in a rational way. But what basis is there for thinking that the world, as we understand it, is true? Why think that we have a grasp of the basic structure of our world? Why think that the contents of our beliefs are true? Given naturalism, at best, we can be agnostic. Hence lies the conflict between naturalism and evolution. If such is the case, as Plantinga has argued, given the reliability of our cognitive faculties and their ability to lead us to true belief, evolution would seem more probable given theism than naturalism.

If, as theists argue, the universe has an ultimate cause and design behind it, and if God serves as a suitable candidate for such an ultimate cause and design, then, it would seem, there is good reason to suppose life given theism. But what of consciousness?

THEISM AND CONSCIOUSNESS

If theism is to explain evil, it must also be able to explain consciousness, given that much of the evil that we see in the world does not result merely

---

33. Ibid., 316–28.
34. Ibid., 328.

from pain but also from suffering, which requires one's ability to reflect on one's pain. Theists believe that consciousness is the result of something like the Judeo-Christian view that God created humans in his image and likeness. I am not saying that every form of theism will hold to this view; rather, that various theisms may hold to something similar to this view, especially certain Christian, Jewish, and Muslim theistic views. The *imago dei*, as Christian theists call it, suggests that God has endowed his human creatures with certain capacities to perform acts, to be intentional, to have beliefs, and to be relational. In order to function in such a way, such creatures would require something like consciousness—an ability to not only understand themselves and their environment but also to reflect on, ponder, and respond to it in such a way that goes beyond a mere instinctual kind of response. So far, so good. Something like consciousness might be expected given theism. But the theistic view of consciousness is not without its own problems, especially when considering the mind/body problem.

As we have seen, the mind/body problem is something that each worldview must work through. This is true of theism as well. With respect to human nature on the mind/body problem, theists hold to a number of different views. Most theists fall into one of two categories: physicalism or some form of dualism. In chapter 2 I argued against physicalism. It is my contention that theistic physicalism is susceptible to some of the same dangers that naturalistic versions face. I will not revisit physicalism here. Rather, I will focus on dualism as a viable option for explaining consciousness, which is, at any rate, the more common position among theists.

When considering dualism, there is more than one variety. There is substance dualism as well as emergent dualism. Among substance dualisms, there is the Cartesian variety as well as the Thomistic sort. Cartesian dualists focus on the mind as distinct from the body, which is an externally related entity that is causally related to the body. Thomistic dualism takes it that the mind is a function of the soul. The soul serves as the primary integrating feature of the person, by which it has certain capacities for both biological and mental functioning.[35] In what follows, I will not discuss each kind and variety of dualism. All that the theist needs to show is that

---

35. J. P. Moreland and Scott B. Rae, *Body and Soul: Human Nature and the Crisis in Ethics* (Downers Grove, IL: InterVarsity Press, 2000), 21.

at least one variety of dualism explains consciousness. My focus here is not to argue for one specific form of dualism; rather, I will only put forth a general argument for mind/body dualism.

What do theists mean when they speak of dualism? If theists believe that there is an ontological distinction between God and the rest of creation, then, at minimum theists are dualists of sorts. God is considered by theists to be something like an unembodied, uncreated mind or entity, without any physical body. With respect to human nature, and perhaps the natures of some animals too, dualists recognize that there is some entity that is distinct from the body or brain. Property-event dualists believe that there is a significant distinction between mental properties and physical properties. Mental events such as thoughts, sensations, beliefs, or desires are all distinct from brain states or events. Substance dualists take this further and recognize that what one calls the "soul," "self," "I," or the "mind" is a distinct entity from the body.[36] Substance dualists, suggest J. P. Moreland and Scott Rae, are committed at minimum "to the claim that the soul is an immaterial entity that could, in principle, survive death and ground personal identity in the afterlife."[37]

There is, yet, one more important distinction that substance dualists make—a distinction between *functional holism* and *ontological holism*. Functional holism recognizes (1) that the soul is in some sense in the body; (2) that the body and soul function as a unity that is both complex and deeply integrated; and (3) that the soul can exist without the body and survive death. Functional holism can work with either Cartesian or Thomistic dualisms. Ontological holism, on the other hand, suggests that the body and soul are so tightly integrated that the soul depends on the body, and when it dies, so, too, does the soul. Disembodiment is impossible. In this case, ontological holism is consistent with property-event dualism, but not with Cartesian or Thomistic versions.[38] I take something like functional holism to be the case, as I will argue below.

What evidence, then, is there for thinking that something like dualism is true? There are, at least, three lines of evidence for thinking that dualism

---

36. Ibid., 20.
37. Ibid.
38. Ibid., 21.

is true: (1) the paradigm-case argument; (2) the near-death experiences (NDEs) and post-death visions argument; and (3) the unity-of-conscious-ness argument. Let us take each one of these arguments in order.

In their book *Body and Soul*, J. P. Moreland and Scott Rae introduce what I will call the "paradigm-case argument." According to this argument, God (and perhaps angels) are paradigm-case persons. Their argument goes as follows:

> If God and, perhaps, angels are paradigm-case persons and since they are immaterial spirits, then it is at least consistent that some-thing be both a person and an immaterial spirit. But more than this, if the paradigm-case persons are immaterial spirits, then this pro-vides justification for the claim that anything is a person if and only if it bears a relevant similarity to the paradigm cases. Arguably, the relevant similarity between other (kinds of) persons and the par-adigm cases is grounded in something all persons have in common and that constitutes that which makes the paradigm cases to be persons in the first place, namely, personhood. Personhood is con-stituted by a set of ultimate capacities of thought, belief, sensation, emotion, volition, desire, intentionality and so forth.[39]

What benefit is there to such an argument? It at least shows that the concept of an unembodied soul is not unreasonable given theism. After all, the chief exemplar of such a notion of person is God, whom theists believe to be something like an unembodied mind. But such a view is not without its critics. Some theistic physicalists will want to argue that per-sonhood is not so much a nature as it is a function of a complex organism realized by the individual. The defender of dualism will answer such a charge by arguing that God is often understood as thinking, feeling, acting, and the like, and that such are descriptions of attributes of God and not some functional states that are in some way external to him. But there is a second reply. As Moreland and Rae put it, "if various mental states are really functional states whose description is neutral to whether the entity realizing that state is a spirit or a brain, then just exactly what is

---

39. Ibid., 25.

the content of 'spirit' when we say that God is a spirit?"[40] This seems to be an issue that theistic physicalists will have difficulty answering if they are adamant about functionalism.

The second line of evidence for dualism comes from the overwhelming data on near-death experiences (NDEs) and post-death visions.[41] For now, I will only be able to cover, briefly, NDEs, though there are some compelling data on post-death visions.[42]

People reporting NDEs generally provide several similar experiences, such as leaving, floating above, and seeing their lifeless bodies. Such experiences are called out-of-body experiences (OBEs). Others claim to have been met by an angel or some other kind of heavenly being, to have encountered a barrier of sorts or a bright light, or to have met deceased loved ones.[43] While not the norm, there have also been some "hellish" cases.[44]

Many NDE reports, while they may be true for all we know (and thus epistemically possible), are not the kinds of experiences that can be empirically verified, and thus they provide little to no import as an explanation for, or reason to believe, the idea that there is such a thing as a soul or an afterlife. After all, as some skeptics claim, many who report NDEs generally interpret their experiences in such a way as to fit their specific cultural and religious biases—for example, Christians claim to have met Jesus or

---

40. Ibid., 26.

41. I came across the term "post-death visions" from Gary Habermas through personal correspondence.

42. For discussions on methodology and veridical cases of post-death visions, see C. D. Broad, "Phantasms of the Living and of the Dead," *Proceedings of the Society for Psychical Research* 50, no. 183 (1953): 51–67; Hilary Evans, *Seeing Ghosts: Experiences of the Paranormal* (London: John Murray, 2002); Erlendur Haraldsson, "Alleged Encounters with the Dead: The Importance of Violent Death in 337 Cases," *Journal of Parapsychology* 73, no. 1 (2009): 91–118; Haraldsson, "Survey of Claimed Encounters with the Dead," *Omega* 19, no. 2 (1988–89): 103–13; Haraldsson, "The Iyengar-kirti Case: An Apparitional Case of the Bystander Type," *Journal of the Society for Psychical Research* 54, no. 806 (1987): 64–67; Ian Stevenson, "The Contribution of Apparitions to the Evidence for Survival," *Journal of the American Society for Psychical Research* 76 (1982): 341–58; Bryan J. Williams, Review of *Phantasms of the Living* (2 Vols) by Edmund Gurney, Fredric W. H. Myers, and Frand Podmore, *Journal of Scientific Explorations* 25, no. 2 (2011): 367–424.

43. For a description of such events, see Raymond A. Moody Jr., *Life after Life* (Harrisburg, PA: StackPole Books, 1976), 19–103.

44. Michael Sabom, *Light and Death: One Doctor's Fascinating Account of Near-Death Experiences* (Grand Rapids: Zondervan, 1998), 165–73.

an angel while Hindus report seeing their deities and so on.[45] According to skeptic, Michael Marsh, NDE researchers need to be more critical of reports given that "NDE accounts are non-identical, non-uniform, and hence personally idiosyncratic."[46] Other skeptics claim that such experiences are nothing more than the firings of synapses in the brain gone wrong or that the persons having said experiences are, in reality, hallucinating.[47]

While the majority are non-evidential, there are a number of such accounts that are veridical[48] and provide empirical evidence for the existence of the soul and an afterlife. But what kind of evidence counts? According to Terence Nichols, there are four lines of evidence that support the genuineness of some NDE accounts: (1) people are capable of describing events that they could not have known beforehand or otherwise; (2) people report meeting dead loved ones or people not previously known to have died; (3) people experienced a change in life perspective as a result of the NDE; and (4) the overall weight of the vast amount of testimony that transcends gender, age, class, and ethnicity, all of which goes beyond that which can be explained by materialist explanations.[49] For our purposes, I will only examine the first kind of evidence.[50]

---

45. Peterson et al., *Reason and Religious Belief*, 232; Michael N. Marsh, "The Phenomenology of the Near-Death Experience (NDE): An Encounter with Eternity—or Simply an Aberrant Brain State?" *Modern Believing* 52, no. 2 (2011): 41–42. See also Moushumi Purkayastha and Kanchan Kumar Mukherjee, "Three Cases of Near Death Experience: Is it Physiology, Physics or Philosophy?" *Annals of Neurosciences* 19, no. 3 (2013): 104–6.

46. Marsh, "Phenomenology of the Near-Death Experience," 41.

47. Skeptic Michael Shermer argues that new evidence supports the belief that NDEs are nothing more than a product of our brains. According to Shermer, neurologist Michael Persinger of Laurentian University in Sudbury, Canada, can induce NDEs by subjecting a person's temporal lobes to varying patterns of magnetic fields. Having subjected himself to Persinger's tests, Shermer claims to have had "a mild out-of-body experience." Michael Shermer, "The Great Afterlife Debate: Michael Shermer v. Deepak Chopra," *Skeptic* 13, no. 4, 2008, 53. See also Peterson et al., *Reasons and Religious Belief*, 231.

48. According to IANDS (International Association for Near Death Studies), "veridical near-death experiences are NDEs in which people reportedly out-of-body have observed events or gathered information that was verified by others upon the experiencer's return to a conscious state." See IANDS: International Association for Near Death Studies, Inc., "Key Facts About Near-Death Experiences," NDEs, last updated August 29, 2017, accessed January 28, 2019, https://iands.org/ndes/about-ndes/key-nde-facts21.html?start=2.

49. Terence Nichols, *Death and Afterlife: A Theological Introduction* (Grand Rapids: Brazos, 2010), 110.

50. Though there is substantive weight on the other three kinds of evidence. For the second type of evidence, see Bruce Greyson, "Seeing Dead People Not Known to Have Died: 'Peak in Darien' Experiences," *Anthropology and Humanism* 35, no. 2 (2010): 159–71; Glynn, *God:*

With respect to the first type of evidence, a variety of collaborative accounts can be adduced.[51] Cardiologist Pim van Lommel provides a veridical account of a man in his forties, who, when he arrived at the hospital, was comatose. The coronary-care-unit nurse on duty reported taking the man's dentures out of his mouth and placing them on a crash cart in order to intubate the patient. Upon seeing the nurse a week later, the man responded to her, "Oh, that nurse knows where my dentures are."[52] He proceeded to tell her, "Yes, you were there when I was brought into the hospital and you took my dentures out of my mouth and put them onto the cart, it had all these bottles on it and there was this sliding drawer underneath and there you put my teeth."[53] From the nurse's perspective, she "remembered this happening while the man was in deep coma and in the process of CPR."[54] After questioning the man further, she reported, "it appeared the man had seen himself lying in the bed, that he had perceived from above how nurses and doctors had been busy with CPR. He was also able to describe correctly and in detail the small room in which he had been resuscitated as well as the appearance of those present like myself."[55]

One NDE that was significantly evidential involves a woman named Pam, who had a brain aneurysm, and who had to have two extraordinary medical procedures back-to-back. During the second procedure, nicknamed "standstill," her body was cooled to 60 degrees and the blood was drained from her head. At this time, her heart was stopped and she had no

---

The Evidence, 117. For the third and fourth types of evidence, see Melvin Morse and Paul Perry, Transformed by the Light: The Powerful Effect of Near-Death Experiences on People's Lives (New York: Villard Books, 1992); Jeffery Long and Paul Perry, Evidence of the Afterlife: The Science of Near-Death Experiences (New York: HarperCollins, 2010), chapters 9–11; Bruce Greyson, "Near-Death Experiences and Spirituality," Zygon 41, no. 2 (2006): 393–414. There have also been cases where people who were born blind have had NDEs and were able to explain visual phenomena that would otherwise be impossible for those who have never had visual experiences before (see Long and Perry, Evidence of the Afterlife, 85).

51. For a variety of cases and extended discussion, see Gary R. Habermas and J. P. Moreland, Beyond Death: Exploring the Evidence for Immortality (1998; repr., Eugene, OR: Wipf & Stock, 2004), 155–72. See also Moody, Life after Life, 94–95.

52. Pim van Lommel, Ruud van Wees, Vincent Meyers, and Ingrid Elfferich, "Near-Death Experience in Survivors of Cardiac Arrest: A Prospective Study in the Netherlands," The Lancet 358 (December 15, 2001): 2041.

53. Ibid.

54. Ibid.

55. Ibid.

brain waves.[56] According to cardiologist Michael Sabom, three clinical tests are administered to determine whether a person experiences brain death. He explains that, "her electroencephalogram was silent, her brain-stem response was absent, and no blood flowed through her brain."[57] Pam had met all three criteria. Sabom, who lays out the medical procedure in detail, reports that Pam, claiming to have had an out-of-body experience, was able to describe the events of her operation, providing specific details, such as the odd shape of the bone saw used on her head and certain conversations had by the medical team. Her descriptions were then corroborated by the medical records from the operation.[58] One interesting aspect of Pam's story is that, while she was not brain-dead at the time of her OBE (though she would be during the second procedure, during which she continued with her NDE), it seems implausible that she could see or hear anything, since her eyes were taped shut and her ears had speakers in them giving clicking sounds, which measured her brainstem activity.[59]

The cases given here only scratch the surface of the many NDEs reported throughout the world. But some question whether these NDEs really do occur or whether there is some naturalistic explanation for NDE phenomena. Though critics have put forth a number of naturalistic explanations, two are prominent: hallucinations and anoxia.[60] Problems attend each of these. Regarding hallucinations, there are some reported cases of people who have had NDEs and who have also experienced drug-induced hallucinations. In such cases, though, serious differences obtained between the two accounts. Further, those who have had hallucinations report that after the fact it was clear that they were experiencing hallucinations. That is not the case with NDEs. Generally, unlike hallucinations, the NDEs are ordered and reality is not distorted, as is often the case with hallucinations. One other significant fact is that when people experience hallucinations, there is no overall life change. But the opposite is the case with respect to

---

56. Sabom, *Light and Death*, 37.

57. Ibid., 49.

58. Ibid., 37–47.

59. Cheryl Fracasso and Harris Friedman, "Near-Death Experiences and the Possibility of Disembodied Consciousness: Challenges to Prevailing Neurobiological and Psychosocial Theories," *NeuroQuantology* 9, no. 1 (2011): 48.

60. For a response to various naturalistic hypotheses, see Glynn, *God: The Evidence*, 120–28.

NDEs. Those who have had an NDE generally report a life change and a significant change in their beliefs and spirituality. But the real difficulty with claiming that NDEs are hallucinations is that hallucinations do not account for those parts of the NDE that can be verified empirically, such as those considered in the two cases mentioned above.[61] But what about anoxia?

Anoxia is a condition that happens when the brain is starved of oxygen, a condition often seen in fighter pilots and mountain climbers. Those who experience anoxia often experience confusion and distortion in their mental processes. The problem with chalking NDEs up to certain physiological explanations, such as anoxia, is that in many of the anoxia cases there is no coherence to a person's thoughts. But that is not what we see with respect to NDEs. Often NDE experiences are crisp and clear, containing vivid details of all that was experienced. The British neuropsychiatrist, Peter Fenwick, has this to say about NDEs and anoxia:

> As the brain becomes anoxic it ceases to function. It becomes disrupted and disorganized, so that you become gradually confused, disoriented, your perception fragments and finally you become unconscious. You do not think clearly, you don't have insights, you don't have clear, coherent visions.... [I]f anoxia is to be the major cause of NDEs we have to postulate a series of very unlikely events. The brain has to be able to synthesize a complex internal world and to be able to remember it, despite a lack of oxygen which is so profound that brain function is widely disrupted so that consciousness is lost.[62]

Lastly, as with hallucinations, anoxia does not account for the kind of veridical experiences shown above.

If acceptable, then, certain phenomena such as NDEs and post-death visions provide veridical evidence not only for the existence of something like the soul, which exists apart from the body, but also for an afterlife. Here, we would concur with Andrew J. Dell'Olio, when speaking of the empirical nature of near-death experiences, "naturalistic materialists, if

---

61. Ibid., 123–24.

62. Peter Fenwick and Elizabeth Fenwick, *The Truth in the Light* (New York: Berkeley, 1995), 214, quoted in Glynn, *God: The Evidence*, 121.

they are to be true to their empiricist heritage, must ... take seriously the phenomenology of experience and its impact on the formation and justification of belief."[63] Having examined such empirical arguments, now we shall turn to our third and last argument for the soul—the unity-of-consciousness argument.

Something like the unity-of-consciousness argument was first put forth by Gottfried Leibniz, but a modern defender of such an argument is William Hasker.[64] Hasker's own view on the mind/body problem is called "emergent dualism." Whether Hasker's emergent dualism fails or succeeds is up for grabs, but the unity-of-consciousness argument is a powerful argument against the physicalist view on consciousness.

The chief difficulty that the materialist or physicalist must face is twofold. On the one hand, the problem lies in the complexity of the physical equipment—that is to say, the brain to physicalism seems to be something like a machine, computer, or the sort, made up of a variety of distinct parts. Yet, on the other hand, it is not at all clear how a unified, complex, conscious experience can be distributed to any one location of the brain or to be distributed among the various parts of such a complex entity. Here, Hasker argues, if we were to take an aspect of our conscious experience, say, our visual field, the information that it yields cannot be contained in something like one single transistor or neuron. Here, the materialist may want to suggest that such a state is broken up into various parts of the brain. Suppose this is the case. The question still remains: *"who or what is aware of the conscious state as a whole?"*[65] Hasker believes that the answer to such a question is obvious: it is the person who is aware of her "conscious state, at any given moment, as a unitary whole."[66] But this leads to a second question for the materialist: "When I am aware of a complex conscious state, what *physical entity* is it that is aware of the state?"[67] Hasker believes that the materialist cannot provide a plausible answer.

---

63. Andrew J. Dell'Olio, "Do Near-Death Experiences Provide a Rational Basis for Belief in Life After Death?" *Sophia* 10 (2010): 115.

64. Hasker first put forth this argument in *The Emergent Self*, 122–46, but later redeveloped it in his article, "Persons and the Unity of Consciousness," in *The Waning of Materialism*, ed. Robert C. Koons and George Bealer (Oxford: Oxford University Press, 2010): 175–90.

65. Hasker, "Persons and the Unity of Consciousness," 181–82.

66. Ibid., 182.

67. Ibid.

The unity-of-consciousness argument, formally stated, is as follows:

1. I am aware of my present visual field as a unity; in other words, the various components of the field are experienced by a single subject simultaneously.

2. Only something that functions as a whole rather than a system of parts could experience a visual field as unity.

3. Therefore, the subject functions as a whole rather than a system of parts.

4. The brain and nervous system, and the entire body, is nothing more than a collection of physical parts organized in a certain way. (In other words, holism is false.)

5. Therefore, the brain and nervous system cannot function as a whole; it must function as a system of parts.

6. Therefore, the subject is not the brain and nervous system (or the body, etc.).

7. If the subject is not the brain and nervous system then it is (or contains as a proper part) a non-physical mind or "soul"; that is, a mind that is not ontologically reducible to the sorts of entities studied in the physical sciences. Such a mind, even if it is extended in space, could function as a whole rather than as a system of parts and so could be aware of my present visual field as a unity.

8. Therefore, the subject is a soul, or contains a soul as a part of itself.[68]

The argument is valid, and I would agree with Hasker that if the materialist were to deny any of the premises, setting aside the notion of the soul in (7), it would be (4). Hasker believes that the materialist, by denying (4), is forced to accept something like holism—but such is not without its own difficulties.

---

68. Ibid., 182.

One potential objection to the unity-of-conscious argument comes from reflection on neurological disunity brought about by commissurotomy and multiple personality disorder. Commissurotomy was once a procedure performed on people who suffered from severe forms of epilepsy, whereby the thick network of connective nerve tissue between the right and left hemispheres of the brain was severed. While such a procedure proved to help with the symptoms of severe cases of epilepsy, it also caused the patients who had the procedure to have a breakdown in communication between the two hemispheres of the brain. At times, it seems as though each hemisphere of the brain was doing its own thing apart from the other, especially when the subject was asked to do a unique or novel task. But, perhaps, more damaging to the notion of a single-unified consciousness is the evidence from multiple personality disorder cases. Those who suffer from multiple personality disorder often display what seem to be two distinct conscious personalities with memories and beliefs of their own.[69] Would such cases, then, count against Hasker's argument? It would seem not. Hasker's argument is more modest in nature. All that he is arguing for is that (1) the various parts of the brain, brain stem, etc. cannot account for the unitary experience of consciousness; and (2) the kind of unity in question is a "modest" kind of unity, "consisting merely in the fact that one has at a given moment a phenomenal field (visual and/or auditory and/or tactual and/or …) which comprises a large amount and variety of data."[70]

If the above arguments are successful, then we have good reason to think that there is something like the soul. If we have a soul, and having a soul is deeply consistent with theism (which seems to be the case), then we have good reasons for thinking that theism succeeds in explaining consciousness. But what of our last categories, the metaphysics of good and evil and human responsibility?

THEISM, GOOD, EVIL, AND RESPONSIBILITY

How surprising is evil given theism? As you might recall, there are two basic kinds of evil, moral evil and natural evil. I will consider each below, along with some attention to the nature of gratuitous evil.

---

69. Ibid., 176–82.
70. Ibid., 183.

Moral evil does not at all seem surprising given theism, especially if God has brought about human creatures who have the capacity to freely perform certain actions. As C. Stephen Layman rightly notes, the ability to love God and neighbor freely, as opposed to some automaton, which is programmed always to do the right thing, is a much higher good.[71] If such choices were not up to the agent, then they would seem emptied of all significance. Therefore, we would expect God, if he were a morally perfect being, to create creatures with such a capacity to choose to love or to do otherwise. Furthermore, on theism, we would expect God to create human creatures with certain desires and the ability to reason and the sort, much like, as noted earlier, we see in the *imago dei*. Many of the moral evils that occur in the world result from an agent's wrongly desiring certain things. Layman provides several examples of this. There is nothing bad per se in a person desiring to eat food for nourishment and enjoyment; however, the evil may come about when the person desires to hoard the food, keeping others from having what they need for nourishment. Again, the desire to control others is not always a bad thing. We want leaders who are capable of leading us in the right way, and sometimes that may require a certain amount of control, but the desire to control others when it is not best for the common good or the individuals controlled can also happen, and too often does.[72]

Now a skeptic might respond by asking whether there might not be instances of wrongdoing without any kind of suffering—such as a person hoarding all the scarce food and God supplying more food so that those in need do not go hungry. Layman thinks that such is logically possible, but I would agree with him that the significance of our choices is intricately and organically connected to the consequences that ensue. On this point Layman argues:

> If we can never benefit or harm others (or reasonably expect to do so), then we haven't been given a significant degree of freedom or responsibility. Furthermore, if our actions never caused harm and suffering, we would surely fail to understand the seriousness of evil. Now, it might be replied that my choices will be significant

71. Layman, "Moral Evil," 10.
72. Ibid.

provided I *believe* I can benefit or harm, even if the basis is false. And I will surely be apt to see the evil I do as egregious if I *believe* it causes others to suffer, even if it really doesn't cause any suffering at all. However, if we believe we can benefit and harm others, when in fact we cannot, then we are systematically deceived about something extremely important and fundamental to our lives, and such massive deception would itself be an evil; hence it is plausible to suppose that a perfectly good God would not set up a world involving such deception.[73]

Deception is often thought of as a kind of moral evil in itself. If God were morally perfect and good, then to set up a world with such mass deception would itself be a great evil. God, in turn, would participate in evil. If God is morally perfect, as theists believe, he could not bring about such a world.

How are theists to respond to the total amount of moral evil and wrongdoing in the world, especially the intensity of certain kinds of evils, which we call horrendous or gratuitous evils? For example, in his article, "The Problem of Evil and Some Varieties of Atheism," William Rowe makes the following argument:

1. There exist instances of intense suffering which an omnipotent omniscient being could have prevented without thereby losing some greater good or permitting some evil equally bad or worse.

2. An omniscient, wholly good being would prevent the occurrence of any intense suffering it could, unless it could not do so without thereby losing some greater good or permitting some evil equally bad or worse.

3. There does not exist an omnipotent, omniscient, wholly good being.[74]

---

73. Ibid., 11.

74. William Rowe, "The Problem of Evil and Some Varieties of Atheism," in *The Evidential Argument from Evil*, ed. Daniel Howard-Snyder (Bloomington, IN: Indiana University Press, 1996), 1–11.

Rowe's argument is a powerful one, and one that theists should not take too lightly. One way of responding to Rowe is by way of skeptical theism.[75] William Alston and Stephen Wykstra, along with a number of other skeptical theists, argue that it is impossible for us to know, given our finite natures and limited cognitive faculties, the reasons that God might have for allowing certain seemingly gratuitous evils. Hence there are no so-called gratuitous (unnecessary) evils in the world. Given our limited cognitive faculties, it is impossible to know what reasons God might have for allowing certain evils in the world.[76] Here I would agree with a number of other theists that it would be unwise to think that every form of evil has a corresponding greater good that is to come about as a result of God's allowing them.[77] Again, I think Layman's insight is correct in thinking that the moral harm and suffering that we humans can inflict is connected intricately to the significance of our choices. He thinks that it is better to consider such instantiations of wickedness as "collateral effects." He suggests that they are "*consequences* of divine creative activity rather than necessary means to divine ends."[78]

One of the chief reasons that theists gravitate toward greater-good type arguments generally has to do with a certain understanding of God's sovereignty. They take it that if such things as gratuitous evils exist, then God is in some sense not sovereign or in control. According to such an understanding of sovereignty, everything that occurs must have a purpose, including evil. But the question theists must ask centers on whether such

---

75. For examples see William Alston, "The Inductive Argument from Evil and the Human Cognitive Condition," in *The Evidential Argument from Evil*, ed. Daniel Howard-Snyder (Bloomington, IN: Indiana University Press, 1996), 97–125; Stephen J. Wykstra, "The Humean Obstacle to Evidential Arguments from Suffering: On Avoiding the Evils of 'Appearance,'" in *The Problem of Evil*, ed. Marilyn McCord Adams and Robert Merrihew Adams (Oxford: Oxford University Press, 1990), 138–60.

76. I will not be able to address Rowe's argument in full in this chapter. But given that I allow for the possibility of gratuitous evils, as will be argued, thereby rejecting Rowe's second point, it would seem that Rowe's argument loses its bite.

77. For theists who hold to this position, see Layman, "Moral Evil," 11; Kirk MacGregor, "The Existence and Irrelevance of Gratuitous Evil," *Philosophia Christi* 14, no. 1 (2012): 165–80; Hasker, *Triumph of God*, 183–98; Bruce A. Little, *A Creation-Order Theodicy: God and Gratuitous Evil* (Lanham, MD: University Press of America, 2005), 99–127; Little, *God, Why This Evil?* (Lanham, MD: Hamilton Books, 2010), 58–79; Ronald H. Nash, *Faith and Reason: Searching for a Rational Faith* (Grand Rapids: Zondervan, 1988), 216–21.

78. Layman, "Moral Evil," 11.

an understanding of God's sovereignty is required or is the best understanding. Must God cause or, at least, allow such evils in the world in order to bring about corresponding greater goods? I think not. The problem with such an understanding leads to a concept of God that is consequentialist in nature when dealing with his creatures. Bruce Little brings this point out clearly:

> Does it necessarily mean that if something happens on this earth without a divine purpose, this somehow strikes at the truth of God's sovereignty? It seems to me that the answer is *No*; to maintain otherwise leads to questionable ends. For example, say a person commits adultery; is it gratuitous evil or is it an evil that God in His sovereignty planned? The plan would have had to be from before creation or at the moment of creation. The end is that God planned for a person to commit adultery, the very thing that God says is sin. God becomes the author of sin. Furthermore, the adultery was planned to bring about a good (under the G-G [greater-good] theodicy), so now sin brings about good and it could be argued that more sin would bring about more good.[79]

In a similar vein, Kirk MacGregor argues that theists who hold to greater-good type arguments are faced with a dilemma. Either evil is necessary for God to bring about some greater good, or it is morally unnecessary. To claim the former goes against divine omnibenevolence—that is to say, to claim that evil is necessary in order for God to bring about greater goods is to say that "God operates according to the principle that the ends justify the means," which, again, goes against a concept of God who is morally perfect and essentially good.[80] But greater-good responses, says MacGregor, would also count against divine omnipotence. It would seem that such an acceptance would lead to the unwanted result that if there are certain goods that can only come about through God's allowance of evils, then there would exist certain "logically possible tasks that God could not perform—namely,

---

79. Little, *God, Why This Evil*, 62.
80. MacGregor, "Existence and Irrelevance," 169.

bringing about various goods in the absence of evils."[81] Such an argument, believes MacGregor, leads to an indirect argument for gratuitous evils.

But there is, I take it, another reason for thinking that something like gratuitous evils exist given significant moral freedom—that God wants for his human creatures to be morally responsible beings. William Hasker calls this the "*principle of divine moral intention*," which he states as follows:

> It is an extremely important part of God's intention for human persons that they should place a high priority on fulfilling moral obligations and should assume major responsibility for the welfare of their fellow humans.[82]

Such a principle, argues Hasker, stands in contradistinction to the idea of God permitting certain evils in order to bring about some greater good or to prevent some greater evil. To think that God is running the world in such a way as to allow certain evils in order to bring about a greater good results in another principle he calls the "offsetting good principle." The principle is stated as follows:

> Any harm resulting from a morally wrong action will be offset by a "greater good" that God could not have obtained without permitting the evil in question.[83]

Hasker believes that if things are really like what the second principle entails, then it would have a serious effect on our motivation to live morally good lives and to take responsibility for the well-being of others. But more than moral motivation, there is a sense in which the two principles are contradictory. Take the following argument:

1. If God prevents all evils that he could without thereby losing some greater good or by bringing about some greater evil, then no gratuitous evils exist.

2. God commands humans to thwart evil.

---

81. Ibid.
82. Hasker, *Triumph of God*, 191.
83. Ibid., 192.

3. If God commands humans to thwart evil, and if no gratuitous evils exist, then God commands humans to thwart those evils which are necessary for bringing about some greater good or for preventing some greater evil.

4. If God commands humans to thwart evils that are necessary for bringing about some greater good or stopping some greater evil, then God is requiring humans to do something that works against the maximal good.

5. To require humans to work against that which brings about maximal good is logically impossible for a morally perfect being to do.

6. Therefore, there exist gratuitous evils.[84]

It seems that God's command to thwart evil runs up against his work in bringing about the maximal good. Our actions really matter and there is a steep responsibility for humans to care for one another. Perhaps, it would be in the theist's interest to give up such greater-good type arguments and rather to recognize that such evils are a part of a world in which humans are given significant moral responsibility and freedom.

Another possible response by the skeptic is to suggest we could still have as much meaning and significance in the world that we do without also having certain types of evils, such as genocide or rape. There is no doubt that there are certain evils, such as the Holocaust, that the world would have been better without (an admission that, by some definitions, again affirms there are gratuitous evils). But the problem with such objections as this one is that if there were no evils such as genocide or rape, then the critic might always find other evils, such as murder, that might come under scrutiny. And when murder is in question, the critic may propose another evil, and this could go on *ad infinitum*. But as Layman suggests, it may be that some people will be perfectly satisfied with a world in which the consequences of our actions would be trivial. Such a world, though it might have its attractions for having fewer risks, would, nevertheless,

---

84. This argument is an adaptation of Kirk MacGregor's argument in "Existence and Irrelevance," 172.

"pale in significance to the world we find ourselves in," says Layman.[85] Nevertheless, such a world does not seem surprising given theism, at least not upon serious and sober reflection. Though our world, as it is, contains many risks, it also contains an abundance of meaning. Our actions really do count. Furthermore, when we demand a world other than the one that has obtained, we are, perhaps unwittingly, wishing for a world with much less significance than our current world now possesses.[86]

In addition to the amount and kinds of moral evils in the world, at least two additional issues merit consideration: (1) what is the basis of morality; and (2) how are theists to understand God's commands? Let us begin with the grounding of morality. What, then, is the basis for good and evil according to theism? Many theists believe that God not only does that which is good and that he always acts justly, but that God is, in God's very nature, something akin to the Platonic notion of "the Good."[87] God in the theistic sense, however, differs in two quite different ways. God is, as Robert Adams suggests, "a concrete individual."[88] God is essentially a person or essentially personal in some significant way. Second, God, as the Good, is not some abstract object; rather, he is a "real being."[89] When theists say that God is "the Good," they do not mean that God, by being the Good, encompasses just anything that a person takes in common language as "good." Rather, Adams, throughout his work, *Finite and Infinite Goods*, couches the notion of *good* in terms of something more along the lines of *excellence*.[90] It is God himself as the Good that grounds any finite goods that

85. Layman, "Moral Evil," 12.

86. Ibid.

87. Not all theists are theistic Platonists; nevertheless, there is overlap between theistic Platonists and other theists in their analysis of moral goodness, namely in the sense that both root it in God. Take, for example, C. Stephen Evans who is a natural law theorist. He recognizes that non-theists can have a good idea of moral obligation (epistemologically), yet moral obligations are ontologically dependent upon God. See C. Stephen Evans, *God and Moral Obligations* (Oxford: Oxford University Press, 2013), 21.

88. Adams, *Finite and Infinite Goods*, 42.

89. Ibid.

90. Adams, *Finite and Infinite Goods*, 14. When speaking of God as the Good, Adams' point is not merely that the Good depends on God; rather, God is the Good, thus endorsing something akin to an identity relation between God and goodness. This is not something that he merely asserts; rather, he offers a principled argument by appealing to value theory. Plato scholars often differ over whether or not the Forms are best understood as *universals* or as *exemplars*. Adams opts for the latter. Desires, too, play a central role in Adam's theory, as

might exist in the world. God, then, is neither dependent on nor looking to anything other than himself with respect to perfect moral goodness. God himself becomes the measure for any commands that he issues. Thus, when God issues commands, those commands are not arbitrary, but have ramifications for flourishing and well-being among his human creatures. However, this doesn't mean God's commands are always for everyone in all times and in all places. It may be that God issues certain commands that are contextually oriented, that is to say, God issues certain commands that are geared toward a specific group for a specific time in history, but which are, nevertheless, in accordance with his divine purposes. These commands would not, however, be arbitrary, so long as they are grounded in God's own moral goodness and are meant for the flourishing of those with whom God gives the command.

Lastly, what about natural evil? Natural evil, I take it, provides the more difficult problem for theists. Not only must theism answer the question of devastation caused by things such as natural disasters or disease, but they must also answer the question of animal pain and suffering.

Before responding to the question of natural evil, it would be helpful to consider some important distinctions. First, it is important to recognize that not everything that appears to be natural evil can rightly be labeled as such. There are many evils that, although they do appear in nature, are, nevertheless, at least a partial result of human doing. Flooding caused by the breaking of dams, damage to the ozone layer and natural habitats due to pollution and human waste, animal death through the changing or destruction of natural habitats, damage to land and animals caused by nuclear explosions and other forms of war, famine caused by the overuse of land, extinction or near-extinction of animals due to poaching, and acid

---

David Baggett and Jerry Walls explain: "The role of our desires ... is to fix the reference of our value terminology to a property or object that has its own nature independent of our desires" (Baggett and Walls, *Good God: The Theistic Foundations of Morality* [Oxford: Oxford University Press, 2011], 94). They continue: "if there is indeed a single best candidate for the role of the Good itself, or the property of goodness," then it is reasonable for one to infer it as the likely essence of goodness. Lastly, for Adams, "whatever best fills the role of Goodness is an object of admiration, desire, and recognition, at least commonly and to some degree" (Baggett and Walls, *Good God*, 94). Without rehearsing the entirety of his discourse, Adams's argument boils down to God as the most plausible candidate for filling this role. For their full summary, see Baggett and Walls, *Good God*, 93-95.

rain due to air pollutants are just some of the kinds of evil that appear in nature, but that, in reality, are a result of human destructive tendencies.

Second, there are other items that must also be taken into consideration, such as human ignorance, neglect, and the choice of risk. Often humans move into areas of the world that are prone to natural disasters, such as hurricanes, tornadoes, and the like. For many of these people, the goods that come from living in such an area outweigh the potential for harm caused by such natural disasters. There have also been reports of people refusing to evacuate a city even knowing that something like a hurricane is coming. It is also understood that sometimes people are ignorant of upcoming natural events, such as tsunamis, that cause vast amounts of destruction. But even in such instances, there may be an element of human responsibility. In the 2004 Indian Ocean tsunami that killed over 250,000 people, there was no tsunami detection system in place, even though the technology had been around for some time. Having such a mechanism in place could have saved thousands of lives.[91] The point here is not to make light of the tragedy that comes with such disasters but only to point out that living in such areas that have an elevated risk factor or refusing to evacuate despite the risk of an impending destruction or the failure to implement strategies for protection despite the capacity to do so are all matters that involve human choice. Our choices are significant and often carry with them certain risks. Making this point does not entail that all evils occurring in nature are a result of human choice; rather, the point is only that some are connected to moral action and choice.

Third, it should be noted that some diseases, which are thought to be forms of natural evil, are either caused by humans or are perpetuated by humans. Some diseases are brought about through neglect of taking care of one's body. Lack of exercise or lack of control in eating certain things can often lead to disastrous effects on the body, such as heart disease or diabetes. Active use of certain drugs can also cause the body's organs to shut down or cause certain cancers. Having multiple sexual partners may lead to sexually transmitted diseases. Sometimes, hospitals, which are to

---

91. Tim Folger, "Will Indonesia Be Ready for the Next Tsunami?" National Geographic (website), updated September 28, 2018, http://news.nationalgeographic.com/news/2014/12/141226-tsunami-indonesia-catastrophe-banda-aceh-warning-science/.

be places of healing, may transmit diseases through acts like blood trans-
fusions, when the blood has not been properly screened. Pollutants in the
water or in the ground where we grow our foods may result in ill effects
on the body. Again, not to make light of these tragedies in the world, but
many of these, again, show that there is a significance to our actions and
choices. Further, this is not to say that all diseases are in some way related
to human freedom; rather, it is only to point out that some are.

Having said that, it is not at all surprising for theism that God would
create such a world as ours. If God exists, then he would have good reasons
for creating, not only human life, but also nonhuman life, such as found
in the great diversity of plants and animals in the world, reflecting his
fecundity. But such a world is the kind of world where we also find a great
amount of natural evil, particularly evils brought about through natural
disasters, predation, disease, and the like. How might the theist explain this?

First, it may be helpful to consider that many of the events that bring
about great destruction are also the same kinds of events that are necessary
for the normal operations of our world and that, often, they bring about
some of the greatest wonders. Take, for example, tectonic plates crashing
together. These are often the cause of such events as earthquakes, tsunamis,
and volcanoes. Yet, without plate tectonics, we would not have the beautiful mountain ranges or tropical islands that we see. But the importance of
plate tectonics goes beyond aesthetics. The earth's climate is remarkably
stable, and this is due, in part, to plate tectonics, which, through volcanoes, cycle out CO_2 into the atmosphere. The release of CO_2 through volcanic activity is important for warming the earth's atmosphere and for
the water cycle. Moreover, plate tectonics is involved in producing the
biodiversity on the earth, which allows complex life to flourish. Without
the effects brought about through plate tectonics, while there may be life,
there could be no human life as we know it.[92]

Second, I am going to suggest something that goes against the intuition
of many who discuss the problem of evil—*not all pain amounts to evil*. It
may be that certain kinds of pain are similar to plate tectonics, in the sense

---

92. Dinesh D'Souza, "Why We Need Earthquakes," *Christianity Today* 53, no. 5, May
2009, 58; Richard Lovett, "Unknown Earth: Why is Earth's Climate so Stable?" *New
Scientist* 199, no. 2675, September 2008, 34, https://www.newscientist.com/article/
mg19926751-900-unknownearth-why-is-earths-climate-so-stable/.

that, without them, our physical bodies would not function properly and flourish as they do. If pain is an important part of proper function, then pain itself may be seen as a good, in the sense that it is better to have certain pains than not to have them. As discussed in chapter 1, there are many great advantages to having pain. When we consider those people suffering from Hansen's disease (leprosy), many of the complications that plague their bodies stem from an inability to feel physical pain. Without pain they do not have the same advantage that I do of feeling certain pains. If I am out walking in the yard and contort my leg in such a way that I sprain my ankle, my body's response is to swell in the area and the result is that I feel pain. Pain, in this instance, is like a warning system telling my body that something is not quite right. The pain that I feel may be a discomfort (given that we all have different tolerances of the pain that we feel, it may be a big discomfort), but even here the pain itself is not the problem—the problem is that one of my body parts has been injured and is not functioning properly. Pain is the consequence of the sprained ankle. Moreover, as noted in chapter 1, people will often put themselves through great pains in order to accomplish goals. Some of the cases considered are athletes who put themselves through great pains to become better or women who choose to experience childbirth naturally apart from any epidurals or pain medicine. Yet, we do not generally classify such pains as evils, especially when they were endured willingly. So, at least to me, it seems that the hedonistic principle that "all pain is evil" is wrong. But someone might object, "What about mental pain?" Even with respect to mental pains, I do not think that we ought to classify all such pains as evil. Perhaps, like physical pain, mental pain, too, functions like a warning system telling us that something is not quite right. For example, suppose I see some heinous act carried out and my immediate response is one of anger and sorrow. At the same time, I feel a great amount of mental pain for the person because of what I saw. If our emotions are in any way connected to our beliefs, then perhaps the pain itself is a way of telling me that something is not quite right. Yet again, there are many individuals who would endure a great amount of mental pain, brought about by ridicule, mental abuse, psychological torture and the like, in order to hold unswervingly to some conviction or to accomplish some task. Here we might think of a POW, who, despite both physical and mental torture, endures a great amount of mental pain for the sake of defending her country. Or, again, we might think of an athlete who willingly takes certain forms of ridicule and embarrassment from a coach or peers in order to achieve the goal of winning or becoming the best that she can be. In each case, the person may be in quite a bit of mental pain but nevertheless show resilience and fortitude. Now, to be clear, that is not to say that there is *no evil involved* in what is going on in either case; rather, the point is that mental pain, much like physical pain, may not itself be evil. The evil is in the fact that there is something that is not quite right that was brought about ultimately through an agent—in the former case the agent using torture and in the latter the person bringing about the ridicule—but the physical or mental pain itself need not be an evil.[93]

Third, the real issue involved in the discussion of the problem from evil is not so much pain as it is in suffering or misery brought about through certain instances of pain. Suffering, as discussed in chapter 1, is closer to a lack of flourishing in the person. Severe pain may be the catalyst for suffering, but it is not necessarily equivalent to suffering. We can think of pain, whether mental or physical, as having a threshold of sorts. Much like any physical object, when enough force or pressure is applied the pain may become so unbearable that the object which feels the pain breaks or becomes debilitated in some way. That is what we often see in some cases of people suffering from certain types of depression. The person's mental pain becomes so unbearable that she cannot function properly. Sometimes, however, the depression is brought about through a physical deficiency, such as a lack in neurotransmitters. In both cases, the person is suffering. In a similar fashion, people who have cancer often experience excruciat-ing pain, which may result in suffering. These are all instances of misery or suffering linked to certain forms of pain. Yet, on the flip side, we can imagine people who have little or no experience of either mental or phys-ical pain but who are, nevertheless, dying from some unknown disease. In such instances, the persons involved do not realize it, but their bodies are no longer flourishing as they should be because they are suffering from the disease.

---

93. For a helpful article that provides insightful discussion on differences between pain and evil, see John Kemp, "Pain and Evil," *Philosophy* 29, no. 108 (1954): 13–26.

Having made the above qualifications, are we now ready to answer the question of natural evil? In order to flesh this out, I will consider an argument first presented by Ed Miller and expanded on by Kirk MacGregor. Miller's argument goes as follows:

> It would be *logically impossible* to have a world without evil: Anything created by God would have to be *less* than God just by virtue of being *dependent* on him, and this means immediately that it must be less than perfect, and *this* means immediately the presence of various sorts of imperfections. How could God create something that was perfect and therefore independent, and therefore uncreated? *It is logically impossible.*[94]

MacGregor expands on Miller's argument in the following way:

> It is logically impossible for God to create a world without evil; if God chose to create anything at all, evil would necessarily come into existence, not because God created or caused it, but because whatever God created would not be God. Notice that all such evils are, in and of themselves, gratuitous or pointless; their only *raison d'être* is the logically unavoidable privation of ontological necessity exhibited by created entities. The only way that any created entity could display perfection is nonessentially, that is, God supernaturally acting to overwhelm or "make up for" its resident imperfections; it could not display perfection in and of itself. Therefore, gratuitous evil is ontologically inescapable for contingent being every bit as much as perfection is essential to Necessary Being. Such immediately explains the existence of gratuitous natural evil; it is logically necessary to the universe, and God simply has to put up with it if he chooses to create a universe at all.[95]

This argument by Miller and MacGregor includes some rather strong statements. On the one hand, there is something right about this argument, and I think that it points the theist in the right direction; however, it needs

---

94. Ed L. Miller, *Questions that Matter*, 3rd ed. (New York: McGraw-Hill, 1992), 356 (emphasis in original), quoted in MacGregor, "Existence and Irrelevance," 173–74.

95. MacGregor, "Existence and Irrelevance," 174.

some qualifications. The central problem with the argument is that we can imagine all kinds of worlds, worlds that might even be metaphysically possible, that would not contain evil. We can imagine a world in which God creates one immutable object and sustains that object in existence everlastingly. While this object is both contingent and less than perfect, it does not seem to me, at least, that such a world requires evil or that evil will inevitably take place due to the contingency and less-than-perfect nature of the thing involved. Neither contingency nor imperfection nor finiteness requires evil in and of themselves. Even if we were to take all these together, as in the case of the finite object, no evil is required. Now whether God has good reasons to create such a world or not is beside the point. Such a world is logically (and metaphysically) possible, and hence the Miller/MacGregor argument fails in that sense. But here is where I think their argument got it right. They grounded their argument in the Creator/creature distinction. There are certain logical limitations to any world that God might create due to the sheer nature of its being finite, imperfect, and contingent. Perhaps they could have qualified their argument to say something to this effect: It would be logically impossible for God to create a world that is dynamic with natural processes *such as ours* without some ensuing evil due to its imperfect, finite, and contingent nature.

Given the above insights form the Miller/MacGregor argument, the theist might put forth an argument for natural evil as follows:

1. If God exists, God would have strong reasons for creating a complex, multileveled world with a great diversity of biological creatures, including creatures that are sentient and intelligent. Some of the highly complex intelligent creatures, namely humans, are capable of having meaningful experiences and entering into significant relationships with God, one another, other creatures, and their environments.

2. Because such creatures are biological and physical in nature, the world had to be ordered according to a set of natural laws or lawlike regulating principles. Given what we know scientifically about the universe, physical life, and especially human

life, life as we know it could not exist unless things were "fine-tuned" in such a way.

3. The universe, as it now stands, consists of a great variety of goods, both in its physical grandeur and beauty and in the flourishing of a great diversity of biological life that it contains. Consequently, such a world also brings with it the possibility that sentient and intelligent life will be negatively affected by the physical processes that govern the formation and operations of the universe, resulting in a great amount of suffering and death.

4. Since we have no reason for thinking that God could have brought about a world with alternative natural laws for supporting life as we know it, and yet a world that consists of great potential for good, or, at least, a balance of good and evil, God is morally justified in creating such a world that contains natural evils.[96]

Perhaps the skeptic might respond in a couple of ways. She might ask, "Why could God not have changed the natural processes in order to bring about a world free of evil?" There are several problems with this response. First, we have no guarantee that, even if God were to change the natural processes, they, too, would not go wrong. How do we know that such processes would not result in much greater natural evils than what we see in the world already? Second, why should we jettison processes that work well most of the time? Take, for instance, our genetic processes. Though genetic processes do sometimes result in mutations, this is not the norm. The same might be said with respect to the case of natural disasters. As noted previously, the same mechanisms that cause these great disasters are also essential for normal operations in the earth. Most of the time these

---

96. This argument is adapted from several other natural order arguments: Reichenbach, *Evil and a Good God*, 101–3; William Hasker, *Triumph of God*, 138; Layman, "Natural Evil," 12. For a similar argument, see Garrett DeWeese, "Natural Evil: A 'Free Process' Defense," in *God and Evil: The Case for God in a World Filled with Pain*, ed. Chad Meister and James K. Dew (Downers Grove, IL: InterVarsity Press, 2013), 53–64.

processes function extremely well.[97] Third, as Bruce Reichenbach argues, changing or altering the natural laws would affect the various constituents that make up the world. He explains,

> The introduction of different natural laws affecting human beings in order to prevent the frequent instances of natural evil would entail the alteration of human beings themselves. Human beings are sentient creatures of nature. As physiological beings they inter-act with Nature; they cause natural events and in turn are affected by natural events. Hence, insofar as humans are natural, sentient beings, constructed of the same substance as Nature and interacting with it, they will be affected in any natural system by lawful natural events. These events sometimes will be propitious and sometimes not. And insofar as man is essentially a conscious being, he will be aware of those events which are not propitious and which for him constitute evils. Therefore, to prevent natural evils from affecting man, man himself would have to be significantly changed, such that he would be no longer a sentient creature of nature.[98]

There is a second response the skeptic might put forward. Since God is omnipotent, as theists believe, why could God not create a world in which he miraculously intervenes to prevent natural evils? There are several responses to this objection. First, could it not be that God is already miracu-lously responding to certain natural evils, such that his working is keeping more natural evils from happening than what we're aware of? Second, a world whereby God always miraculously intervenes would result in crea-tures who are incapable of understanding the significance of their actions. It is only in a world such as ours, one with natural processes and governed by natural lawlike features, that human freedom can be exercised in a meaningful way.[99] Third, such a world would be highly unpredictable and irregular. As Reichenbach further explains:

> But without the regularity which results from the governance of natural laws, rational action would be impossible. Without

---

97. Feinberg, *Many Faces of Evil*, 196–97.
98. Reichenbach, *Evil and a Good God*, 111–12.
99. Feinberg, *Many Faces of Evil*, 200–201.

regularity of sequence, agents could not entertain rational explanations, make predictions, estimate probabilities, or calculate prudence. They would not be able to know what to expect about any course of action they would like to take. Whether or not such action would be possible, what they would have to do to have God bring it about, whether it could occur as they planned (supposing agents could plan, which is doubtful), what the consequences would be—all this would be unknown and unknowable. Hence, agents could not know or even suppose what course of action to take to accomplish a certain rationally conceived goal. Thus rational agents could neither propose action nor act themselves.[100]

Moreover, it is highly doubtful that humans could be fully functioning moral agents in such a world since being a moral agent requires not only the ability to act but also to propose some course of action. A highly irregular world would prevent both proposing a course of action and acting on it.[101] But suppose the critic responds by suggesting that there is a middle ground, so to speak, that is to say, a world partially ruled by natural processes and partially ruled by miraculous intervention. Again, Reichenbach is insightful on this point:

But what would such a world be like? Presumably, a world which was only partially operated by miracle would be one in which God would allow events at some times to follow a "regular pattern," and at other times not. That is, sometimes causal conditions x and y would result in effect z, and at other times they would be followed by an effect of a different sort. For example, heavy snowfall in the mountains and collapse of snow walls will cause an avalanche to proceed down the mountain slope according to the law of gravity when no sentient creatures is in its path; but should a climber be present, either that which causes the avalanche "regularly" will not have this effect this time, or the avalanche will still occur but will swerve around the climber or halt at his feet. But natural laws such as the law of gravity assert universal and necessary connections

---

between phenomena. Then if events sometimes followed a "regular pattern" and sometimes not, there would be no natural laws regarding that particular event. But then the appeal to a "regular pattern" is specious, for "regular pattern" presupposes that there are normative natural laws which describe or govern the course of events, so that one can distinguish what is regular from what is irregular. "Regular pattern" has meaning only within the context of natural laws. Furthermore, if this absence of universal and necessary connections is widespread, as would seem to be required in order to prevent all natural evils, the world would have few if any natural laws; it would, in effect, be governed by miraculous intervention. Thus, though this so-called middle ground would remove the contradiction with respect to the possibility of human action vis-à-vis being free, the consequences of it still would be such as to make rational prediction and rational action impossible, and hence to make moral action impossible.[102]

It would seem, then, that theists have good reasons for supposing the need for a world such as ours.

Before moving on to a comparison between the four metaphysical systems on explaining evil, it would be helpful to consider one last issue—the difficult problem of animal pain and death. How might the theist respond?

Unlike its metaphysical rivals, theism provides within it the resources for thinking that there might be some kind of compensation for animal life in the end. Many theistic traditions hold to something like an afterlife, and all three major theistic traditions hold to the resurrection of the dead. Christianity and Judaism both take it that there will be a future restoration of creation. Now, there are differences of opinion on what things will be like in the end times, and each theistic tradition will have to work this out. All that I am suggesting, here, is that there is a significant possibility for animal compensation and that theism, if God is omnipotent, could bring about such a state.[103]

---

102. Ibid., 107–8.

103. It is beyond the scope and purpose of this chapter to consider with any kind of detail this important but difficult problem. For recent theistic responses to animal pain and suffering, see Christopher Southgate, *The Groaning of Creation: God, Evolution, and the Problem*

EVALUATION OF THEISM

As we have seen, each of the three non-theistic systems have some difficulties explaining the facts regarding evil. Of the three examined thus far, process panentheism fares better than either pantheism or naturalism. But what of theism? It seems that theism has no significant difficulties explaining moral evil, especially given libertarian freedom. Perhaps, the greatest difficulty for theism is in explaining the existence of natural evil, and particularly animal pain, although a world that operates according to certain stable natural laws is better than one ruled by unpredictable miraculous intervention. Furthermore, as argued in this chapter, such a world that has elements of risk, as our world does, has greater significance than ones without such risks. Lastly, theists recognize that such a world—finite, dynamic, and limited—inevitably leads to imperfection, especially if God has granted the creation to have a certain amount of freedom to be and to operate as *he created it to be*. This understanding demonstrates an important metaphysical principle recognized by theists that there is a significant difference between the Creator and the creature, which theists base on the contingency of the world (whether logically or temporally) and the necessity and eternality of God. Regarding animal pain, while theists face difficulties, there are resources within theism that provide partial explanations of the facts. For example, animals, like humans, are part of a dynamic, contingent, and limited system that, while on the whole operates and functions properly, may, nevertheless result in some destruction when animal and human life are affected by such processes. Furthermore, as we saw, theists might rightly reject the hedonistic principle that all pain is evil. Pain though it may lead to suffering, is an important part of the proper function of certain forms of biological life. In addition, pain may even lead to certain forms of flourishing (e.g., when someone perseveres through a rigorous physical routine in order to achieve a goal). While no doubt animal pain and predation provide difficulties for theists, and there is much more work that needs done in this area, there is reason to believe, however, that (1) pain in humans is quite different than pain in animals

---

of Evil (Louisville, KY: Westminster John Knox, 2008); Ronald E. Osborn, *Death Before the Fall: Biblical Literalism and the Problem of Animal Suffering* (Downers Grove, IL: InterVarsity Press, 2014); Trent Dougherty, *The Problem of Animal Pain: Theodicy for All Creatures Great and Small* (New York: Palgrave Macmillan, 2014).

and (2) that theism likely features resources to redeem animal suffering that exceed those of this world.

Regarding logical consistency, theism, like naturalism, is a straightforward system, though it is more complex. Despite its complexity, theism is, nevertheless, overall consistent. Most attacks on theism come from the phenomena of evil in the world. As I have argued, given something like human libertarian freedom and a natural order that is governed by laws or lawlike regularities, and given the finite and dynamic nature of the world that is other than God, there is nothing logically inconsistent about God's existence and evil in the world. Furthermore, Alvin Plantinga, in *God, Freedom, and Evil*, has shown that there is no logical inconsistency between the existence of God and the existence of evil in the world, something to which most atheists will agree. This still leaves important questions to ask concerning evil, to which distinctive aspects of Christian theology, I believe, can answer quite well.

How well does theism fare at providing explanatory power and explanatory scope? Unlike the other systems, theism had no difficulties explaining life. It does not run into the problem of infinite regress as the other three metaphysical systems do. How about theism and consciousness? As with naturalistic and pantheistic views, any attempt at adopting a physicalist form of consciousness fails; however, most theists hold to dualism, the view whereby the mind is in some sense distinct from the body. In this chapter, three lines of argument were given in support dualism. First, if God himself is an unembodied mind, then theists have as an exemplar or paradigm-case of what an unembodied mind is like. Second, theists have at their disposal certain empirical evidence from NDEs and post-death visions. Third, and lastly, theists have the unity-of-consciousness argument. As argued, all that one need to show is a minimalistic version of dualism in order to have consciousness, which theists can do. Finally, regarding the metaphysics of good and evil and moral responsibility, again, theism fares quite well. For theists, humans were created with libertarian freedom, and, hence, they generally have the capacity to do otherwise. Process panentheists, on the other hand, recognize that freedom is a basic feature of all actual entities, and especially human creatures, who have a greater capacity of freedom. Regarding good and evil, as I have argued throughout, neither is surprising given theism. There is reason to expect certain forms of moral evil given human libertarian freedom. Furthermore, based on the Creator/creature distinction, the finite and limited nature of the world, the various processes needed to sustain biological life, and that the world is dynamic, it is not at all surprising that certain kinds of natural evil may result. Theists also believe that God is the good, or at least perfectly good, and the ground for all moral action, both our source and moral *telos*. For theists, not only is God the ground for good, but God has also established a moral order that humans are to abide by. Lastly, theists believe that not only does God have the power to overcome evil, but eventually he will do so, carving out important room for rational hope in the face of the problem of evil.

Some might charge theists with ad hoc-ness in their system, especially pertaining to the afterlife. The notion of an afterlife is an important aspect of the theistic system, without which it would be difficult to make sense of God's bringing the world to rights and final justice. What reason is there for thinking that something like the afterlife is true? How might the theist respond? There are at least two lines of argument a theist might give regarding an afterlife. First, as discussed earlier in this chapter, there is veridical evidence for both near-death experiences and post-death visions. Furthermore, there are modern documented cases of people returning to life after having been prayed for.[104] While the evidence does not conclusively guarantee an afterlife, it does give theists reasons for thinking that there might be something like an afterlife. Second, if God is omnipotent, there is reason to believe that he could do something like bring people back from the dead, as in the notion of the resurrection. For example, Christians take it that God raised Jesus from the dead. They base this on a variety of historical evidences.[105] Now, if the Christian theist can show that God raising Jesus from the dead makes better sense of the historical data than do the best naturalistic theories, and if they can show that miracles are possible in a world such as ours, then theists are within their epistemic right to

---

104. For a detailed discussion of raisings of people both in antiquity and the present, see Craig S. Keener, *Miracles: The Credibility of the New Testament Account* (Grand Rapids: Baker Academic, 2011), 1:536–79.

105. This historical data for the disciples seeing Jesus after his crucifixion is quite strong. See Gary R. Habermas, *The Risen Jesus and Future Hope* (Lanham, MD: Rowman & Littlefield, 2003), 3–51; Michael R. Licona, *The Resurrection of Jesus: A New Historiographical Approach* (Downers Grove, IL: InterVarsity Press, 2010); N. T. Wright, *The Resurrection of the Son of God* (Minneapolis: Fortress, 2003).

believe in something along the lines of an afterlife. Taken together, these reasons for thinking there is such a thing as an afterlife can do much to dispense with the charge of ad hoc-ness in theism.

To what extent is theism a plausible system in itself and in comparison to the other systems? Of the four systems, theism can genuinely explain evil based on its major tenets. It can do so without redefining good and evil, and it can do so by understanding those terms in the way most people understand the words, that is, without equivocal or idiosyncratic meanings. Furthermore, theism adequately answers each of the four areas: life, consciousness, the metaphysics of good and evil, and human freedom. This does not mean that there are no difficulties for theism. There are still many areas that theists must work out. The areas of consciousness and the problem of animal pain are just two key areas that need further attention. That additional work is needed does not hinder theism from providing a partial explanation to such issues.

Moreover, theists believe that God has created the world with a moral order, and it is God himself who is the standard for the good that we see in this order. If we take it that God made humans to be like him in certain respects (e.g., the Christian and Jewish understanding of the *imago dei*), we have good reason for thinking that the world and its order is knowable and understandable. It is because of the established moral order and God's creating humans to be like him that people can recognize that certain things are right and wrong. They can see the moral order of things, even if they choose not to follow it.

Additionally, the God of theism can genuinely do things about the evil in the world. While God may have general policies in place such as libertarian freedom with respect to his human creatures and lawlike regulatory processes in nature, it does not mean that God is inactive or can do nothing about the evil in the world. Furthermore, given the theistic understanding of an afterlife, it does seem that there is something akin to eschatological payoff for God's creatures when it is all said and done (e.g., resurrection, restoration of creation, and so on). Lastly, there is the possibility of final justice for the evils committed in this world. In all, it seems that theism not only provides a more plausible explanation given the other metaphysical systems when it comes to explaining evil, but theism provides a plausible explanation in and of itself.

Finally, how livable of a system is theism compared to the other metaphysical systems? Naturalism, pantheism, and panentheism each face the same fate—the pending doom of the universe. As William Lane Craig so forcefully puts it:

> And the universe, too, faces a death of its own. Scientists tell us that the universe is expanding, and the galaxies are growing farther and farther apart. As it does so, it grows colder and colder, and its energy is used up. Eventually all the stars will burn out, and all matter will collapse into dead stars and black holes. There will be no light at all; there will be no heat; there will be no life; only the corpses of dead stars and galaxies, ever expanding into the endless darkness and the cold recesses of space—a universe in ruins. This is not science fiction. The entire universe marches irreversibly toward its grave. So not only is the life of each individual person doomed; the entire human race is doomed. The universe is plunging toward inevitable extinction—death is written throughout its structure. There is no escape. There is no hope.[106]

For the naturalist, there is no escaping that such an outcome is the conclusion of all our human efforts to achieve greatness. What, in the end, have our scientific progress and discoveries accomplished? For the pantheist, the same organizing force lying behind all of life, animating the very world we live in, ultimately leads the world to its final demise. It is hard to see how a God that is not all-powerful could turn things around for the hope of the world. In the end, would such a God—indifferent as it may be—care? What of the God of process panentheism? Could such a God do any better? Here, it would seem, the mad scientist strikes again. Just as there is no guarantee that the world will turn out with more good than evil, so too is there no guarantee that the world will avoid its impending doom. What, then, becomes of all of God's work? What becomes of God? Would God, then, begin the whole evolutionary process over again, keeping at it until all things finally turn out as planned? In the end, we might forecast

---

106. William Lane Craig, *Reasonable Faith: Christian Truth and Apologetics*, 3rd ed. (Wheaton, IL: Crossway, 2008), 72.

the eschatological payoff of each metaphysical system as follows: bleak (process panentheism); bleaker (pantheism); and bleakest (naturalism).

Of the four systems, only theism provides a metaphysical system that is livable in the face of evil. Theism provides within it the resources needed to not only explain why the world is in the shape that it is, but it also provides a solution to the evil in the world. Theism recognizes that there is something wrong with the world. It is not how it should be. As Stephen Davis rightly points out, "The world is not worthwhile as it stands: it needs to be redeemed."[107] Only a God who is powerful enough to act in the world and who is religiously available to his creatures can bring about the kind of changes needed to thwart evil. Moreover, theists believe that the world will eventually be put to right. There will be final vindication for all wrongs committed, and many of God's creatures will share in a blissful afterlife. Lastly, if God created all things, including the entire four-dimensional space-time universe, as theists believe, then there is no reason to think that God could not stop the impending doom that lies in store for the universe. Only a God who is infinite in power can keep the universe from reaching its ultimate doom and restore it to its original intended goodness.

---

107. Davis, "God of Process Theology," 131.

CHAPTER 6
A GOD WHO LOVES

I n the previous chapter I argued that theism explains life, consciousness, the metaphysics of good and evil, and human responsibility better than its metaphysical rivals. Moreover, I argued that theism is livable in the face of evil and provides an overall thicker worldview response. Despite this, theism is not off the hook and must answer a significant challenge. To see this challenge, it will be helpful to consider a quote from H. P. Owen summarizing Charles Hartshorne's critique of classical theism:

> Hartshorne maintains that the self-sufficient, changeless God of classical theism cannot possess the property of love that Christian theists attribute to him. If God is love he must be a "social" being. He (like any member of human society) must be affected by the objects of his love; he must be pained by their sufferings and enriched by their achievements. If he did not need his human creatures for the completion of his being he would not have any reason for creating them. "A being which contains, in sheer independence of others, all possible perfection and value must surely know better than to clutter up existence with beings which can add nothing to the value that would exist without them" (50).[1]

There is much going on here, and I cannot consider the entirety of this Hartshornean type of objection in this chapter. I will consider parts of this objection in the final two chapters. For now, I would like to focus on the

---

1. Owen, *Concepts of Deity*, 82. Owen is quoting Hartshorne from page 50 of his book *Reality as Social Process*.

point that if God is love, then it necessitates that God be a social being. If Hartshorne is correct, then it raises a fundamental problem for the theist. Either God needs the world to demonstrate his love or God does not have love as an essential attribute. Many if not most theists recognize that love is an essential attribute of God. Moreover, if God were not loving, as the preponderance of theists believe, then could theists provide an adequate answer to the problem from evil? But for God to feature love as an essential property, there must be something for God to love. Theists will want to avoid saying that God must create in order to love something other than himself since such an admission suggests that God is not complete in and of himself, and hence deficient, lacking *aseity* (that is, absolute self-existence). In other words, God would need something other than God's self for his completion, resulting in a form of panentheism.

As I argue below, there is a way out for theists. We can make a distinction between "Unitarian" theism and "Trinitarian" theism. Unitarian theists believe that God consists of only one person. Trinitarian theists, on the other hand, recognize that God is more than one person (presumably three). By this, they do not mean that there is more than one God or being; rather, they mean that within this one God there exists more than one person (Father, Son, and Holy Spirit). If one were to accept a Trinitarian understanding of God over a Unitarian view, as most Christian theists do, one can avoid either horn of the Hartshornean-style dilemma. This is the move that I will pursue and argue for in the pages that follow.

This chapter, then, will accomplish three purposes. First, it provides a response to the Hartshornean-style critique, showing how God can be an essentially loving being without comprising divine aseity and without slipping into panentheism. Second, this chapter aims to give support for one stripe of theism over others, namely Christian theism, which takes God to be tri-personal in nature, opposed to other theistic views that understand God as mono-personal. As will be shown in the remainder of the book, and especially the last chapter, taking God to be Trinitarian has certain advantages, giving, in my estimation, a more robust response to the reality of evil in the world. Third, and finally, this chapter prepares the way for a uniquely Christian response worked out in chapter 8, which is primarily grounded in the Christian doctrine of the economic Trinity.[2] I begin by sketching out a basic objection to Unitarian theism, which requires making sense of divine aseity and what is meant by God as being essentially loving, followed by a positive case for the doctrine of the Trinity. Having shown why Trinitarian theism makes better sense of God's aseity and being essentially loving, I respond to two potential objections to the doctrine of the Trinity.

TOWARD A TRINITARIAN GOD

When theists speak of aseity, they refer to God's "uncreatedness, self-sufficiency, and independence of everything else."[3] James Beilby defines God's aseity in the following way:

> God is independent, self-existent, and fully self-sufficient. He does not need anything outside of himself to exist, be satisfied, be fulfilled, or (to borrow an overused phrase from contemporary psychology) be "self-actualized." Whether Exodus 3:14 is translated "I am who I am" or "I will be what I will be," the meaning is the same: God's existence and character are determined by him alone.[4]

Beilby goes on to distinguish between two senses of divine aseity. The first is *ontological aseity*, by which he takes it to mean that God is "uncaused, without beginning, not dependent on an external person, principle, or metaphysical reality for his existence."[5] The second is *psychological aseity*, whereby he means God to be "fully self-satisfied" and without any need or want for something outside of himself. God is, in this sense, happy and fulfilled in God's self.[6]

What, then, do we mean when we speak of God as being essentially loving? First, let us begin with the idea of an essential property. Though the topic of theological essentialism is considered in more detail in the

---

2. When Christians speak of the "economic" Trinity, they mean the outworking of the Trinity in the world as God acts, reveals, and communicates through the work of the divine persons of the Godhead.

3. Alvin Plantinga, "Does God Have a Nature?" in *The Analytic Theist: An Alvin Plantinga Reader*, ed. James F. Sennet (Grand Rapids: Eerdmans, 1998), 225.

4. James Beilby, "Divine Aseity, Divine Freedom: A Conceptual Problem for Edwardsian-Calvinism," *Journal of the Evangelical Theological Society* 47, no. 4 (2004): 647.

5. Ibid., 648.

6. Ibid.

next chapter, to say that some property is essential for God means that God exemplifies that property in every possible world and could not have lacked it in any possible world in which God exists, as Alvin Plantinga explains:

Something has a property essentially if and only if it has it and could not possibly have lacked it. Another way to put the same thing is to say that an object x has a property P essentially if and only if x has it in every possible world in which x exists.[7]

Second, to say that something is loving means, minimally, that it is other-concerned or other-directed. But most theists will understand divine love as more than sheer benevolence or a general concern for the other in that there is also an element of self-giving or sharing in love, as philosopher Richard Swinburne explains:

Love involves sharing, giving to the other what of one's own is good for him and receiving from the other what of his is good for one; and love involves co-operating with another to benefit third parties. This latter is crucial for worthwhile love. There would be something deeply unsatisfactory (even if for inadequate humans sometimes unavoidable) about a marriage in which the parties were concerned solely with each other and did not use their mutual love to bring forth good to others, for example by begetting, nourishing, and educating children, but possibly in other ways instead. Love must share and love must co-operate in sharing. The best love would share all that it had.[8]

Though Swinburne is a Christian theist, something similar is found in other theistic views on divine love.[9] Having established above what we mean by aseity and God's being essentially loving, we now turn to the central problem of Unitarian theism. In order to see this, it would benefit us

---

7. Alvin Plantinga, "Essence and Essentialism," in *A Companion to Metaphysics*, ed. Jaegwon Kim, Ernest Sosa, and Gary S. Rosenkranz (Oxford: Blackwell, 2009), 232.

8. Richard Swinburne, *The Christian God* (Oxford: Oxford University Press, 1994), 177–78.

9. For example, Jacob Neusner argues that it is precisely God's love that models how Jewish people are to respond to others in love. See Neusner, "Divine Love in Classical Judaism," *Review of Rabbinic Judaism* 17 (2014): 121–44.

to first visit an argument for the Trinity from J. P. Moreland and William Lane Craig:

1. God is by definition the greatest conceivable being.

2. As the greatest conceivable being, God must be perfect.

3. A perfect being must be a loving being.

4. If God is perfectly loving by his very nature, he must be giving himself in love to another.

5. The other cannot be a created person.

Therefore

6. The other to whom God's love is necessarily directed must be internal to God himself.[10]

They conclude,

God is not a single, isolated person, as unitarian forms of theism like Islam hold; rather, God is a plurality of persons, as the Christian doctrine of the Trinity affirms. On the unitarian view God is a person who does not give himself away essentially in love for another; he is focused essentially on himself. Hence, he cannot be the most perfect being. But on the Christian view, God is a triad of persons in eternal, self-giving love relationships. Thus, since God is essentially

---

10. This argument is adapted from J. P. Moreland and William Lane Craig, *Philosophical Foundations for a Christian Worldview* (Downers Grove, IL: InterVarsity Press, 2003), 594–95. Similarly, Richard of St. Victor argues:

> On the basis of these considerations, it is clearly impossible that any one person in the divinity could lack the fellowship of association. If he were to have only one partner, he would not be without anyone with whom he could share the riches of his greatness. However, he would not have anyone with whom he could share the delights of love. There is nothing which gives more pleasure or which delights the soul more than the sweetness of loving. Only someone who has a partner and a loved one in that love that has been shown to him possesses the sweetness of such delights. (Richard of St. Victor, *Of the Trinity*, in *The Christian Theology Reader*, 4th ed., ed. Alister E. McGrath [Malden, MA: Blackwell, 2011], 178)

For similar arguments, see Stephen T. Davis, *Christian Philosophical Theology* (Oxford: Oxford University Press, 2016), 65–68; Swinburne, *The Christian God*, 177–80.

loving, the doctrine of the Trinity is more plausible than any unitarian doctrine of God.[11]

Most theists would not doubt that God is the greatest conceivable being,
nor would they doubt that God is love and that love belongs to divine perfection. But why think that (6) is true, that the object of God's love cannot
be (merely) directed toward something outside of God himself, say, his
creatures? Craig and Moreland respond with the following thought experiment. Creation is a free act of God. God was neither compelled nor caused
to create. But we can think of a possible world in which God exists without having created. If love is essential to God's nature, then God must be
perfectly loving. Yet, in such a world, no humans, angels, or other agents
exist. Thus, created agents cannot sufficiently explain God's love.[12]

I find Moreland and Craig's argument quite convincing; however,
defenders of Unitarian theism (UT) may not be happy with it. They might
object in one of two ways. First, the defender of UT might simply bite the
bullet and acknowledge that God does indeed demonstrate his love through
his interaction with his creatures. But why is that such a problem? Such a
move brings with it a significant theological cost. It would force the theist
to deny God's aseity, which means that God could not be the greatest conceivable being.

7. If God is the greatest conceivable being, then aseity is essential to God's nature.

8. If aseity is essential to God's nature, then God is not one person.

9. God is the greatest conceivable being.

10. If God is the greatest conceivable being, then God is not one
    person (Hypothetical Syllogism from 7, 8).

11. God is not one person (Modus Ponens from 9, 10).

---

11. Moreland and Craig, *Philosophical Foundations*, 595.
12. Ibid.

Why should we think (8) is true, that is, if God has aseity that he could not be one person? As noted above, for God to be *a se*, that is, to have aseity, God must find fulfillment or fullness or completeness in the divine life and not in something external to that life. But if God is essentially loving, as defenders of UT affirm, then God must give his love away to some external "other." But to accept this, the defender of UT ends up denying God's aseity and would no longer be espousing theism, but something more akin to panentheism, whereby God needs creatures to love for divine self-actualization, fulfillment, or completion.

There is, perhaps, a second way out for UT. Why could God not be perfectly happy and loving *sans creation*, and, yet, his love be directed toward himself in eternal bliss? Wouldn't this salvage God's aseity? This is precisely the move taken by Dale Tuggy. Consider the following scenario:

> A perfect, divine person exists but doesn't create (or otherwise generate or give existence to) anything else. He's just there, timelessly beholding and loving himself, but not anyone else. He's a perfectly loving being—just as much as he would be were he to whip up some creatures, so as to have an object of love beyond himself. He's all-knowing, and so can perfectly imagine what it's like to love another. But, he doesn't experience any such relationship, as only he exists. This god is perfect, yet perfectly alone.[13]

In order to move his argument forward, Tuggy gives the following reasoning:

> We're told that a completely perfect being must be "perfectly loving." I agree. But what is it to be "perfectly loving"? Perfection is a matter of a thing's intrinsic condition, and so the perfection of being perfectly loving is a certain state of character, being disposed to think, feel, and act in loving ways. In principle, it seems that one can be perfectly loving without actually loving perfectly, or without ever actually loving anyone else in any way.[14]

---

13. Dale Tuggy, "On the Possibility of a Single Perfect Person," in *Christian Philosophy of Religion: Essays in Honor of Stephen T. Davis*, ed. C. P. Ruloff (Notre Dame, IN: University of Notre Dame Press, 2015), 135.

14. Ibid., 136.

In his attempt to disambiguate between being "perfectly loving" and "loving perfectly," Tuggy ends up equivocating on his use of the word "loving." He wants to argue that, on the one hand, God loves himself *sans creation*, yet, on the other, God can be perfectly loving without loving perfectly. Which is it? How is it that one can love one's self without actually loving perfectly? To put it differently, if one is perfectly loving, and if one loves one's self, as Tuggy believes is possible per his scenario, then one must love one's self perfectly, unless, of course, Tuggy means that loving perfectly is something that's true of God only when directed toward his creatures or someone other than himself. If that's the case, then it's not at all clear how, given UT, God can love himself at all, or, at least, love himself perfectly. Tuggy, it would seem, is making the point for the Trinitarian. The more robust kind of love is one that is other-centered and other-directed.

But let's suppose that the God of UT can love himself as a single person, as Tuggy proposes. What would that look like? To flesh this out, let's consider a scene from C. S. Lewis' book *Perelandra*, the second part to his beloved space trilogy.

In *Perelandra*, C. S. Lewis writes of a world where the sole inhabitants of the world have not yet fallen into sin. The main antagonist, a space traveler named Weston, who happens to be possessed by the devil, has been working toward causing the Green Lady—a woman reminiscent of Earth's Eve—to turn against God's commandment. In one of his attempts, Weston, or the un-man, as he is called, offers the Green Lady a mirror. Upon looking in the mirror, she shrieks back in horror. When asked by un-man what is fearful about the mirror, she exclaims: "Things being two when they are one."[15] She continues, "That thing," as she points to the mirror, "is me and not me, ... It comes to mind, Stranger, ... that a fruit does not eat itself, and a man cannot be together with himself."[16] Surely, that thing in the mirror, the image of the Green Lady, is an image of herself, but it's not really who she is. The Green Lady in Lewis' story has been looking for her beloved, the King, and when she looks in the mirror, she sees only herself. Seeing herself "out there" in the mirror is such a horror to her because she cannot see herself apart from her relationship to the King. When we focus

---

15. C. S. Lewis, *Perelandra* (New York: Scribner, 1996), 137.
16. Ibid.

on ourselves only, or when our love is directed inwardly to ourselves, it forms an illusory perspective of our true self and identity, and we become self-absorbed, unconcerned for the other.

While directed at humanity, Lewis' point is helpful at getting to the deficiency of the Unitarian view of God. We can imagine a God who contemplates and enjoys himself, much like Aristotle's God, but why think such a God is loving at all? Surely, there is an element of enjoyment that comes with love, and we can imagine God enjoying the divine self. After all, aren't we commanded in Judaism and Christianity to love our neighbors *as ourselves*? But it is not at all clear that what's being commanded here is to love ourselves. Rather, the loving of the self is assumed. The whole point of the command is that the way in which we love ourselves should be, at bottom, the standard, or to put it in the words of Francis Howard-Snyder, "the blueprints," by which we love others.[17] But moreover, why think that such a God would be interested in something other than himself? What reason do we have for thinking that such a God wouldn't be self-absorbed, and upon creation wanting to look out for the good of his creatures? Here's Lewis' insight: the deepest kind of love is only had when had in relation to another; in other words, love is relational. A God who is essentially loving, who demonstrates the deepest kind of love, is a God who is also essentially relational. It's a love that gives of itself to another. It is selfless. No wonder Jesus tells us that the greatest love a man can have for his friends is to lay down his life for them (John 15:3). A Trinitarian God provides not only the ontological grounding for other-directed love but also for relationship itself.

TRINITY AND PERICHORESIS

If God is, as Craig and Moreland argue, "a triad of persons in eternal, self-giving love,"[18] then within the Triune God is the deepest relationship in all of reality. This relationship—the perichoretic relationship between the Father, Son, and Holy Spirit—forms the heart of Christian theism. But how are we to understand the doctrine of **perichoresis**?

---

17. Francis Howard-Snyder, "Christian Ethics," in *Reason for the Hope Within*, ed. Michael J. Murray (Grand Rapids: Eerdmans, 1999), 388.

18. Moreland and Craig, *Philosophical Foundations*, 595.

John of Damascus employed the word "perichoresis" in order to describe "the mutual indwelling" or "mutual interpenetration" between the Father, Son, and Spirit.[19] He borrowed the word from Gregory of Nazianzus who used the concept largely in connection to Christology.[20] For John and other Eastern Fathers, perichoresis was an important theological concept for expressing "the conjunction of unity and distinction, stability and dynamism, symmetry and asymmetry."[21] They noted that perichoresis gave insight into three key areas: the Trinity, the incarnation, and life in the kingdom.[22]

In recent years, theologians have rediscovered the importance of perichoresis. Karl Barth describes perichoresis in the following way:

> The triunity of God obviously implies, then, the unity of Father, Son and Spirit among themselves. God's essence is indeed one, and even the different relations of origin do not entail separations. They rather imply—for where there is difference there is also fellowship—a definite participation of each mode of being in the other modes of being, and indeed, since the modes of being are in fact identical with the relations of origin, a complete participation of each mode of being in the other modes of being.[23]

Barth disliked the modern understanding of "person," that is, an autonomous and isolated individual. As a corrective measure, he preferred the term "mode." [24] The significance of Barth's notion of perichoresis within

---

19. S. M. Smith, "Perichoresis," *Evangelical Dictionary of Theology*, 2nd ed., ed. Walter A. Elwell (Grand Rapids: Baker Academic, 2001), 906–7.

20. Verna Harrison, "Perichoresis in the Greek Fathers," *St. Vladimir's Theological Quarterly* 35, no. 1 (1991): 55.

21. Ibid., 63.

22. Ibid., 63–65.

23. Karl Barth, *Church Dogmatics*, vol. I.1 *The Doctrine of the Word of God*, ed. G. W. Bromiley and T. F. Torrance, 1st pbk. ed. (London: T&T Clark, 2004), 370.

24. Barth is not buying into the older heretical notion of modalism, as some have falsely misunderstood him. Rather, Barth's emphasis on "modes" was an attempt to break away from the modern notion of person found in theological liberalism of his time. Barth continues to express differentiation within the Godhead while continuing to emphasize oneness of essence. The notion of perichoresis is essential to Barth's understanding of the divine relation within the Triune God. However, many modern theologians find Barth's rejection of the word "person" as unfortunate and his use of "mode" inadequate for bringing about a robust understanding of the Trinity.

the Triune God is his emphasis on "fellowship" and "complete participation" among each of the "modes," or, in the terms of classical Christianity, the "persons."

The notion of perichoresis, however, is not merely a theological concept, but one that is grounded within the language of Scripture. In the Gospel of John, the apostle provides for us glimpse of the internal relationship of God, when he tells us that the "Word was *with* God" (John 1:1). The preposition *pros* could be translated, literally, as "toward." The expression itself is difficult to translate in the Greek, but roughly has the understanding of "accompaniment and relationship."[25] According to Andreas Köstenberger, *pros* "indicates a place or accompaniment, but also a disposition and orientation." This goes beyond mere co-existence to express "active relationship," or more radically put, "intercourse 'with'."[26] Not only is John showing that the Word *was* God, but that there is differentiation and movement toward the other within the Triune God. John elsewhere records Jesus' words, indicating, not only his oneness with the Father, but his being "in" the Father. Take the following statement from Jesus, "the Father is in me, and I in the Father" (John 10:38; cf. John 14:20; 17:11, 21–23), or more strikingly, Jesus' words to Phillip, "Anyone who has seen me has seen the Father. ... Don't you believe that I am in the Father, and that the Father is in me? ... Believe me when I say that I am in the Father and the Father is in me" (John 14:7–11). The Father's presence in Jesus is such that Jesus can declare to his disciples that seeing him is the same as seeing the Father.[27]

An analogy may be helpful to demonstrate the concept of perichoresis. We can think of three tuning forks, say, Tuning Fork A (TFA), Tuning Fork B (TFB), and Tuning Fork C (TFC), that are tuned to the exact pitch. Now imagine placing the tuning forks in such a way that each can equally penetrate the others. TFA is placed in such a way that it is directed toward TFB and TFC. TFB is placed so that it is directed toward TFA and TFC. Lastly, TFC is placed so that it is directed at TFA and TFB. When simultaneously struck, each individual pitch of the tuning forks mutually penetrates the others. On the one hand, the three tuning forks are putting forth distinct

---

25. Leon Morris, *The Gospel According to John* (Grand Rapids: Eerdmans, 1995), 67.

26. Andreas Köstenberger, *John* (Grand Rapids: Baker Academic, 2004), 25.

27. J. Scott Horrell, "Toward a Biblical Model of the Social Trinity: Avoiding Equivocation of Nature and Order," *Journal of the Evangelical Theological Society* 47, no. 3 (2004): 407.

sounds, yet, on the other, the pitch from each tuning fork is exactly the same, interpenetrating one another. Now, all analogies break down, and surely this one has its limitations. For instance, tuning forks are not personal kinds of things. Moreover, in order for a tuning fork to work, it needs an agent to strike it for the sound to release. Furthermore, with respect to the Trinity, the persons are not in some way separate from one another, as are the tuning forks. But what's key is the picture of interpenetration that takes place. Each pitch is distinct, yet unified as they penetrate one another. Here, we may think of each person of the Trinity as distinct (not separated), yet mutually indwelling the other. Each person is open up to, and moving toward, the other in mutual interpenetration.

But how might we understand this complete participation with respect to the relationship between the persons of the Trinity? Here I would like to suggest that at the deepest level of the perichoretic relation is the notion of interpenetrating love between each of the persons of the Trinity. Not only is God one in essence, but God is also one through love toward the other. This is the deepest love possible. It is a love that is active and self-giving; whereby the persons of the Trinity each eternally give of themselves to the others.

Given the doctrine of perichoresis, we can now see how John of 1 John could claim that "God is love" (1 John 4:8). God is love is not merely a statement about God's character, nor is it a statement primarily about how God acts toward his creatures; rather, it is a claim about the very nature of the inner life of the Triune God. The very nature of God is such that the three persons of the Trinity exist in eternal self-giving love toward the "other." There is complete indwelling and mutual interpenetration between the persons of the Trinity. As philosopher Stephen T. Davis suggests with respect to perichoresis,

> The core of God's inner being is the highest degree of self-giving love. The Persons are fully open to each other, their actions *ad extra* are actions in common, they "see with each other's eyes", the boundaries between them are transparent to each other, and each ontologically embraces the other.[28]

---

28. Davis, *Christian Philosophical Theology*, 72.

At the core of all of existence is a dynamic "loving relationship among persons."[29]

THE PROBLEM OF MONOTHEISM

Having considered the doctrine of the Trinity and perichoresis, let us now consider two objections to the doctrine of the Trinity. First, an objector might claim that the doctrine of the Trinity contradicts the very concept of monotheism. Take, for example, this Christian claim: the Father is God, the Son is God, and the Holy Spirit is God. Would not such a claim lead to something like tri-theism—the view that three divine beings exist—instead of monotheism? Would not the acceptance of more than one divine person contradict the Jewish understanding of monotheism? How might the Christian theist respond?[30]

To begin with, it may be helpful to consider just what it is that one means by "monotheism." Traditionally philosophers of religion have understood monotheism to mean something like: there is only one God who exists and that this God alone is ultimate.[31] Yet, if not careful, certain other expectations might be read into this understanding of God, such as any being who is considered to be God must have a certain property X. In the case of Christian theism, critics often assume that for some being to be classified as God, such a being must have the characteristic or property of being only one person. Therefore, trying to understand Jesus and the Holy Spirit as God would be a violation of basic monotheism, and especially Jewish monotheism. But as recent investigations into early Judaism, particularly Second Temple Judaism, have shown, we must be careful not to impose categories upon a Jewish understanding of monotheism that were not necessarily a part of it, while at the same time, we must allow that some development has taken place in Jewish thinking as it pertains to monotheism.[32] There has been much in recent discussion on just what

---

29. Stephen T. Davis, "God's Action," *In Defense of Miracles*, eds. R. Douglas Geivett and Gary Habermas (Downers Grove, IL: InterVarsity Press, 1997), 176.

30. In this first part I will consider the question of monotheism. In the next section, I will focus more on the question of unity between the divine persons.

31. For a discussion on various kinds of monotheistic views, see Keith Yandell, *Philosophy of Religion: A Contemporary Introduction* (New York: Routledge, 1999), 86–97.

32. See Alan Segal, *Two Powers in Heaven: Early Rabbinic Reports about Christianity and Gnosticism* (Leiden: Brill, 2002).

Jewish monotheism entails.[33] Just what is it that sets the God of Judaism apart from other deities?

In his work on monotheism during the Second Temple period, Larry Hurtado has argued that what set the God of Christians and Jews apart from other conceptions of deity in the ancient world was a radical devotion to and exclusive worship of this one God. Early Christians and Jews during this period held to a diversity of heavenly beings, "whom they regarded very positively, typically as part of the entourage of the one God (e.g., angels)."[34] But these beings were not the recipients of worship. Hurtado contends that such devotion "means that the 'God' of the NT is posited, not as one among others, or as one member of a divine genus, but as *sui generis*, unique and solely worthy of worship."[35] Hurtado claims that within the New Testament documents, Jesus received the same devotion that was reserved for God alone. Early on there was a binitarian shape to worship among Christians, which began after Jesus' death and resurrection. Some of the earliest Christological materials in the New Testament are hymns and confessions embedded within the New Testament documents, giving primacy and devotion to Jesus (John 1:1–18; Rom 1:3–4; 3:24–26; 1 Cor 15:3–5; Gal 3:26–28; Eph 5:14; Phil 2:6–11; Col 1:15–20; 1 Tim 3:15; Heb 1:3).[36]

---

33. See especially Richard Bauckham, *God Crucified: Monotheism and Christology in the New Testament* (Grand Rapids: Eerdmans, 1998); Bauckham, "Monotheism and Christology in the Gospel of John," in *Contours of Christology in the New Testament*, ed. Richard N. Longenecker (Grand Rapids: Eerdmans, 2005), 148–66; Bauckham, *Jesus and the God of Israel: God Crucified and Other Studies on the New Testament's Christology of Divine Identity* (Grand Rapid: Eerdmans, 2008); Larry W. Hurtado, *One Lord, One God: Early Christian Devotion and Ancient Jewish Monotheism* (Philadelphia: Fortress, 1988); Hurtado, "First-Century Jewish Monotheism," *Journal for the Study of the New Testament* 71 (1998): 3–26; Hurtado, *Lord Jesus Christ: Devotion to Jesus in Earliest Christianity* (Grand Rapids: Eerdmans, 2003); Hurtado, *How on Earth Did Jesus Become God? Historical Questions about Earliest Christian Devotion* (Grand Rapids: Eerdmans, 2005); Hurtado, *God in New Testament Theology* (Nashville, TN: Abingdon Press, 2010); James D. G. Dunn, *Did the Early Christians Worship Jesus?: The New Testament Evidence* (Louisville, KY: Westminster John Knox, 2010); Peter Hayman, "Monotheism—A Misused Word in Jewish Studies?" *Journal of Jewish Studies* 42, no. 1 (1991): 1–15; Paul A. Rainbow, "Jewish Monotheism as the Matrix for New Testament Christology: A Review Article," *Novum Testamentum* 33, no. 1 (1991): 17–91; Michael S. Heiser, "Monotheism, Polytheism, Monolatry, or Henotheism: Toward an Assessment of Divine Plurality in the Hebrew Bible," *Bulletin for Biblical Research* 18, no. 1 (2008): 2–4.

34. Hurtado, *God in New Testament Theology*, 28.

35. Ibid., 29.

36. Within the body of the New Testament, there are numerous creedal, hymnic, and confessional materials. These statements are often short, pithy statements; however, there are some longer statements, as well. In addition, these early creedal and hymnic formulas were

Richard Bauckham, too, has done significant work in the area of Second Temple monotheism. Rather than focusing on either a "functional" or "ontic" Christology, as many biblical critics and theologians are often prone to do,[37] Bauckham begins his investigation by working from within the category of, what he calls, "Christology of divine identity."[38] A Christology of divine identity, which was the Christology of the earliest Christian communities, "was already the highest Christology."[39] Making such distinctions as "ontic" and "functional," Bauckham thinks, distorts our understanding of how the earliest Christians understood God and how they did their Christology. On this point, Bauckham asserts:

> When we think in terms of divine identity, rather than divine essence or nature, which are not the primary categories for Jewish theology, we can see that the so-called divine functions which Jesus exercises are intrinsic to who God is. This Christology of divine identity is not a mere stage on the way to the patristic development of ontological Christology in the context of a Trinitarian theology. It is already a fully divine Christology, maintaining that Jesus Christ is intrinsic to the unique and eternal identity of God. The Fathers did not develop it so much as transpose it into a conceptual framework more concerned with the Greek philosophical categories of essence and nature.[40]

often used within a variety of settings and contexts, such as baptism, exorcism, worship, and instruction. The reason that such formulas are important to discussions in Christology is that the writers of the New Testament utilized these sources in developing their material. Thus, such formulas predate the actual writings in which they are found. See Oscar Cullmann, *The Earliest Christian Confessions*, trans. J. K. S. Reid (London: Lutterworth Press, 1949), 18–34; J. N. D. Kelly, *Early Christian Creeds*, 3rd ed. (Burnt Mill, UK: Longman Group Ltd., 1972), 13–29; Vernon H. Neufeld, *The Earliest Christian Confessions* (Grand Rapids: Eerdmans, 1963), 1–12; Richard N. Longenecker, "Christological Materials in the Early Christian Communities," in *Contours of Christology in the New Testament*, ed. Richard N. Longenecker (Grand Rapids: Eerdmans, 2005), 68–74; Ralph P. Martin, *Worship in the Early Church* (Grand Rapids: Eerdmans, 1974), 39–65; Gary R. Habermas, *The Historical Jesus: Ancient Evidence for the Life of Christ* (Joplin, MS: College Press, 1996), 143–70.

37. For a detailed discussion of functional Christology, see Millard J. Erickson, *The Word Became Flesh: A Contemporary Incarnational Christology* (Grand Rapids: Baker, 2000), 215–41, 507–30.

38. Bauckham, *Jesus and the God of Israel*, x.

39. Ibid.

40. Ibid.

There are two basic ways that one can approach monotheism during the Second Temple period. The first is to argue that the monotheism of the postexilic period was strict in such a way that it would have been "impossible to attribute real divinity to any figure other than the one God."[41] Within the context of Jewish monotheism, there is no way that Jesus could have ever been considered divine. The second is a revisionist approach to understanding Jewish monotheism during the Second Temple period. According to Bauckham, this second approach, which places focus on intermediary figures, such as principal angels, exalted patriarchs, and personifications of divine attributes, tends toward blurring the distinction between the one true God and "all other reality."[42] Bauckham recognizes that both approaches are somewhat misguided. With the first view, Bauckham believes that Jewish monotheism is indeed strict. The Jews during the Second Temple period were self-consciously aware of their monotheistic beliefs, and, for them, there was a clear distinction between the one true God of Israel and all other reality. Despite an abundance of intermediary figures within the literature of postexilic Israel, and the fact that such figures had some relevance within the matrix of the Israelite worldview, it is a major point of contention as to whether such figures provide any key insight into the study of Christian origins. A high Christology developed within such a context not because the Jews applied to Jesus a "semi-divine intermediary status" but because they identified "Jesus directly with the one God of Israel."[43]

According to Bauckham, what has been lacking in the whole discussion is a proper understanding of how the Jews during the Second Temple period understood the uniqueness of the true God of Israel. When a proper understanding of what made the God of Jewish monotheism unique is rightly considered, then can one appropriately assess and understand just exactly what the early Christians were doing with Jesus when they included him in the unique identity of the one true God of Israel. How, then, are we to understand "divine identity"?[44]

---

41. Ibid., 2
42. Ibid.
43. Ibid., 3.
44. Ibid., 4.

"Identity" is a term that Bauckham used to describe his findings in the literature of the Second Temple period.[45] For Jews during the Second Temple period, their entire worldview revolved around a certain pattern of "cultic worship" which was "formed by exclusive allegiance to the one God."[46] Yet, this presupposes that God was in some way "identifiable," that is, this God had a unique identity. Bauckham says,

> Since the biblical God has a name and a character, since this God acts, speaks, relates, can be addressed and, in some sense, known, the analogy of human personal identity suggests itself as the category with which to synthesize the biblical and Jewish understanding of God.[47]

This is not to say, however, that Jews were unconcerned with metaphysical statements about God. It is clear from some of the literature of the Second Temple period that certain writers, for example Josephus and Philo, adopted Greek metaphysical language and applied it to God. Moreover, one of those aspects that distinguishes the true God from all other reality is the belief that he is eternal, which is a metaphysical statement about God. But this was not the predominant conceptual framework from which Jews

---

45. It is important not to equivocate and confuse Bauckham's use of "identity" with the philosophical notion of the "is" of identity (usually distinguished from the "is" of predication). As I discuss below, rather than making an identity claim, Bauckham is perhaps doing something more like making an "is" of predication claim despite his use of the word "identity," that is to say, Jesus belongs to the category of divine. It is interesting to note that Jesus and the Spirit are rarely called "God" in the New Testament. Instead, and especially in the Pauline literature, the word "God" is generally reserved for the Father. But a bit more reflection on the New Testament formulas will reveal that New Testament authors had other ways of speaking of someone as divine. Paul most often uses the following triadic formula to speak of the divine persons: Father = God; Son = Lord; Holy Spirit = Spirit (Rom 1:7; 1 Cor 1:2; 8:6; 12:4; 15:24–28; 2 Cor 1:2; Gal 1:3; Eph 1:2; 4:4–6; Phil 1:2; 2:9–11; Col 1:2–3; 1 Thess 1:1; 2 Thess 1:2; 1 Tim 1:2; 2 Tim 1:2; Titus 1:4; Phlm 3). First Corinthians 8:6 is a significant passage in which Paul takes the *Shema* and reformulates it to account for both the Father and the Son: "Yet for us there is one God, the Father, from whom are all things and for whom we exist, and one Lord, Jesus Christ, through whom are all things and through whom we exist" (ESV). This passage takes place within the context of a discussion of idolatry. Paul is assuring the Corinthians that though there may be many so-called "gods" and "lords," Christians serve one God and Lord, which is a reaffirmation of the *Shema*—as clear of an affirmation of monotheism as one can get—except in this context Paul is applying it (the *Shema*) to both the Father and the Son. Both the Father and the Son belong, to use Bauckham's word, to the unique "identity" of the one true God.

46. Bauckham, *Jesus and the God of Israel*, 6.

47. Ibid.

during this time period worked out their understanding of God. They were not so much concerned with *what* deity is but rather with *who* the one true God is. But what are those characteristics that distinguish the one true God from all other reality, including the gods of the nations?

Bauckham recognizes two sets of identifying features that distinguish the God of Jewish monotheism. The first set includes features that speak to God's relationship to his people Israel. It was to Israel that God revealed his divine name Yahweh. Moreover, it was Yahweh, the God of Israel, who made a covenant with his people, who delivered his people out of the hands of Egypt, and who gave them a law. The second set of identifying features—the set that Bauckham is most concerned about for his argument—focuses on how Israel's God relates to the rest of creation. Concerning this second category, there are two underlying themes seen throughout the literature—that God is the creator of and the sovereign ruler over all things. It is these two distinguishing factors (being creator and sovereign) that set apart the God of Israel from all other reality, including the gods of the nations. As the sole creator and ruler over all of reality, God employs a variety of servants to do his bidding. He is envisioned in the Second Temple literature as the great and supreme emperor ruling over all of reality.[48]

There is a third aspect that one must consider in connection with God as creator and sovereign ruler—**monolatry**, the view that God alone should be worshiped, even if other deities exist. Unlike the gentiles, who thought that one could worship a high god, and, yet, at the same time worship lesser deities, the Jews during the Second Temple period reserved worship for the one true God alone.[49]

When one takes these three aspects of Second Temple Judaism together, one can further differentiate between three main categories of Jewish monotheism: *creational*, *eschatological*, and *cultic* monotheism. God alone is the sole creator of all reality. He accomplished this without help or advice from any other. Yet, stemming from this first category of *creational*

---

48. Ibid., 7–10; Richard Bauckham, "The Worship of Jesus in Philippians 2:9–11," in *Where Christology Began: Essays on Philippians 2*, ed. Ralph P. Martin and Brian J. Dodd (Louisville, KY: Westminster John Knox, 1998), 129.

49. Bauckham and Hurtado are in agreement on this and find it to be a central feature of Jewish monotheism during the Second Temple period.

monotheism comes the second category of *eschatological* monotheism by which God, as the sole ruler over all creation will ultimately fulfill his promises, establish his eschatological kingdom, and make his lordship known to the nations. Only the sole ruler and lord over all things should be worshiped—this is his third category of *cultic* monotheism.[50] What Bauckham finds striking is that the earliest Christians applied these same categories to Christ, making up, what he calls, *Christological Monotheism*.[51] Perhaps the strongest evidence of this is the widely used expression found in Psalm 110:1, in which Christ is seated on God's cosmic throne (Phil 9:11; cf. Isa 45:22–23). Within the earliest Christian literature, Jesus is depicted as "the one who will achieve the eschatological lordship of God and in whom the unique sovereignty of the one God will be acknowledged by all," and, moreover, he is "included in the unique rule of God over all things, and is thus placed unambiguously on the divine side of the absolute distinction that separates the only Sovereign One from all creation."[52] God does not share his throne with any other. Yet, by taking a place on the cosmic throne of God, by participating in the sovereign rule and lordship of God, and by receiving worship due to God alone, Christ was depicted in the earliest Christian literature as sharing in the unique identity of the one true God, and thus he was given the highest status that could have possibly been given (Phil 2:6–11). The earliest Christians attributed to Jesus the highest Christology possible within the Jewish monotheistic context. Moreover, in the earliest Christian formulations, Jesus is depicted not only as sovereign ruler but also as creator of all things (John 1:1–3; 1 Cor 8:6; Col 1:15–17; Heb 1:2–3), which implies his pre-existence (Phil 2:6–8). Lastly, we see within the literature that Jesus is given the divine name (Phil 2:9).[53]

Given studies like Hurtado's and Bauckham's, Jewish monotheism can accommodate for more than one person within its overarching schema, especially given Bauckham's notion of "identity." Holding to a concept of a tri-personal God in no way contradicts the concept of Jewish monotheism, unless, of course, one loads upfront what monotheism means and insists

---

50. Bauckham, *Jesus and the God of Israel*, 184.

51. Ibid.

52. Ibid.

53. Ibid.

on saying more than what those during Second Temple Judaism would say. The early church, then, found themselves with the task of translating ideas and concepts from one way of thinking to another. It is precisely because of what they found within the pages of the Scriptures that the early Fathers of the church wrestled through working out a formula that faithfully expressed their findings and did so in such a way that expressed the language and concepts found within the matrix of their own religious and cultural contexts.

PROBLEM OF IDENTITY

While there is room within Jewish monotheism for something like more than one person belonging to the unique identity of the one true God, there is still yet another problem that critics raise—the problem of identity.[54] How is it that the Father, Son, and Holy Spirit are understood by Christians to be identical? After all, the Father is God, the Son is God, and the Holy Spirit is God. Would not this imply that the Father is identical to the Son and to the Spirit which is an apparent contradiction?

In order to answer this, it will be helpful to consider the aforementioned distinction between the "is" of identity and the "is" of predication. When speaking of the "is" of identity, one aims at asserting that some object or person can be understood in at least two ways. For example, Ronnie Campbell is the father of Abby, Caedmon, Justus, and Zeke or Superman is Clark Kent. In each case, one could insert the words "the same thing as" or the "same person as." The "is" of predication, on the other hand, is used to express that whatever is located on the left side of the equation has the property of that which appears on the right. "Superman is superhuman," "Jack is furry," and "Caspian is feline" are all examples of the "is" of predication.[55]

With respect to God, then, what is it that Christians are claiming? If by "is God" the Christian had something like the "is" of identity in mind, then she would be caught in a contradiction since it would follow that the Father is identical with the Son and with the Spirit; however, if she takes

---

54. Here, again it must be emphasized that we should not equivocate on Bauckham's use of "identity" with how philosophers intend it.

55. Thomas D. Senor, "The Incarnation and the Trinity," in *Reason for the Hope Within*, ed. Michael J. Murray (Grand Rapids: Eerdmans, 1999), 247–48.

"is God" to mean something like the "is" of predication, then she is saying something more along the lines of person P "is divine," which would be much less thorny of an issue when it comes identity. But the Christian is not yet clear. It seems that for Christians to predicate of each of the persons "divinity" would render them susceptible to the charge of tri-theism, the heretical view that three gods exist. Moreover, such a view would clearly contradict the Christian adherence to monotheism (that only one God exists). Prima facie, Christians are stuck with the following juxtaposition: God is one and God is three. But the critic will point out that nothing can be both exactly one thing and three things without holding to a view that is logically incoherent. To such a critic, the doctrine of the Trinity would seem as logically incoherent.[56] But as Thomas Senor has rightly suggested:

> When the creeds say that God is three and yet one, they should not
> be understood as asserting that God is three and *one of the same*
> *thing*. That would be contradictory and obviously so. Rather, what
> is being claimed is that there is an important unity in the godhead
> as well as plurality.[57]

Christians have long recognized the tension between the threeness and the oneness of the Trinity. Steering too much toward the threeness leads to tri-theism; whereas, steering too much toward the oneness leads to modalism—the view that God manifests himself in different modes of existence (at one time the Father, at another the Son, or at another the Spirit). Both views were judged by the early church as heretical. So, how might the Christian make sense of the unity and plurality within the Trinity?

Traditionally Christians have put it this way: God as being three individuals (*hypostases*) or persons (*personae*) in one substance (*homoousios*).[58] Thomas Torrance expresses the classical Christian understanding of the Trinity in the following way:

---

56. Bauckham, *Jesus and the God of Israel*, 255–56.

57. Ibid., 256.

58. Richard Swinburne, "A Defense of the Doctrine of the Trinity," in *Philosophy of Religion: A Reader and Guide*, ed. William Lane Craig (New Brunswick, NJ: Rutgers University Press, 2002), 562–64. I find Swinburne's use of the word "individual" to be less than adequate. We're not suggesting that the persons of the Trinity are separate or apart from one another, or that they do their own thing, as the modern understanding of the word "individual" might imply. There is only one being of God, not separate beings or individuals, in that case.

In our understanding of the New Testament witness to God's revelation of himself, "the Father", "the Son", and "the Holy Spirit" are
unique and proper names denoting three distinct Persons or real
Hypostases who are neither exchangeable nor interchangeable
while nevertheless of one and the same divine Being. There is one
Person of the Father who is always the Father, distinct from the Son
and the Spirit; and there is another Person of the Son who is always
the Son, distinct from the Father and the Spirit; and another Person
of the Holy Spirit who is always the Holy Spirit, distinct from the
Father and the Son. In this three-fold tri-personal self-revelation
of God one Person is not more or less God, for all three Persons are
coeternal and coequal. They are all perfectly one in the identity of
their Nature and perfectly homoousial or consubstantial in their
Being. Each of the three Persons is himself Lord and God, and there
is only one and the same eternal Being of the Father, the Son and
the Holy Spirit. The Holy Trinity of three divine Persons is thus
perfectly homogeneous and unitary, both in the threeness and oneness of God's personal activity, and in the threeness and oneness of
his eternal unchangeable personal Being. *Three Persons, one Being.*[59]

Though Christians speak of the three persons as distinct, that must not
be confused with separateness. As Torrance further explains, "No divine
Person is who he is without essential relation to the other two, and yet
each divine Person is other than and distinct from the other two."[60] In
this sense, then, it is this relatedness of each divine person to the other
divine persons that constitutes what and who they are. The Father cannot
be the Father apart from his relation to the Son and the Spirit, and the Son
cannot be the Son apart from his relation to the Father and the Spirit, and
the Spirit cannot be the Spirit apart from his relation to the Father and the
Son. According to Torrance,

The relations between the divine Persons are not just modes of existence, but hypostatic interrelations which belong intrinsically to

59. Thomas F. Torrance, *The Christian Doctrine of God: One Being Three Persons* (London:
T&T Clark, 1996), 155.
60. Ibid., 157.

what Father, Son and Holy Spirit are coinherently in themselves and in their mutual objective relations with and for one another.[61]

Thus, when thinking of the doctrine of the Trinity, Christians cannot think of God apart from the interrelatedness of the three persons. If one of the persons were absent, then we would not have the Christian God but something like ditheism.

What is it, then, that constitutes the unity between the divine persons? Here, something like the doctrine of perichoresis might provide a way forward. Before considering perichoresis as it relates to my proposal, it may first be helpful to consider Social Trinitarianism.

There are two main views on the doctrine of the Trinity—the so-called Latin view (LT) and the so-called Social Trinitarian view (ST). I will not here defend either view, since this is an in-house debate. For now I will assume something like the ST view is true in order to defend against the charge of incoherence.

ST is usually described as beginning with the threeness of God instead of God's oneness. Most versions of ST hold to each of the three persons as existing as a society or community (perhaps a better understanding is that God is community-like) and each having something like a generic divine nature. The notion of person for defenders of ST carries the idea of having a distinct mind and will or distinct center of consciousness. The word "God" then carries the notion of "the Godhead."[62]

In order to explain their version of ST, J. P. Moreland and William Lane Craig use the example of the Greco-Roman mythological creature, Cerberus.[63] Cerberus is a dog-like creature with three heads. Given that Cerberus has three heads, we may assume that it has three brains with three distinct centers of consciousness. Yet because of its biology we might also assume that there is no one center of consciousness, suggesting that for Cerberus to function properly it would require a significant amount of cooperation between each of the minds. Despite there being three distinct heads with three centers of consciousness, given that it is a single

---

61. Ibid.

62. Davis, *Christian Philosophical Theology*, 61.

63. Moreland and Craig, *Philosophical Foundations*, 593.

biological entity we would still think that there is only one dog-creature, so say Moreland and Craig. To flesh this out a bit more, the authors assign to each of the heads the following names: Bowser, Rover, and Spike. They then give the example of Hercules attempting to enter Hades when one of the heads, Spike, snarled at him. In such a case, they explain, Hercules could accurately report that Cerberus snarled at him. They then ask their readers to suppose further that Cerberus is not merely canine but has minds much like our own, endowed with rationality and self-conscious-ness and that each of the heads has personal agency. Would we not, then, have something like a tri-personal being? If Cerberus were to die in battle and its soul were to persist in the afterlife, might not we have something like what is pictured in the Trinity prior to the incarnation—three unem-bodied distinct centers of consciousness united as one being? The authors take it that God is a soul or is soul-like. Here we would have not one person; rather, we would have one being (a soul) with three distinct centers of consciousness.[64] Does this model of ST work?

I find Moreland and Craig's proposed analogy appealing, allowing for the "three-in-one" model that ST Trinitarians hold, showing a deep unity between the persons and divine nature; however, I would like to bolster their view with some reflection on the doctrine of perichoresis.

In working through his own model of the Trinity, which he calls "peri-choretic monotheism," Stephen Davis suggests the following are needed to show the Trinity to be a single individual (unity):

(1) Each of the Persons equally possesses the divine essence in its totality. (2) The three necessarily share a marvelous unity of pur-pose, will, and action; that is, it is not possible for them to disagree or to be in conflict. (3) They exist in *perichoresis* (circumincession, co-inherence, permeation). That is, each is "in" the others; each ontologically embraces the others; to be a divine Person is by nature to be in relation to the other two; the boundaries between them are transparent; their love for and communion with each other is such that they can be said to "interpenetrate" each other.[65]

---

64. Ibid.
65. Stephen T. Davis, *Christian Philosophical Theology*, 61.

Davis has provided a helpful grid for working through an ST under-standing of the Trinity. One of the chief difficulties when working through this doctrine, and particularly the ST version, is that it would seem we have something like four persons: God the Father, God the Son, God the Holy Spirit, and the Godhead. Getting back to our earlier distinction between the "is" of identity and the "is" of predication, the defender of ST will want to suggest that what is taking place is the "is" of predication. In other words, "God" is a reference to the divine essence (1). When we speak of "God," there is a sense in which we have in mind a single being. That is not disputed; however, it must remain clear that it is more accurate to speak of God as *personal* rather than saying that God is *a person*. When the defender of ST says "God" has done X, she means that the entire Godhead (or, perhaps, one of the divine persons) has accomplished X.

Davis's emphasis on perichoresis (3) allows the defender of ST to accom-modate for an even greater unity between the persons working from the Moreland and Craig analogy. Not only do each of the persons share a divine essence, each divine person is completely open to and penetrates the other persons. It is a moving toward the other in divine love. Thomas Torrance provides a helpful portrait of what this perichoretic love looks like within the Trinity:

When we turn to the First Epistle of St John we learn that "God is Love", and that this Love is defined by the Love that God bears to us in sending his Son to be the propitiation for our sins, and indeed for the sins of the world. That is to say, the very Being of God as Love is identical with his loving, for he is himself the Love with which he loves; his Being and his Act are one and the same. This very love that God is, therefore, is identical with Jesus Christ who laid down his life for us, and who in his own Being and Act as the Son of the Father embodies the Love of God. The self-giving of the Son in sacri-ficial love and the self-giving of the Father in sacrificial love are not separable from one another, for the Father and the Son dwell in one another, together with the Spirit of God, whom we know through his witness to the Son, and through whose dwelling in us God dwells in us. This means that we are to understand the Love that God is in his being-in-act and his act-in-being in a Trinitarian way. The

Father, the Son and the Holy Spirit who indwell One Another in the
Love that God is constitute the Communion of Love or the movement
of reciprocal Loving which is identical with the One Being of God.
It is as God the Father, God the Son, and God the Holy Spirit that
God is God and God is Love. As one Being, three Persons, the Being
of God is to be understood as an eternal movement of Love, both in
himself as the Love of the Father, the Son and the Holy Spirit for
one Another, and in his loving Self-giving to others beyond himself.[66]

Divine love, as Torrance explains, does not involve merely God's being
or merely his act but God's "being-in-act" or "act-in-being." It is precisely
this dynamic and active eternal movement toward the other—being-in-
act, which Torrance borrows from Barth—that makes for a strong unity. It
is also this perichoretic love relationship between the persons that allows
for a complete knowing of the Other because of the interpenetration and
mutual indwelling of that relationship. The intimate knowledge between
the Father, Son, and Spirit is nothing like anything a created being can
experience. Each of the persons of the divine Trinity knows the others
intimately. It is such an intimacy that a divine person is completed by the
other persons, so much so that he cannot be himself apart from them. Yet,
the knowledge that the divine person experiences is not merely a complete intimate knowing of the divine self in relation to the others but a
complete knowing of the others as they exist in relation to one another.
Here we might think of it as something like "omnisubjectivity" whereby
each divine person shares fully his mental states with the other divine
persons—complete and total vulnerability.[67]

Given the above, I suggest that we understand the persons of God as
three distinct (but not separate) unembodied centers of consciousness, all
of whom are personal agents, having something like an intellect, emotion,

---

66. Torrance, *The Christian Doctrine of God*, 165.

67. For an interesting discussion on the possibility of divine omnisubjectivity, see Linda
Zagzebski, "Omnisubjectivity," in *Oxford Studies in Philosophy of Religion*, vol. 1, ed. Jonathan L.
Kvanvig (Oxford: Oxford University Press, 2008), 231–48. Zagzebski coined the term "omnisubjectivity," but she uses it quite differently from how I am applying it here. Her version has
to do with whether God has something like omnisubjectivity as it relates to his knowledge of
his creatures. I am taking it only in the sense of how each of the divine persons might know
the other divine persons.

and will of their own, but not apart from the other. The persons are coequal, sharing fully those properties of the divine nature in oneness of being and substance, while existing eternally in divine perichoretic and interpenetrating relationship. This perichoretic relationship allows for full and complete unity and for each of the persons fully to indwell, embrace, and intimately know the Other. The giving up of the divine self in self-giving love to the divine Other reassures that all the acts of the divine Trinity are one. Taking something like the above understanding of the Trinity answers, to my satisfaction, the critic's charge of incoherence based on identity.

CHAPTER 7
A GOD WHO ACTS

S o far, I have argued that of the four metaphysical systems, theism best explains the phenomena of evil in the world and provides an overall thicker worldview response to the reality of evil; however, as we saw in the previous chapter, minimalistic theism in and of itself falls short since a concept of God that is Unitarian or mono-personal in nature cannot explain both God's aseity and his being an essentially loving person. I argued that something more is needed, which a Trinitarian understanding of God provides. As we continue to respond to the Hartshornean-type objection proposed in the previous chapter, there is still, yet, another question that Christian theists must answer: Can the God of Christian theism act in the world? To put it more specifically, given the classical Christian conception of God, is it coherent to believe that the Triune God discussed in the previous chapter can act in the world, work miracles, stop evil, and answer prayers? Is this God not only loving, but can he respond to his creatures in a loving way?

Process theologians have long criticized the classical theistic conception of God as being static and without concern for the suffering of his creatures. Such a view of God, they claim, is unbiblical. Instead the Whiteheadian/Hartshornean view of God is more in line with the biblical teaching that God is love. In light of such objections, I now take up the challenge of sketching out a Christian conception of deity whereby, on the one hand, God is religiously available to his people, that is to say, the God of Christian theism can receive and answer prayers, while also being aware of what is going on in the world. Yet, on the other hand, I argue for a conception of deity whereby God can act within the world, doing things such as performing miracles, delivering his people, bringing about final justice, restoring creation, and putting the world to rights. This God, claims the Christian theist, does so without also being contained by or enmeshed in the world, as we might see in process thought. What I am here advocating for is a form of theological essentialism. Theological essentialism can accommodate many of the criticisms against classical theists, yet without also giving up the central tenets of the Christian understanding of God. Furthermore, I contend that the theological essentialist can maintain a position that is true to Scripture while also remaining within the Anselmian tradition of Greater Being theology.

To accomplish this, I begin by sketching out three options available to Christian theists—classical theism, open theism, and neoclassical theism.[1] I will then argue that of the three something like neoclassical theism best fits with the biblical view of God. Moreover, not only does the neoclassical view adequately answer those concerns raised by process theologians, it avoids the difficulties of process theism itself, while also providing a robust and coherent view of the God/world relation, which is vital if the Christian God is to do something about evil in the world.

CHRISTIAN CONCEPTIONS OF GOD

There is nothing more crucial to a Christian theist than her concept of God. For the most part, Christians agree on certain central truths concerning God: that God has certain attributes (e.g., omniscience, omnipotence, omnibenevolent), that he is the creator of the world (in some sense or another), that he is religiously available, and that he acts in the world to redeem and reconcile his people to himself.[2] Despite these points of convergence, Christians often disagree on their understanding of what God is like. Stephen Davis distinguishes between three systems: the classical theory (that is, classical theism), the openness theory (or openness theism), and the neoclassical theory (or neoclassical theism). Davis considers each view a live option for the Christian theist today.[3] Below, I follow Davis' basic

---

1. Stephen T. Davis, "Three Views of God, Which is Correct?" in *Disputed Issues: Contending for Christian Faith in Today's Academic Setting* (Waco, TX: Baylor University Press, 2009), 206.

2. Ibid., 205.

3. Ibid., 206–7.

outline for each of these views while making nuances that fit with the purposes for the rest of the chapter.

CLASSICAL THEISM

Classical theism (CT) has been the traditional view, held by such thinkers as Augustine, Anselm, and Aquinas. Modern adherents to this view include Brian Leftow, Eleonore Stump, and Paul Helm. CT affirms that God is not only omnipotent, omniscient, and omnibenevolent but also metaphysically simple, that his temporal mode of existence is timeless, and that he is immutable and impassible. What adherents of CT mean by affirming that God's temporal mode of existence is timeless is that God does not have temporal location or extension. God no more exists in time than in space—God transcends all created space-time. God's timelessness entails *absolute* immutability and *vice versa*. By absolute immutability, adherents of CT hold that, not only does God not change, but he also could not change in any sense. In the words of Paul Helm, "It is not that God is immutable because he is unwilling to change, but because his perfect nature is such that he need not and cannot change."[4] Similarly, Thomas Aquinas argued that "it is evident that it is impossible for God to be in any way changeable."[5] As impassible, God does not suffer, nor is he affected by anything outside of himself. Lastly, metaphysical simplicity refers to God's not having parts. Defenders of CT would argue that based on God's simplicity one cannot in reality speak of God as having more than one property. It is acceptable to say that God is loving and omnipotent, but these are not separate properties. God *just is* his properties.[6]

OPENNESS THEISM

Not all Christians, of course, are happy with CT. One alternative is openness theism (OT), sometimes referred to as open theism, openness theology, or the open view of God. Adherents of OT, such as William Hasker, John

---

4. Paul Helm, "Divine Timeless Eternity," in *God and Time: Four Views*, ed. Gregory Ganssle (Downers Grove, IL: InterVarsity Press, 2001), 35. See also Helm, *Eternal God*, 20.

5. Aquinas, *Summa Theologica*, I, Q. 9, Art. 1.

6. Davis, "Three Views of God," 207.

Sanders, Clark Pinnock, Gregory Boyd, and David Basinger,[7] find the idea of God held by adherents of CT to be too greatly influenced by Greek philosophical thought. They agree with classical theists that God is, say, eternal, omnipotent, and the Creator of all things; however, they believe such doctrines as divine simplicity, immutability, impassibility, and divine timelessness do not fit with the picture of God painted in the Bible. Consider the words of OT defender, Clark Pinnock:

> Aristotle spoke of God as an unmoved mover, which contrasts sharply with the God of Abraham, Isaac, and Jacob. Aristotle believed God moves other beings by being an object of desire and thought, without moving itself. God serves as the final cause for worldly activities, while remaining completely unchangeable in itself. Echoing Plato, Aristotle denied any kind of change in God, because, he thought, any change in a perfect being would have to be change for the worse. The only activity, therefore, which God could engage in would be the "activity" of self-contemplation. How very different is this immobile substance from the living God of biblical revelation.[8]

Instead, the God of the Bible is dynamic and active, open with respect to the future, and takes greats risks in creating. On the OT understanding of the biblical God, Pinnock writes:

> Our understanding of the Scriptures leads us to depict God, the sovereign Creator, as voluntarily bringing into existence a world with significantly free personal agents in it, agents who can respond positively to God or reject his plans for them. In line with the decision to make this kind of world, God rules in such a way as to uphold the created structures and, because he gives liberty to his creatures, is happy to accept the future as open, not closed, and a relationship with the world that is dynamic, not static. We believe that the Bible presents an open view of God as living and active, involved

---

7. Clark Pinnock et al., *The Openness of God: A Biblical Challenge to the Traditional Understanding of God* (Downers Grove, IL: InterVarsity Press, 1994); Gregory A. Boyd, *God of the Possible: A Biblical Introduction to the Open View of God* (Grand Rapids: Baker, 2000).

8. Clark Pinnock, *The Most Moved Mover: A Theology of God's Openness* (Grand Rapids: Baker Academic, 2001), 7.

in history, relating to us and changing in relation to us. We see the universe as a context in which there are real choices, alternatives and surprises. God's openness means that God is open to the changing realities of history, that God cares about us and lets what we do impact him. Our lives make a difference to God—they are significant. God is delighted when we trust him and saddened when we rebel against him.[9]

Defenders of OT reject the classical Christian view of divine omniscience, which suggests that God has exhaustive foreknowledge of the future. For them, God knows all things past and present perfectly; yet, the future is open because God does not have knowledge of certain events that will take place in the future. Surely, they claim, God might know his own purposes and what he will indeed bring about and accomplish; however, it is logically impossible for him to know what creatures with libertarian freedom will or would indeed do, given their free choice. In other words, if humans are free in the libertarian sense, that is, their actions are not coerced, determined, or caused by God (or something else), then the future is not something that is fixed or set in place, and therefore it cannot be known by God or anyone else. Here, defenders of OT agree with determinists or compatibilists that if determinism was true, then God would, indeed, know the future. He would know it because he determined it. Instead, they maintain that determinism and libertarian freedom are incompatible with one another. Because determinism is false and because humans have libertarian freedom, they would argue, it is metaphysically impossible for God to know these future contingents.

NEOCLASSICAL THEISM

Neoclassical theism (NCT) finds much in agreement with CT but disagrees with respect to the doctrine of divine timelessness, opting for an understanding of God's mode of existence as temporal (e.g., everlasting, omni-temporal, or relatively timeless). Some defenders of NCT deny that God is immutable and impassible, but others maintain both, opting for

---

9. Clark Pinnock, "Systematic Theology," in *The Openness of God: A Biblical Challenge to the Traditional Understanding of God* (Downers Grove, IL: InterVarsity Press, 1994), 103–4.

a nuanced understanding of each. Adherents of NCT usually reject the notion that God is simple, at least as Augustine and Aquinas understood it. However, most in this camp agree with CT that God knows the future and opt for either something like middle knowledge or simple foreknowledge. Defenders of NCT include Alvin Plantinga, Nicholas Wolterstorff, William Lane Craig, and Stephen Davis, just to name a few.

Of the three views, I find something like NCT to be more in line with the biblical understanding of God. Not all theists agree, of course. Certainly, advantages and disadvantages persist with any theological view, and no matter which way one goes, there are always theological tradeoffs. In what follows, I will briefly state the chief difficulties I have with OT, and then will focus the rest of the chapter on CT. It will be impossible to consider each of the core tenets of CT—divine timelessness, immutability, impassibility, and simplicity—in a single chapter. Instead, the thrust of the remainder of the chapter places emphasis on the CT doctrines of divine timelessness and absolute immutability (I will consider divine impassibility in the final chapter).[10] I do not think that the divine timeless view is incoherent; however, it does come with certain theological costs that I believe outweigh the theological costs of a God who is temporal—at least *in some sense temporal*. Instead, I argue that something like Alan Padgett's Relative Timelessness view provides a more robust understanding of God's relationship to time, whereby it makes sense of the biblical understanding of a God who can act in the world, answer prayers, and be religiously available to his creatures.

---

10. While I do not consider the doctrine of divine simplicity in detail, this attribute has been an important feature of CT. What one does with divine simplicity will often set the course for how one interprets the divine attributes of eternity and immutability. This was especially true for Aquinas in his *Summa Theologica*. If God is timelessly eternal, then God is immutable in the absolute sense, impassible, and metaphysically simple. These four characteristics of CT are significantly interconnected and might properly be labeled *eternalism*. As will be shown, I reject eternalism, opting for a view of God's temporal mode of existence as relative timelessness or omnitemporality. Such a view does not allow for a doctrine of divine simplicity *as understood by defenders of CT*. The view of NCT I am advocating for in this chapter doesn't deny the doctrine of divine simplicity but only a certain understanding of divine simplicity. For my own position, I agree with CT that God does not consist of parts; however, it is not at all clear from this that there are no distinctions between divine perfections. For a fuller discussion on different ways of understandings divine simplicity, see Morris, *Our Idea of God*, 113–18. Finally, I will consider divine impassibility in the last chapter. I do not deny the impassibility doctrine; however, I reject the stricter or absolute understanding of divine impassibility espoused by eternalism.

SOME DIFFICULTIES WITH
OPENNESS THEISM

There is much within the OT position that is commendable and with which I agree. Defenders of this view take the Bible seriously and aim to understand God as portrayed in the biblical record. They are keenly aware of how Greek philosophical thought has impacted the way defenders of CT have often interpreted Scripture.[11] Moreover, in contrast to process theology, the OT position holds affirmatively to God's creation of the world *ex nihilo* and that there's an ontological distinction between the Creator and the creature. Finally, they maintain that God is dynamic and active in the world.[12] He can hear our prayers, know our thoughts, and respond to his people—though, I'm not sure any classical theist would deny this, even though they might understand God's knowledge of and response to his creatures differently than defenders of OT. Having considered some strengths, let us now consider some difficulties with OT.

First, in my estimation, OT limits God's omniscience by denying God's foreknowledge. While defenders of OT often are quick to point out how Greek philosophical views affect one's interpretation of the Bible, they must admit, too, that their own philosophical conclusions, such as their understanding of libertarian freedom, affect how they interpret certain passages within Scripture and how God interacts with the world. As one who is sympathetic to libertarian freedom, I find it difficult to square with Scripture that God is ignorant of the future, whether by metaphysical impossibility or by divine choice to lay aside the ability to know the future.[13]

---

11. While I agree this is certainly true, we must tread cautiously here. Just because some idea is a Greek way of thinking does not mean it is false. Furthermore, we cannot suppose that simply because something is a Greek way of thinking that it doesn't cohere or fit with the biblical view and understanding.

12. Pinnock, "Systematic Theology," 107–11. I don't think, as Pinnock and others have suggested, that the CT view of God represents a God who is static and unresponsive, especially since many defenders of CT hold to God as always in act (*actus purus*). Though, I certainly concur with them that, perhaps, God's activity in the world may be different from the way in which Thomas Aquinas and other classical theists have understood it.

13. Richard Swinburne argues that God limits his knowledge of the future in order to preserve both his freedom and the freedom of his creatures. Consider the following:

In choosing to preserve his own freedom (and to give others freedom), he (that is, God) limits his own knowledge of what is to come. He continually limits himself in this way by not curtailing his or men's future freedom. As regards men, their choices are much influenced by circumstances and this makes it possible for a

Defenders of the openness view take certain passages of Scripture, such as Genesis 6:5–6 (which indicates at the time of the flood God regretted or was sorry for having created human beings), to mean that God was ignorant of how things would turn out in such instances. But opponents of OT readily recognize that the Bible often uses divine accommodation and employs anthropomorphisms to tell us truths about God. In such places what's really being recorded is God's responses and actions as understood from the human perspective.[14] Davis sums up this point well:

> Accordingly, the fact that God is sometimes depicted as being ignorant of how things will turn out and as later regretful when they turn out badly is a function of how God's actions appeared to human observers of the events in question or how they seemed to the biblical writers at the time they wrote. Such texts do not describe God's inner life, nor ... are they meant to do so. Since they describe God's actions in the world, they describe not God as God is in himself but God as seen in God's work.[15]

The use of anthropomorphism and divine accommodation does not mean no action took place, nor does it mean God has no mental states. Surely, something really happened. There was, indeed, a divine response to the actions of human beings. Yet, such responses and actions are depicted in human terms and written down as they were perceived. But isn't such a response a cop-out, the defender of OT might object? How are we to know when to take a passage in a straightforward manner or figuratively? This is a legitimate question. On this Paul Helm provides a helpful hermeneutical principle: Christians should interpret those passages that paint God as ignorant and changing his mind in light of those passages that demonstrate God's maximal knowledge and power.[16]

So why, then, should the Christian believe that God has knowledge of the future? Moreover, wouldn't God's knowledge of the future mean

---

being who knows all the circumstances to predict human behavior correctly most of the time, but always with the possibility that men may falsify those predictions. (Swinburne, *The Coherence of Theism*, 174)

14. Davis, "Three Views of God," 214–15.

15. Ibid., 215.

16. Paul Helm, *The Providence of God* (Downers Grove, IL: InterVarsity Press, 1993), 90.

determinism is true? Let's begin with the first question. David Hunt identifies four prima facie reasons for thinking that God has foreknowledge: (1) it is firmly rooted in Scripture; (2) God as a supreme and perfect being demands this; (3) divine sovereignty and providence require it; and (4) a consensus of the church's leading thinkers supports it.[17] Hunt rightly warns that critics may object to any one or all of these points. Of the four, the strongest reason is (1). Both (2) and (3) somewhat hang on (1), though independent arguments for each can be given. As for (4), though a consensus of church teaching should cause us to heavily consider some doctrine before abandoning or jettisoning it, I take it that final authority rests in Scripture. Nevertheless, these reasons, taken together, provide a strong cumulative case. For our purposes, however, I will focus only on (1).

Given (1), what biblical support do we have for divine foreknowledge? Scripture teaches that God foreknows the future in a general way (Isa 44:6–8; 46:9–10; Dan 2, 7; Matt 24, 25; Acts 15:8), predicts the rise of Cyrus (Isa 44:26–45:7), and foretells Christ's coming (Mic 5:2) and his crucifixion (Acts 2:23; 3:18).[18] Moreover, the Gospels paint Jesus as having knowledge of future events, especially in reference to his passion, death, and resurrection (e.g., Mark 8:31; 9:31; 10:32–34), but also in connection to a variety of other events (Matt 17:27; Mark 13; 14:13–15, 18–20, 27–30; Luke 17:22–37).[19] We should also consider the nature of prophecy itself. As William Lane Craig has argued extensively, the overarching sweep of prophecy in both the Old and New Testaments requires God's knowledge of the future. On this Craig says,

> God's knowledge of the course of world history and his control over it to achieve his purposes seem fundamental to the biblical conception of history and are a source of comfort and assurance to the believer in times of distress. …
>
> God's knowledge of the future seems essential to the prophetic pattern that underlies the biblical scheme of history. The test of

---

17. David Hunt, "The Simple-Foreknowledge View," in *Divine Foreknowledge: Four Views*, ed. James K. Beilby and Paul R. Eddy (Downers Grove, IL: InterVarsity Press, 2001), 68–69.

18. Henry C. Theisen and Vernon D. Doerksen, *Lectures in Systematic Theology*, rev. ed. (Grand Rapids: Eerdmans, 2000), 47; William Lane Craig, *The Only Wise God: The Compatibility of Divine Foreknowledge and Human Freedom* (1987; repr., Eugene, OR: Wipf & Stock, 1999), 26.

19. Craig, *Only Wise God*, 35–36.

the true prophet was success in foretelling the future: "When a prophet speaks in the name of the LORD, if the word does not come to pass or come true, that is a word which the LORD has not spoken" (Deut 18:22).[20]

Perhaps, one of the strongest passages affirming God's foreknowledge, especially as it relates to God's providential role in salvation history, comes from the prophet Isaiah:

Set forth your case, says the LORD;
  bring your proofs, says the King of Jacob.

Let them bring them, and tell us
  what is to happen

Tell us the former things, what they are,
  that we may consider them,

that we may know their outcome;
  or declare to us the things to come.

Tell us what is to come hereafter,
  that we may know that you are gods;

do good, or do harm,
  that we may be dismayed and terrified.

Behold, you are nothing,
  and your work is less than nothing;
  an abomination is he who chooses you. (Isa 41:21–24)

In this passage, God himself lays down the gauntlet, making knowledge of the future the test that distinguishes the one true God from all the gods of the nations.[21]

---

20. Ibid., 27.

21. Ibid., 29. I do not claim to have shown extensively God's foreknowledge. For a fuller treatment, I recommend the reader to Craig's excellent work on divine foreknowledge in *The Only Wise God*. See also Millard Erickson, *What Does God Know and When Does He Know It?: The Current Controversy Over Divine Foreknowledge* (Grand Rapids: Zondervan, 2003), 39–85.

But what of our second question? If God knows the future, doesn't that mean the future is determined? This is known as the argument from fatalism. Stated formally:

1. Necessarily, if God foreknows *x*, then *x* will happen.

2. God foreknows *x*.

3. Therefore, *x* will necessarily happen.[22]

So, *x* cannot be a contingent feature of the world, since it happens necessarily, so the argument goes. However, it is a non sequitur since (3) does not properly follow from (1) and (2). Instead, (3) should read more like:

3. Therefore, *x* will happen.[23]

Yet, as Craig has argued, there's no reason to think that *x* will *necessarily* happen (i.e., that it *must* happen), but only that it *will* happen. Why is that? Because it is possible for *x* not to happen. Yet, if *x* fails to happen, continues Craig, then God would have foreknown it to be the case that *x* fails. Craig believes we can make sense of God's knowledge as it relates to human free choices without resorting to fatalism. Consider the following:

> The fact that Jones will actually mow the lawn is the reason why God foreknows that Jones will mow the lawn. Jones does not mow the lawn because God foreknows; God foreknows because Jones will mow the lawn. Now this does *not* mean Jones's action *causes* God's foreknowledge. The word *because* here indicates a logical, not causal, relation, one similar to that expressed in the sentence "four is an even number because it is divisible by two." The word *because* expresses a logical relation of ground and consequent. God's foreknowledge is *chronologically* prior to Jones's mowing the lawn, but Jones's mowing the lawn is *logically* prior to God's foreknowledge. Jones's mowing is the ground; God's foreknowledge is its logical

---

22. Craig, *Only Wise God*, 73; Craig, "The Middle Knowledge View," in *Divine Foreknowledge: Four Views*, ed. James K. Beilby and Paul R. Eddy (Downers Grove, IL: InterVarsity Press, 2001), 126.

23. Craig, "The Middle Knowledge View," 126.

consequent; Jones's mowing is the reason why God foreknows that Jones will mow the lawn.[24]

Craig, it seems to me, has adequately responded to the problem from fatalism. But friends of OT might object by raising a philosophical problem regarding God's foreknowledge and creaturely free acts. How is it, they claim, God can know the future free actions of his creatures since there is nothing there for God to know? To put it differently, it is logically impossible for God to know future contingencies or the counterfactuals of creaturely freedom since there is nothing yet (out there in the future) for God to know.[25] If something like the above were true, then it would mean that God could not know beforehand whether tomorrow morning I will freely mow the lawn or not. Such statements as "Tomorrow morning Ronnie Campbell will freely mow the lawn" ultimately have no truth value. However, by denying the truth value of future events, defenders of OT end up denying the Principle of Bivalence, which states that for any proposition p, p is either true or it is false.[26]

In my own estimation, denying the Principle of Bivalence in connection to future propositions runs into several difficulties and absurdities, as Craig has adequately shown.[27] But, moreover, it seems to me that the burden of proof is on defenders of OT (and determinists, too) to show why God can't know counterfactuals of creaturely freedom.

But let's suppose that defenders of OT are right—God is often surprised by or disappointed in his creatures and doesn't know the outcomes of future creaturely actions. If that were the case, then God's being surprised or disappointed by what people do (e.g., the amount of evil caused by people before the flood) results in a God who holds to erroneous beliefs. How so? Before an event, say before the flood, God had the erroneous belief that people would not do x or, at least, they would not be as bad as x. But to God's surprise, things didn't go quite as he had expected. In other words,

---

24. Craig, The Only Wise God, 74.

25. Ibid., 56.

26. Davis, "Three Views of God," 215; Craig, "A Middle Knowledge Response," in Divine Foreknowledge: Four Views, ed. James K. Beilby and Paul R. Eddy (Downers Grove, IL: InterVarsity Press, 2001), 56.

27. See Craig, The Only Wise God, 55–60.

mental states, such as being surprised or disappointed, argues Stephen Davis, could only have been had by God if only prior to those states God had expected otherwise.[28] Davis continues,

> Now beliefs are not the same things as expectations, but it is hard to see how someone can have an expectation that an event will occur without having some sort of belief (however strongly or weakly held) that it will occur. Accordingly, if God was surprised and disappointed at what eventually occurred, then before the event occurred, God had a false belief.[29]

Surely, defenders of OT will not deny that surprise and disappointment are true representations in Scripture of God's mental states. To state otherwise would go against their hermeneutic.

A second difficulty I have with OT is that it severely limits God's sovereignty, and this is especially important as it relates to the problem of evil. In some ways, OT has a certain advantage over those views that affirm divine foreknowledge. After all, if God's human and angelic creatures have libertarian freedom, then God is not responsible for the choices he did not know they would make, and hence God is not responsible for evil. But this also shows the severity of this view. In creating the world God took a great risk. There was no guarantee that anyone in the end would have been saved. How could he have known? Surely, those who refuse God do so according to their own will, and it is because of their own choosing that they end in eternal separation from God. But given OT, why think God would have had any guarantee that even one of his creatures would have accepted him, followed his ways, and made it through in the end? There is no reason to think that such would have been the case at all. Contra OT, Scripture indicates that God does indeed know who will in the end be saved, and he knows this even before the foundation of the world (Rev 13:8).[30] Now we shall consider classical theism.

---

28. Davis, "Three Views of God," 216.
29. Ibid.
30. Ibid., 215.

THEOLOGICAL ESSENTIALISM AND
OBJECTIONS TO CLASSICAL THEISM

Traditionally, Christians have understood God to have a certain (logical) set of core attributes. By *core* attribute is meant that God has a certain essential property without which he would cease to be himself.[31]

Before moving on to discuss some objections to CT, it would be helpful to distinguish an essential property from a nonessential property. An essential property is the kind of property that belongs to a thing's nature. Essential properties are such that they can neither be changed nor given up. If an essential property of a thing was altered, then that thing would no longer be what it is. In contrast, nonessential properties are the kinds of properties where their change would not affect the nature of the thing in question.[32]

As noted, God's attributes are essential properties. Yet, many predications made of God refer to his nonessential properties, which often have to do with God's relationship to his creatures. Ronald Nash helps to clarify this point when he says,

> Relational predicates like "creator," "ruler," and "reserver" do not denote core divine attributes. A property like "being Lord of Israel" is likewise a nonessential property. It is logically possible that God might not have had this property. He might never have created Israel, or Israel might never have accepted Yahweh as its God. Being Lord of Israel is not essential to the being of God.[33]

This distinction is crucial. Take the following propositions about God:

1. God is creator of the universe.

2. God is sustainer of all things.

3. God is redeemer of his people.

Most Christians theists would agree that each property is nonessential for God to have. God was neither obligated to create the world nor sustain

---

31. Nash, *The Concept of God*, 16.
32. Ibid.
33. Ibid.

it. He could have chosen to exist, happily, without a world. In contrast, take the following propositions:

1. God is immaterial.

2. God is eternal.

3. God is omnipotent.

4. God is omniscient.

5. God is love.

Unlike the previous set of properties, most Christians would agree that the latter are essential to the nature of the God of Christian theism, even if they have differences on what those properties entail.

Not all predicates applied to God concern his essential attributes, for example, the propositions "God is the God who acts in the world" or "God is the God who performs miracles." Such properties are nonessential to God's nature. Yet these nonessential qualities are dependent on God's essential attributes. To put it more clearly, in order for God to be the God who acts in the world or the God who performs miracles or the God who responds to the cries of his people, his nature must be such that he *could* act in the world and perform miracles, become incarnate, stop evil, and the like.

But it is at this point that some critics have difficulty with the CT understanding of God. For instance, physicist Paul Davies, who is himself a panentheist of sorts, raises the following objection:

> The problem about postulating a God who transcends time is that ... many of the qualities which most people attribute to God only make sense within the context of time.... Is he not continually active in the world, doing work, "oiling the cogs of the cosmic machine" and so on? All of these activities are meaningless except in a temporal context. How can God plan and act except in time?[34]

Later, Davies presents another objection:

---

34. Paul Davies, *God and the New Physics* (New York: Simon and Schuster, 1983), 38.

A God who is in time is subject to change. But what causes that change? If God is the cause of all existing things ... then does it make sense to talk about that ultimate cause itself changing? ... A God who is in time is, therefore, in some sense caught up in the operation of the physical universe. Indeed, it is quite likely that time will cease to exist at some stage in the future. ... In that case God's own position is obviously insecure. Clearly, God cannot be omnipotent if he is subject to the physics of time, nor can he be considered the creator of the universe if he did not create time. In fact, because time and space are inseparable, a God who did not create time, created space neither.[35]

Both of Davies' objections charge the Christian view of God of incoherence. Is the God of Christianity incoherent?

DAVIES' FIRST OBJECTION

Concerning Davies' first objection, if God transcends time, how is it that God acts in time? The kinds of actions that are often attributed to God require that he be temporal or, at least, that such actions take place within time. Take the following example:

Smith prays to God at t^1 to answer x, and

God answers x at t^2

For God to answer Smith's prayer, three things are required of God: 1) God must know that Smith uttered a prayer; 2) God must know that Smith uttered a prayer at some time t^1; and 3) God must know that t^2 is a time different from t^1. But if God transcends time, how is it that he knows what time it is in the world or at what time he should act in the world? Prima facie, this raises a significant problem for the defender of CT. CT holds that God is timelessly eternal, which entails that God is absolutely immutable. But to say that God is absolutely immutable requires that God cannot change in any sense. Thus, God cannot be aware of what is taking place in the world at any time. For, if God knows now, or any other time,

---

35. Ibid., 133.

what is going on in the world, then it would require that God's knowledge in some way changes. But if God experiences change in any sense, then he could not be timeless.

One possible out for the defender of CT is to argue that all points of time are equally real and available to a timeless God.[36] He is as equally present to Abraham as he is to the apostle Paul. But is this view coherent? It depends on whether a stasis theory of time is true.[37]

Philosophers of time propose two broad theories concerning the nature of time. The first is the process theory of time (dynamic or A-theory). This view argues that there is a real movement, or process, from the past to the present to the future. The past no longer exists while the future has not yet come into existence. Both the past and the present are ontologically different from the future. The stasis theory of time (static or B-theory), on the other hand, suggests that all moments of time within the space-time universe coexist. In order to capture the notion of the stasis theory of time, physicist Russell Stannard invites his readers to stop thinking of time as something in addition to or outside of the other three dimensions. To give an analogy, he suggests thinking of the four-dimensional space-time universe as if one were holding up four fingers of one's hand in the air. Three of the fingers represent space, whereas the fourth one represents time. He explains,

That fourth finger is time. What it means is that four-dimensional space-time does not change. Something can only change *in time*. But space-time is not in time. *All* of time is here in this fourth finger. One point on my finger is the moment you walked into the lecture theater. The knuckle is this particular instant in time. Towards the end of my finger is the moment when you can thankfully head for the doors and go to lunch and take an aspirin after all these mental gymnastics. It's all there: *past, present, and future*. It's static. We call it a *block universe*. Just as each point in space exists on an equal footing with any other, so does each point in time. We are accustomed to think that all of space exists at each point of time. So, for

---

36. Wayne Grudem, *Systematic Theology: An Introduction to Biblical Doctrine* (Grand Rapids: Zondervan, 1994), 171.

37. See DeWeese, *God and the Nature of Time*, 4.

example, at this instant in time not only does Portsmouth exist, but also New York, Hong King, planet Jupiter, and distant galaxies. So all of space exists at each point in time. What *this* is saying is that likewise at each point in space, all of time exists. At this point of space here—in this hall—all of time exists: the day work started on building the hall, the instant you entered it this morning, this present moment, your leaving it, the day the hall gets demolished. It all exists here—in some sense. I stress "in some sense." This finger assures us that this is so—but *how*? It defies the imagination; it is all so counterintuitive.[38]

The past, then, is just as ontologically real as the future. Therefore, time, for the static theorist, exists in earlier-than and later-than relations. There is no objective process of becoming nor is there any coming into or going out of being. All temporal passage is merely mind dependent.

The stasis theory, when held in conjunction with the timeless view of God, brings with it several theological difficulties, as some Christian theists have recognized. For instance, it renders impotent the traditional doctrine of creation *ex nihilo*.[39] On this view, there is no temporal beginning to the universe (as the traditional understanding of creation *ex nihilo* suggests); rather, God, from all eternity, has tenselessly (changelessly without any temporal extension) produced the entire space-time universe.[40] Consider the words of William Lane Craig:

> A robust doctrine of creation therefore involves both the affirmation that God brought the universe into being out of nothing at some moment in the finite past and the affirmation that He thereafter sustains it in being moment by moment.

---

38. Russell Stannard, "On the Developing Scientific Understanding of Time," in *What God Knows: Time, Eternity, and Divine Knowledge*, ed. Harry Lee Poe and J. Stanley Mattson (Waco, TX: Baylor University Press, 2005), 52.

39. Craig, *Time and Eternity*, 210–15.

40. Helm makes this point clearly when he says,

> A timeless being may not act within the universe, yet it makes sense to say that such a being produces (tenseless) the universe. The production of the universe is thus not the production of some event or complex of events in time; it is the production of the whole material universe, time included. (Helm, *Eternal God*, 69)

Now the static theorist can ingenuously make only the second affirmation. For him *creation ex nihilo* means only that the world depends immediately upon God for its existence at every moment. The static time theorist's affirmation that God brought the universe into being out of nothing at some moment in the past can at best mean that there is (tenselessly) a moment which is separated from any other moment by a finite interval of time and before which no moment of comparable duration exists and that whatever exists at any moment, including the moments themselves, is timelessly sustained in being immediately by God. All this adds to the doctrine of ontological dependence is that the tenselessly existing block universe has a front edge. It has a beginning only in the sense that a yardstick has a beginning. There is in the actual world no state of affairs of God existing alone without the space-time universe. God never really rings the universe into being; as a whole it co-exists timelessly with Him.[41]

In addition to problems surrounding creation, if the stasis theory is true, one must wonder if evil is ever defeated. If all time coexists and is equally real, then Christ's pre-incarnate state is just as real as his resurrection and our future resurrection bodies. When does God ever conquer death? The pangs of death are as objectively coexistent with the elimination of death.[42] Lastly, such a view leads to an odd view of the incarnation of the Son of God. In one real sense, if the stasis view of time is correct, the divine nature of the Son of God has timelessly, or tenselessly, been united to the human nature.[43]

There are other non-theological reasons for rejecting the stasis theory of time. For instance, the Second Law of Thermodynamics points to time as moving in a direction. Furthermore, astrophysicists note that the universe is expanding. This implies that the universe had a beginning and will slowly come to an end, in what scientists call a heat-death. Lastly, it is hard

---

41. Craig, *Time and Eternity*, 212–13.

42. Ibid., 214.

43. See Eleonore Stump and Norman Kretzmann, "Eternity," *Journal of Philosophy* 78, no. 8 (1981): 453; Helm, "Divine Timeless Eternity," 54.

to defend the belief that the process of time is merely mind dependent and separate from objective becoming in the real world.[44]

The defender of CT, at this point, might suggest that God could bring it about that he produce all effects at all times through one, changeless eternal act. One can imagine God timelessly willing that some action a take place at some time t in response to some event e. In his omniscience, God knew that Smith would utter a prayer at t^1, and thus timelessly willed his response to Smith's prayer to occur at t^2. This is not only true of this one event, but for all events at all times within the space-time universe. Yet this act is one unchanging act produced by God from all eternity with scattered effects throughout the space-time universe.[45]

Alan Padgett doesn't find such an approach helpful. God, says Padgett, is the ultimate cause behind all things that exist within the universe, including all matter and energy and the laws of nature. Furthermore, for the essential property that any object has, God is the cause of its existence at every episode of its life. Now this does not mean that God causes every effect that takes place in the world. My typing on this keyboard is not caused by God. Yet, God is the one who sustains the essential nature of what makes me who I am and the essential nature of what makes this keyboard what it is. Moreover, the universe and all that exists within it is in constant dependence upon God for its existence.[46] If God were to remove his sustaining power, the universe would cease to exist because

---

44. See Davies, *God and the New Physics*, 10–11; Alan G. Padgett, *Science and the Study of God* (Grand Rapids: Eerdmans, 2003), 123, 135; Craig, *Time and Eternity*, 197–98. Padgett, "Divine Foreknowledge and the Arrow of Time: On the Impossibility of Retrocausation," in *God and Time: Essays on the Divine Nature*, ed. Gregory E. Ganssle and David M. Woodruff (Oxford: Oxford University Press, 2002), 65–75; John Polkinghorne, "Time in Physics and Theology," in *What God Knows: Time, Eternity, and Divine Knowledge*, ed. Harry Lee Poe and J. Stanley Mattson (Waco, TX: Baylor University Press, 2005), 65–66.

45. Paul Helm explains as follows:

> The correct way to think of God's eternally willing something in time is to think of one eternal act of will with numerous temporally scattered effects. As an analogy, we may think of a person's action in setting the timer on her central heating system. This is (we may suppose) one action, analogous to God's eternal willing. But this one action has numerous temporally scattered effects, analogous to the effects in time of God's one eternal act of willing; as a result of the one act, the system fires at 7:00 a.m., goes off at 12:00 noon, fires again at 2:00 p.m., goes off again at 10:30 p.m. day after day. The basic point is: there can be one decision to bring about different effects at different times. (Helm, "Divine Timeless Eternity," 53)

46. Padgett, *God, Eternity and the Nature of Time*, 19–20.

the universe does not possess aseity. Padgett notes, "The act by which God sustains each moment of creation is a direct act."[47] By "direct act," Padgett means "an act whose immediate effect is brought about without the intervention of any other causal sequence."[48] A direct act excludes any kind of "created causal chain between the divine cause and its effect."[49] All direct acts produced by God are what Padgett calls "Zero Time Related," that is to say, no moment of time occurs between God's direct act and its "immediate effect."[50] Two events are considered Zero Time Related if and only if there is no duration that takes place between them. Padgett demonstrates his point by considering two episodes, B and C:

> Say that God acts such that, at some time $T4$, some episode B of an object was sustained. Further, at the present time, $T5$, God acts so as to sustain a different object's episode, C which is in the same place as B. Now $T4$ and $T5$ are some distance apart in time, and not Zero Time Related. Can the same divine, eternal, immutable act sustain both B and C? Since $T5$ is not, B no longer exists, and so is not being sustained, either in our time or in eternity, by any act of God. Since God's sustaining of C is direct, he cannot (logically cannot) sustain C by an act whose effect is dated at $T4$, and by some causal chain indirectly sustains C-at-$T5$. Furthermore, the present effect of God's eternal act at $T5$ is Zero Time Related with the eternal intention of God; but this same eternal intention and act cannot also be Zero Time Related to B, since B and C are not themselves Zero Time Related. By a single, timeless act God can sustain C and any episode Zero Time Related to C. But since the divine sustaining is a direct act which must be Zero Time Related to its effect, the same divine act cannot sustain both C and B. At the present time ($T5$) B is not real, and so a different act (different, that is, than the act which sustained B) is now called for if God is to sustain C. The particular intention

47. Ibid., 20.
48. Ibid.
49. Ibid.
50. Ibid., 21.

plus power-to-act, such that B-at-$T4$ is sustained, can only sustain episodes Zero Time Related to $T4$.[51]

The proponent of CT might unhappily object, arguing that God timelessly wills that a certain effect take place at a certain time. This might work, claims Padgett, if all one means by "wills" is that God designs such-and-such effect to occur. But if by "will" one "includes design, intention and power-to-act, and if the stasis theory of time is false, then God cannot timelessly 'will' that a certain effect take place at some future time, since the effects of his 'will' do not yet exist."[52]

Padgett forcefully shows that the act of God's power that produced B is not the same act of power that he used to produce C. At $T4$ God was not producing C. But since God is now producing C and is no longer producing B, it is safe to say that God has changed from his relation of sustaining one episode to his relation to now sustaining another.[53]

If Padgett's objection stands and the process theory of time is true, can we rationally hold to the CT view? After all, if God stands in a causal relationship to a temporal creation, wouldn't that mean that God is temporal by virtue of that relation? Yet, if, say, the stasis theory of time is true, then one could coherently hold to CT, though it may bring with it certain theological costs.

DAVIES' SECOND OBJECTION

But what of Davies' second objection? If God is the creator of time, how could it be that God exists in time? Existing in time requires that one change. But how does the ultimate cause of all things change? Furthermore, if God is subject to time how does God escape the processes of time? If temporal, would not God be dependent on something other than himself for his existence?

In order to escape Davies' objection, the Christian theist must demonstrate four things regarding God and his temporal mode of existence. First, the Christian theist must show that God transcends created space-time.

---

51. Alan G. Padgett, "God and Timelessness," in *Philosophy of Religion: A Reader and Guide*, ed. William Lane Craig (New Brunswick, NJ: Rutgers University Press, 2002), 240–41.

52. Ibid.

53. William Lane Craig, *God, Time, and Eternity* (Dordrecht: Kluwer Academic, 2001), 59.

If God is the creator of the space-time universe, including all energy and matter, then he cannot be limited to or bound by it. Second, the Christian theist must demonstrate that God's temporality does not make him dependent on something outside of himself. Third, it must be shown that if God does change in any sense, such changes do not increase or decrease his metaphysical stature. Fourth, and lastly, the Christian theistic concept of God must be compatible with a God who acts in space-time and who is religiously available (e.g., answers prayers, performs miracles, etc.).

Before moving on, it would be helpful to consider what one means by the phrase "God is in time." Much confusion hinges on two items: (1) What is "time"? and (2) What does one mean by the preposition "in"? Garrett DeWeese helpfully points out that philosophers of time distinguish between four different kinds of time: physical clock time, psychological time, cosmic time, and metaphysical time.[54] The first kind of time, physical time, refers to the time of any world in which the laws of nature are such that they allow for measurement of time by some kind of physical clock or instrument. Such time is relative to a "local reference frame."[55] Psychological time, unlike physical time, refers to a person's subjective experience of the passage of time, which varies from individual to individual. For some, the passage of time of an event may have seemed short while for others it may have seemed long. A third kind of time is cosmic time. Cosmic time differs from physical time in that it is not limited to a local reference frame. Instead, cosmic time refers to the duration of the entire cosmos or universe. The fourth, and final kind of time, is metaphysical time. Metaphysical time is that which grounds all other kinds of time.[56] If God in some way "experiences succession in his being," says DeWeese, "then metaphysical time would be equivalent to God's time."[57]

Thus, when a theist argues that God is temporal, or at least that God's eternal nature has a temporal element to it, she doesn't mean that God exists in some kind of time outside of himself—either a time that is coexistent with his being or a time that was created by him. As a necessary

54. DeWeese, *God and the Nature of Time*, 9–11.
55. Ibid., 9.
56. Ibid., 10–11.
57. Ibid., 10.

being, God doesn't depend on anything outside of himself for his existence. Metaphysical time, then, is God's own time, which is grounded in God's own conscious life and in his causation. DeWeese states:

> What constitutes metaphysical temporality is the same relation that constitutes any other temporality: causation. ... [T]he causal succession of mental states in God's conscious life grounds the flow and direction of metaphysical time. And, given that God is creator and sustainer of the contingent order, his causal sustenance of every world will ground the time of that world.[58]

But the critic might object that if God is temporal, he experiences change. Any being that changes, changes either for the better or for the worse. But if God is already perfect, how could he change for the better? He would continually become more and more perfect, which is absurd. God cannot grow in his perfection; he is already perfect. Yet, if God changes for the worse, he would no longer be God since such a change would mean that he is no longer perfect. In response to the critic, why should we think that all changes be changes in value? It doesn't seem to be the case. There can be, as Thomas Morris explains, changes that are "value-neutral," that is to say, there are changes that do not necessitate an increase or decrease in a person's intrinsic value or metaphysical stature whatsoever, such as my moving my fingers across this keyboard to form words on the computer screen. "If there are value-neutral changes," says Morris, "it will not follow from the fact that God cannot change for the better or for the worse that God cannot change at all."[59] Morris' insight seems correct. It doesn't

---

58. Ibid., 253

59. Morris, *Our Idea of God*, 127. Bruce Ware makes a similar argument when he says:

> A good number of theologians throughout the history of the Church had denied of God any change whatever because they conceived of change as always and only for either the better or the worse. That there might be some sort of change that involved no such qualitative increase or decrease was not always given due consideration. ... God is made neither better nor worse by his relational changes. He neither increases nor decreases in excellence since he is, as already stated, the fullness of all excellence. Indeed, God cannot change for the better or the worse, but he can change in some sense nonetheless. He changes from anger to mercy, from blessing to cursing, from rejection to acceptance. Each of these changes is real in God, though no such change affects in the slightest the unchangeable supremacy of his intrinsic nature. God's relational mutability only expresses in time and in personal relationship the changelessness of his intrinsic nature and free word.

follow that God's awareness of what is going on in the world today or that God's changing in his power-to-act at different times in any way affects his metaphysical stature. God remains changeless in his essential nature.

But what of those places in Scripture that seem to indicate that God changes in his relationship toward his creatures, say, going from wrath to mercy toward a repentant sinner? While God's attitude changes toward the sinner, it does not mean that God has somehow gained value in his metaphysical stature. Bruce Ware makes the important distinction between God's "onto-ethical" immutability and his "relational" mutability. It is not that God's essential nature changes. God's ethical immutability is grounded in God's ontological immutability. Thus, when God changes in his attitude toward a repenting sinner, it is not so much that God has changed in his metaphysical stature; rather, because of God's ontological nature, he must always respond relationally to his creatures in accordance to his moral nature.[60] God's relational mutability always expresses God's ontological unchangingness,

> because God's intrinsic moral nature is unchangeable it must always and without fail express in ways appropriate to the moral state of any given human situation. Thus, when the human moral state changes (e.g. from rebellion to repentance) the immutable divine nature must now reflect itself in ways that are appropriate to this new situation.[61]

The objector might retort: if God is aware of what is going on in the world, then his knowledge is constantly changing. Would this not limit his omniscience? But this too does not follow. For, what God is aware of by temporal relation to the world is nothing more than what was already contained in his omniscience—on the assumption that his omniscience is inclusive of free future choices. The only difference is that now the content of God's knowledge has become actualized and, therefore, relational.

(Bruce A. Ware, "An Evangelical Reformulation of the Doctrine of the Immutability of God," *Journal of the Evangelical Theological Society* 29, no. 4 [1986]: 440–41).

60. Ware, "Evangelical Reformulation," 434, 436, 438.

61. Ibid., 440.

The world is in reality the actualization, or the "coming into being," of his divine plan, which contains the free decisions of human creatures.[62]

FORMULATING A COHERENT
CONCEPTION OF GOD

So far, I have argued that the CT view, that is, the view that God is timeless and absolutely immutable while coherent (assuming that the stasis theory of time is true), is difficult, though not impossible, to reconcile with the belief that God acts in the world today. It is possible to argue for this view only with some significant theological costs. Nevertheless, suppose that the stasis theory turns out to be true and that God is timelessly eternal and absolutely immutable, it would not render the Christian theistic concept of God unintelligible. Nor would it be incoherent with a Christian view of the God/world relation and with a God who performs miracles, redeems his people, and the like. Yet, if, as has been argued throughout, God's eternality has a temporal element to it, it doesn't mean that God exists in created space-time or that he is somehow caught up in the processes thereof. Rather, arguably God has his own time—metaphysical time. All other time, then, is grounded in God's metaphysical time (causation). In the remainder of this chapter, can we now construct a coherent view of the God/world relation which allows for the possibility of God's acting in the world to defeat evil in the world?

TRANSCENDENCE AND IMMANENCE

In working out a proper understanding of the God/world relationship, Christian theists must keep in view Scripture's portrayal of God as both transcendent and immanent. These two doctrines keep Christian theism from collapsing into deism, pantheism, or panentheism. On the one end of the spectrum, Scripture portrays God in his holiness as completely other than and beyond creation (Ps 97:9; Isa 55:8–9; Eph 4:6; 1 Tim 6:16). As argued in the previous chapter, God is *a se* or self-existent, that is to say, he is complete in and of himself and does not depend on anything outside of himself for his existence. Thought on God's aseity stems from reflection on God

---

62. I assume a form of Molinism (middle knowledge). But one need not adhere to Molinism to make this point. One could just as easily make a similar move and hold to simple foreknowledge.

as the creator of all things, who brought all things into existence out of nothing (Gen 1:1; Ps 33:6, 9; John 1:1–3; Col 1:15–16; Heb 1:2; 11:3). Yet, on the other end, God is seen as the one who hears the cries of his people (Exod 3:7). He is the one who delivers his people out from the hands of Pharaoh (Exod 14:30) and who delivers his people from their sin (Gal 1:4). He knows his creation intimately and is everywhere present (Matt 10:29; Ps 139:7–13). Also, God the Son became incarnate (John 1:1–14; Col 1:19–20; 2:9) and was raised from the dead by the Father (Rom 8:11; 10:9, 10). There are passages, too, that demonstrate both God's transcendence and immanence together (Ps 139:7–13; Isa 6:1; 57:15).

RELATIVE TIMELESSNESS

If God is not timeless and absolutely immutable in the traditional sense, then how ought the theist to understand God's temporal mode of existence, while yet remaining faithful to the doctrines of divine immanence and transcendence? One possible route is Alan Padgett's view that God's temporal mode of existence is that of relative timelessness (RT). What distinguishes RT from the traditional view of timelessness is that with RT there is a sense in which God is temporal. Padgett says,

> Because the universe is an ever-changing reality, things do change in their fundamental ontological status at different times—a change we must ascribe to God, and cannot ascribe to the objects themselves, since this has to do with their very existences.[63]

If God does things at different times, then God is temporal.[64] Like the CT view, RT takes into consideration the intuition that God transcends created space-time. According to Padgett, something is considered to be timeless if such a being's existence is "somehow beyond or above time."[65] Yet, one can distinguish between two kinds of timelessness. The traditional view says that something is timeless if such an entity lacks any temporal location or extension. The RT view, on the other hand, argues that some entity is timeless if it does not exist in any kind of measured time. Therefore, no

---

63. Alan G. Padgett, "God and Time: Toward a Doctrine of Divine Timeless Eternity," *Religious Studies* 25, no. 2 (1989): 209.

64. Ibid.

65. Ibid., 210.

kinds of measured time words could apply to such an entity. The former kind of timelessness Padgett calls "absolute" timelessness while the latter he calls "relative" timelessness.[66]

There are three important elements to RT. First, God does not exist in measured time. This does not mean that God is unrelated to our time. He sustains our space-time universe. Yet, God is not in any way bound by the laws of nature. The second element is that God's life does not occur in our own space-time universe. At no time can we locate God in our own time. While God grounds our space-time universe, he nevertheless is free not to enter into it. God is spaceless, that is to say, he is without spatial location. As an incorporeal being, God does not have a physical body. He is immaterial. Yet, if God so chooses, he could enter into our space-time universe and take up a body, as in the incarnation. But this does not mean that he becomes contained by space-time. The third element is that God is not vulnerable to those negative aspects within time. No amount of time limits him. He is the Lord over time.[67] As Padgett sums it up,

> God is the Lord of heaven and earth, of time and eternity. Any changes that happen on earth do so because of the will and power of God, which sustain all changing things in their being. ... Because of his infinite wisdom and power God is not limited in the amount of things he can accomplish, nor problems he can work through, in a limited period of time. Nothing happens outside of his will, knowledge and power. In this way God's time is radically different from our human experience of time and its limitations upon us.[68]

The advantage of a view such as RT is that God is temporally aware of what is going on in the universe, yet, like the traditional view, God is not caught up in creation's physical processes. He can act within the world, perform miracles, and be religiously available to his creatures without being contained by or caught up in the processes of the world. Lastly, RT fits well with the language of Scripture. Consider the psalmist's words in

---

66. Ibid.

67. Ibid., 211–14.

68. Ibid., 214. I am in agreement with Padgett, here, but one clarification is needed. It is clearer to state that nothing happens outside of God's *permissive* will. Surely things contrary to God's *perfect* will do occur, like when people sin.

Psalm 90:2, "Before the mountains were brought forth, or ever you had formed the earth and the world, from everlasting to everlasting you are God." Or, in a few verses following, the psalmist declares, "For a thousand years in your sight are but as yesterday when it is past, or as a watch in the night" (Ps 90:4).

Having considered a version of theological essentialism and a conception of God in this chapter, whereby he can act in the world, perform miracles, and be religiously available to his creatures, I now turn to the final chapter, where I argue for a God who defeats evil.

CHAPTER 8
A GOD WHO DEFEATS EVIL

Any adequate discussion on the problem from evil must not only answer why there is evil in the world but must also wrestle with the existential problem from evil. People are deeply concerned about all the evils that affect them. They want to know if God hears their cries of pain, if he joins with them in the midst of their sufferings, and whether he's actually doing something about all of the evil in the world. In this final chapter, I seek to address this existential dimension to the problem from evil.

So far, I have argued that (1) theism explains evil better than its metaphysical rivals, (2) Christian theism, against other theisms, makes better sense of a God who is essentially loving, and (3) the God of Christian theism is a God who can act in the world, perform miracles, and stop evil. Below I argue that the God of Christian theism isn't a God who sits idly by, doing nothing about evil; rather, the Triune God is a God who, in the midst of the pain and suffering in the world, acts to bring about evil's ultimate defeat.

I begin by considering the Christian understanding of God as light and love. God as light and God as love provide the vision and grounds for Christian ethics. As will be argued, God's goodness grounds God's love and God's love directs God's goodness. This has significant application for human interaction in the face of moral evil. Following this, I consider whether God suffers. Many theologians and philosophers believe that only a suffering God can relate to the sufferings that humans go through. Much of this turns on what one means by suffering. I will argue that God does indeed relate to us in our sufferings, yet he does so without becoming debilitated or diminished in his being. Having discussed divine suffering, I turn to the topic of divine action, especially the work of the Son of God in his death and resurrection to defeat sin and death. This is followed by reflection on the church's responsibility in and through the power of the Spirit to be a force for stopping evil in the world. Finally, I consider God's ultimate defeat of evil, first by responding to the problem of hell, followed by reflection on the Christian's final hope.

LIGHT, LOVE, AND FELLOWSHIP

The brief New Testament letter of 1 John makes two striking claims about God—"God is light" and "God is love." These claims provide for John a theological framework and ethical vision for the small community of believers.[1]

Throughout Scripture, "light" is often used as a metaphor to reflect certain characteristics of God, his revelation, or salvation.[2] Discernable from the context of 1 John, John uses "light" as a metaphor to reflect God's flawless perfection, truthfulness, impeccability, and moral goodness. Immediately following the words "God is light," the author of 1 John clarifies what he means by reminding his readers that in God "there is no darkness at all" (1 John 1:5). John is setting up for his readers a strong contrast between God, who is light, and darkness. As noted by I. Howard Marshall,

> The contrast between God and darkness is expressed as strongly as possible. The point is not so much that God did not create darkness but rather that living in darkness is incompatible with fellowship with God. This makes it clear that the writer is thinking of light and darkness predominately in ethical terms.[3]

I take it that when John says, "God is light," he is making an important claim with respect to God's nature, though, couched in metaphor, which in turn, grounds how we are to live in relation to God and others. "God is light," then is a reference to God's perfect moral goodness. The negative

---

1. Robert W. Yarbrough provides four reasons for thinking this is the case. First, it has the ring of a summary statement. It is the message that John heard "from him" and declares to his readers. Second, the verse comes after four introductory statements, which would seem to indicate, based on positioning, its overall importance. Third, when John speaks of the Son, he *ipso facto* speaks of the Father since it is the Son who came from the Father and reveals him to us (a major theme in the Johannine writings John 1:1-2, 18; 14:8-11; 1 John 1:2-3). Fourth and, perhaps, most critically, the language is deeply rooted in Old Testament theology. See Yarbrough, *1-3 John* (Grand Rapids: Baker Academic, 2008), 46-47.

2. I. Howard Marshall, *The Epistles of John* (Grand Rapids: Eerdmans, 1978), 109.

3. Ibid.

that follows, that "there is no darkness at all," serves to intensify the previous point. In other words, John is saying that God is morally perfect.[4]

There is another important aspect with respect to the proposition "God is light" that needs to be addressed, namely, that "light" also has to do with, in the words of Millard Erickson, God's "integrity" or "truthfulness."[5] With respect to truthfulness, Erickson lists three dimensions: "(1) genuineness—being true; (2) veracity—telling the truth; and (3) faithfulness—proving true."[6] That God always tells the truth (veracity)[7] and that God never breaks his promise (faithfulness)[8] are grounded in God's genuineness.[9]

Here we may conclude that John's reference to God as light contains within it a close connection between God's perfect moral goodness and his genuineness or integrity, which would also indicate for humans that there is a close connection between moral goodness and truthfulness in character and living. As Yarbrough reminds us, the theme of the epistle, then, "is not dominated first of all by his [John's] teaching, his commands, or his encouragement to love, or even the occasions that call all these forth"; rather, "It is dominated ... by his vision of God—God's light, his moral excellence and efficacious purity."[10] A proper vision of God provides for us a proper framework for ethical thinking and living.

The second claim that "God is love" also weighs significantly in the thought of John. As noted with "God is light," "God is love" is a statement about the very nature of God. The reason that God demonstrates his love toward us is because God's very nature is love. This idea that God is love is

---

4. For a different perspective, see Daniel L. Akin, *1, 2, 3 John* (Nashville, TN: Broadman & Holman, 2001), 65.

5. Millard J. Erickson, *Christian Theology*, 2nd ed. (Grand Rapids: Baker, 1999), 316.

6. Ibid.

7. Scripture repeatedly emphasizes that God cannot tell a lie (1 Sam 15:29; Titus 1:2). Moreover, Jesus speaks of God's word as truth (John 17:17).

8. See Hebrews 6:18.

9. Erickson, *Christian Theology*, 316. See 2 Timothy 2:13. Within the context of 1 John, claiming to have fellowship with God, while walking in the darkness, results in the person lying and not living by the truth. Further, to claim that one is without sin means that one is deceiving oneself and that truth is absent from one's life. Yet, walking in the light results in a person's having fellowship with God and with fellow believers (1 John 1:6–8). Given the contrast, here, it would seem that walking in the light has a quality of being truthful. If walking in the light has within it a quality of being in the truth, then we can assume that God as light involves truthfulness.

10. Yarbrough, *1–3 John*, 50.

not an abstraction. In Hebraic and Christian thought, God is personal. Love is essential to the very nature of the tri-personal God. As argued in chapter 6, the core of all of existence is a dynamic "loving relationship among persons."[11] In other words, God's act of love toward us is predicated on the fact that the tri-personal God is love.

"God is love" (as with "God is light") also provides further theological grounding for ethical living (1 John 4:7-12). The reason that John's readers should love one another is because love "comes from God," who "is love" in his very essence. Those who love God "know God" and have "been born of God." Those who do not love do not know God.[12] But what does John mean by "love"? He gives his readers a clue earlier in the epistle when he says, "This is how we know what love is: Jesus Christ laid down his life for us" (1 John 3:15, NIV). Jesus, who is God incarnate, exemplifies love in the giving of himself for others. For this reason, believers are to lay down their lives for one another; loving not merely in word but by action "in truth" (1 John 3:17-18). God, too, shows his love toward us in that he sent his Son. God sent his Son, not because we loved God, but because of his love for us. "God's love is," as Millard Erickson points out, "an unselfish interest in us for our sake."[13]

Similarly, C. S. Lewis speaks of God's love in the following way: "He can give good, but cannot need or get it. In that sense all his love is, as it were, bottomlessly selfless by very definition; it has everything to give and nothing to receive."[14] Thus John's understanding of God as love suggests

---

11. Stephen T. Davis, "God's Action," *In Defense of Miracles*, eds. R. Douglas Geivett and Gary Habermas (Downers Grove, IL: InterVarsity Press, 1997), 176.

12. See 1 John 4:7-12. Yarbrough elaborates on John's thought:

> Love, John seems to be saying, is to be sought, hollowed, nurtured, and guarded simply by virtue of its inherent God-rootedness. ... In a sense, "all things" are from God (1 Cor. 11:12). But love for John is not merely one among many things finding distinctive rootage in God. It is rather a primary attribute of God. ... John will go on to state that to fail to love aright is to belie one's Christian confession (4:20). Love among Christian believers (and, judging from Jesus's example, love for non-believers too) is a nonnegotiable necessity in the household of faith. (Yarbrough, *1-3 John*, 235)

13. Erickson, *Christian Theology*, 319.

14. C. S. Lewis, *The Problem of Pain* (New York: HarperSanFrancisco, 1996), 43.

that in God's very essence is a sense of selflessness or giving up of one's self toward the "other."[15]

"God is love" and "God is light" are two sides of the same proverbial coin. John is painting a vision of God which informs how we humans ought to be—a life lived in truth, in harmony with God, and with the other's best interest in mind. Yet John's reasoning for our living this way is grounded in the very nature of God. As light, God cannot do anything that is morally evil. As love, God seeks out the best for the "other." It is God's moral character that grounds his love, and it is his love that seeks out what is best and good and holy for the "other." Hence God's loving actions toward his creatures are always for their best; he cannot do otherwise. His desire is for his creatures to be in fellowship with him because he is the source of all that is good, true, and holy.

Since God is light, what God desires for his children is for them to "walk in that light" and to be in fellowship with him (1 John 1:7). What does walking in light and fellowship with God consist of? First, John reminds us that walking in the light means that we are to be truthful with ourselves. To deny that we have sin in our lives or to claim that we have fellowship with God when we are walking in the darkness causes us to be liars and the truth not in us. When we acknowledge sin in our lives before God, God forgives and purifies us through the blood of Jesus (1 John 1:6-10).

Second, one must have true beliefs about God and his Son (1 John 2:22–23; 3:23; 4:2-3; 5:1-5). At face value, this may seem a bit odd. Why must one have true beliefs about God and his Son? A significant aspect of being in the light and having harmony with God is living in truth. To deny truth about the Son results in having a false belief about God. Jerry Walls presents a similar argument when speaking of belief in Jesus as necessary for one's salvation. According to Walls, salvation is "about a perfect relationship with God."[16] He goes on to argue:

> If God is a Trinity and Jesus is God the Son incarnate, as Christians
> teach, then a perfect relationship with God entails knowing Jesus
> is God the Son. Not to believe Jesus is God the Son would involve a

---

15. For now, I will leave our discussion on God as love as selflessness toward the other, but I will resume the discussion below.

16. Jerry L. Walls, *Heaven: The Logic of Eternal Joy* (Oxford: Oxford University Press, 2002), 48.

fundamentally mistaken understanding of God, which would be incompatible with a perfected relationship.[17]

God has given humans revelation about himself that is clear about Jesus' identity as the Son of God. Furthermore, the "revelation is sufficiently clear," says Walls, "that those who have access to it are responsible to believe."[18] Further, when rejecting Jesus, one is not only rejecting the source of truth (Colossians 2:3; John 14:6), but also the source of all life. Both the Gospel of John and 1 John provide pictures of Jesus as being the source of truth and of life.[19]

Since God is love, believers are to love one another, as noted earlier, with self-giving love. This kind of love looks out for the benefit of the other. Love that is selfless is the same kind of love that God has. John points out that those who fail to love their brothers remain in death (1 John 3:14). Death, here, does not refer to physical death, but it points to a lack of life and of fellowship with God and with others (1 John 2:9; 3:15). Moreover, one cannot claim to love God and not love one's brother. In doing so, that person becomes a liar. Love for God and love for one's brother are closely connected. Those who love God must also love one's brother. Yet, John makes it clear that the reason brothers can love one another is that God first loved us (1 John 1:19-21). It was out of our need that God responded to us. It is not that we initiated it but only that we responded to it. Receiving God's love is transformational, for in it, God demonstrates to us what love truly is (1 John 3:16; 4:9). Lastly, believers are to love God above all, doing his will, not loving their own worldly desires, which, as part of the world, pass away (1 John 2:15-17).

Before moving on, it would be helpful to consider what Christians mean by loving one's neighbor since the command is potentially ambiguous and often misunderstood. In modern Western culture, love is often associated with an emotion or affection. C. S. Lewis found such an understanding of love inadequate:

---

17. Ibid., 49.

18. Ibid.

19. John 17:3—"Now this is eternal life: that they may know you, the only true God, and Jesus Christ, whom you have sent." Eternal life—abundant life—is ultimately found in having personal knowledge of God and of the Son.

Charity means "Love, in the Christian sense". But love, in the Christian sense, does not mean an emotion. It is a state not of the feelings but of the will; that state of the will which we have naturally about ourselves, and must learn to have about other people.[20]

It seems that Lewis is on to something important here. Love cannot be equated merely with an emotion. Based on 1 John, having pity on a brother or sister in need requires also loving through actions "in truth" (1 John 3:17–18). However, one must proceed with caution not to chalk loving one's neighbor up solely to a matter of the will or to some sort of loving behavior. In 1 Corinthians 13:3, Paul tells us that "If I give all I possess to the poor and surrender my body to the flames, but have not love, I gain nothing." Given Paul's words, love cannot be equated merely with acting in such a manner. One's inner state is at least as important as one's actions.[21] Francis Howard-Snyder believes that loving one's neighbor requires, at minimum, some amount of benevolence; however, it cannot be limited to that. She writes,

The second great commandment is like the first. It is fair to assume that the love we owe our neighbor is of the same kind as the love we owe God. Our love for God ought to include an appreciation of him and a desire for union with him, in addition to a desire that his will be done. If our love for our neighbor is to be like the love we owe God, this suggests that the love we have for our neighbors should involve the same elements. Indeed, it makes sense that our love for other people should not be simply benevolence or sheer concern for their well-being, but should also involve desires to be related to them, and an appreciation of what is valuable in them, and enjoyment of them. For if one's attitude toward others was solely that of benevolence, it would seem that one wouldn't want anything they have to offer. Sheer benevolence looks like a kind of arrogance, an attitude of independence and inequality vis-à-vis our neighbors.[22]

---

20. C. S. Lewis, *Mere Christianity* (New York: HarperSanFrancisco, 1980), 129.

21. Francis Howard-Snyder, "Christian Ethics," in *Reason for the Hope Within*, ed. Michael J. Murray (Grand Rapids: Eerdmans, 1999), 386.

22. Ibid., 387–88.

Similarly, Alexander R. Pruss suggests that the biblical concept of love includes three "intertwined aspects."[23] Not only must one show benevolence but also an appreciation for and "a striving for union" with the other.[24] Pruss argues that benevolence without appreciation turns toward "a proud and superior philanthropic attitude."[25] We pursue union with the other because of the value that we see in the other. In seeking union with the other, the benefactor becomes not merely the giver of good things but places herself "on a more equal plane with the beloved, and is vulnerable to being rejected by the beloved."[26] Yet, the recipient of the goods cannot take the actions of the benefactor for granted. If the benefactor seeks union with the other, it breaks down the barrier of the recipient's feeling shame for being helped.[27] Pruss continues by arguing that appreciation is not enough. Appreciation without union is bankrupt since a failure to "possess" or to be "joined with the beloved" results in an inability to fully appreciate the other. Lastly, pursuing union and appreciating the other is not enough. One must also seek the other's good. Failure to do so results in "a self-defeating selfishness."[28] Pruss continues,

> For genuine union with the other involves pursuit of the other's goals, and an appreciation of goods is incomplete when it does not motivate us to further those goods. And it is only if, with a mixture of humility and surprised joy, we see our being united with the other as good for the other that we can hope that the other will fully (and not merely by being deceived, say) be joined to us.[29]

Lastly, the expression "love your neighbor as yourself" in Jesus' command implies an element of self-love. This does not demand, however, that one fall into vanity or nihilism. As C. S. Lewis aptly puts it, love for

---

23. Alexander R. Pruss, "One Body: Reflections on Christian Sexual Ethics," 2, accessed November 12, 2012, http://bearspace.baylor.edu/Alexander_Pruss/www/papers/OneBody -talk.html.

24. Ibid.

25. Ibid., 3.

26. Ibid.

27. Ibid.

28. Ibid.

29. Ibid.

ourselves "means that we wish our own good."[30] Further, self-love, suggests Howard-Snyder, should serve as a blueprint for how we ought to respond to others. While we often find ourselves having greater love for those we find attractive or find deserving of our love, self-love, on the other hand, is generally not as temperamental. While the object of our focus in self-love may change, say from being upset with some performance or being glad when we do well at some goal, our overall concern, whether being upset or glad, is for our well-being. Sadness and gladness point to that same desire.[31] Further, union with the "other" is not merely what's best for them, but it is also what's best for the self. Lastly, it is not selfish or wrong to appreciate one's self. The self's identity is found in relationship to others. Appreciation for the self, then, is formed through one's relatedness with others within the community. The self is an important part of the community, which without the community would not be what it is.

The New Testament concept of love, then, is unconditional in nature. Jesus' parable of the Good Samaritan exemplifies unconditional love.[32] Unconditional love is an overall attitude and movement toward the other, looking out for the best interest of the other while also seeking union. It is directed toward all, whether or not the other responds back in the same manner, or even if the other retaliates in hostility or in hurt.[33]

EVIL AND DIVINE SUFFERING

As argued above, as well as in chapter 6, love is at the center of who God is. This love is not a passive kind of love; rather it is an active love that is selfless and seeks out the good for the other. This love is grounded in God's goodness; yet, this love also directs God's goodness. Divine goodness and divine love ground how humans should respond to one another. Furthermore, as argued in chapter 7, the God of Christian theism is a God who can act in the world to stop evil, in contrast to the god of pantheism or the god of process panentheism, who is impotent in defeating evil.

---

30. Lewis, *Mere Christianity*, 130.
31. Howard-Snyder, "Christian Ethics," 388.
32. Luke 12:25–37.
33. Howard-Snyder, "Christian Ethics," 388.

Some Christian theists have argued that not only can God act in the world but that God also suffers along with his creatures. Take, for example, the words of Alvin Plantinga:

God's capacity for suffering, I believe, is proportional to his great-ness; it exceeds our capacity for suffering in the same measure as his capacity for knowledge exceeds ours. Christ was prepared to endure the agonies of hell itself; and God, the Lord of the universe, was prepared to endure the suffering in order to overcome sin, and death, and the evils that afflict our world, and to confer on us a life more glorious than we can imagine.[34]

A variety of theologians, too, take it that God is passible and capable of suffering. Regarding God's suffering, Clark Pinnock believes that God's "suffering or pathos ... is a strong biblical theme."[35] The German theologian Jürgen Moltmann takes the suffering of God to be central to any theodicy:

If God were incapable of suffering in every respect, then he would also be incapable of love. He would at most be capable of loving himself, but not of loving another as himself, as Aristotle puts it. But if he is capable of loving something else, then he lays himself open to the suffering which love for another brings him; and yet, by virtue of his love, he remains master of the pain that love causes him to suffer. God does not suffer out of deficiency of being, like created beings. To this extent he is "apathetic." But he suffers from the love which is the superabundance and overflowing of his being. In so far he is "pathetic."[36]

Baptist theologian Millard Erickson, too, thinks that God suffers. Time and again, says Erickson, we see in the Old Testament that God is aban-doned by his people, Israel. Furthermore, in passages such as Genesis 6:6 and Psalm 103:13, we are told that God "grieves" over human sin and "pities

---

34. Alvin Plantinga, "Self-Profile," in *Alvin Plantinga*, ed. James Tomberlin and Peter van Inwagen (Dordrecht: Kluwer Academic, 1985), 36.

35. Clark Pinnock, "Systematic Theology," 118.

36. Moltmann, *The Trinity and the Kingdom*, 23. It should be noted, here, that by "pathetic," Moltmann does not refer to how we usually understand the word; rather, it has to do with the capacity for suffering.

his children." There is no doubt some anthropomorphism is going on in such passages, but we must not dismiss such images as having no import with respect to God's nature. But most importantly for Erickson is the incarnation. It is in the incarnation of the Son of God where we see, most clearly, God's experience of evil. Jesus weeps over the death of his friend Lazarus (John 11:35). Through this he experienced sorrow. Moreover, Jesus experienced abandonment, suffering, ridicule, physical abuse—and, ultimately, death on the cross.[37] When we consider the incarnation, says Erickson, it is difficult to escape the conclusion of divine suffering.

> Some theologians have sought to avoid this conclusion and to preserve the impassibility of God by maintaining that Jesus' suffering was a function only of his human nature. Gregory of Nyssa, for example, held that as God, the Son is impassible. Augustine maintained that "passion," suggesting disturbance and changeableness, is incompatible with the divine nature. This, however, seems not only to impose upon Jesus a set of conceptions not based upon clear biblical witness, but to divide the unity of the two natures in the one person. It may in effect be a variety of incipient Nestorianism.[38]

Erickson cautions that any suffering that God partakes in is endured voluntarily. God, says Erickson, has chosen at several points certain imposed self-limitations (e.g., creation, making covenants with his people, incarnation). None of these self-limitations, however, leads to any kind of deficiency in the divine nature.[39] God's suffering is never more clearly seen than in the Son's death upon the cross, the ultimate outworking of his love toward us. Moreover, it is through the suffering on the cross that God makes possible for his free creatures to be reconciled to him. Reconciliation does not come without great cost. As Erickson further explains:

> Reconciliation, the restoration of relationships that have been broken, always requires some cost, some pain. In quarrels there is an exchange of harsh statements. Each is followed by a similar or perhaps more bitter response. If the quarrel is to cease, someone

---

37. Erickson, *The Word Became Flesh*, 607–9.
38. Ibid., 609–10.
39. Ibid., 611–12.

must decline to respond or retaliate. This means forgoing the satisfaction of returning the pain to the other: And this decision means absorbing the pain into oneself.[40]

Erickson suggests this is what God, through Christ, has done on our behalf. He has absorbed the pain and suffering brought about by human sin.[41]

Unlike these theologians and philosopher, I take caution in saying that God suffers, especially if we understand suffering to mean that God in some sense would not flourish.[42] How could the giver of all life not flourish? Such an understanding of God would imply that there was a deficiency in the divine nature. Yet, we must deal with the biblical evidence. Are such passages merely anthropomorphic? How might we resolve this?

On the one hand, there is some bite to the above arguments. There is a real sense in which God experiences the full effects of evil, and, perhaps, pain, particularly through the incarnation. Yet, on the other hand,

---

40. Ibid., 616.

41. Not everyone agrees that God can suffer. There has been much written in recent years on the important topic of divine immutability and impassibility. A helpful article addressing the topic is Ware, "An Evangelical Reformulation of the Doctrine of the Immutability of God," 431–46. For additional discussion on the doctrines of God's immutability and impassibility, see Terence E. Fretheim, *The Suffering of God: An Old Testament Perspective* (Philadelphia: Fortress, 1984); Richard E. Creel, *Divine Impassibility: An Essay in Philosophical Theology* (New York: Cambridge University Press, 1986); Issac August Dorner, *Divine Immutability: A Critical Reconsideration* (Minneapolis: Fortress, 1994); Michael J. Dodds, *The Unchanging God of Love: Thomas Aquinas and Contemporary Theology on Divine Immutability*, 2nd ed. (Washington, D.C.: The Catholic University of America Press, 2008); James F. Keating and Thomas Joseph White, eds., *Divine Impassibility and the Mystery of Human Suffering* (Grand Rapids: Eerdmans, 2009); Rob Lister, *God is Impassible and Impassioned: Toward a Theology of Divine Emotion* (Wheaton, IL: Crossway, 2013).

42. In chapter 1 I distinguish between physical pain, mental pain, and suffering. While both mental pain and physical pain might lead to suffering, nevertheless one might experience suffering apart from either kind of pain altogether. So, in that sense, suffering belongs to a different category. Furthermore, following Stump, I argued that human suffering has to do primarily with what a person most cares about. There are two sides to suffering, as considered in the first chapter, one objective and one subjective. The objective side has to do with someone being kept from flourishing, but the subjective element has mostly to do with the desires of a person's heart not being met. If we take suffering to mean something as we defined it in chapter 1, then it would seem that God is excluded from it. It seems more reasonable to think that God might experience pain than thinking of God as suffering. The experience of pain, as I have argued in both chapter 1 and chapter 5, does not require that one suffer. The experience of pain does not require that one become debilitated by it nor does it cause a lack of flourishing, both of which are impossible for God.

we should proceed with caution in calling the experience of these effects of evil suffering. I believe it is precisely because of God's impassibility—the inability to suffer—in his essential nature that God can withstand the evils in the world. When the Fathers spoke of impassibility, they primarily meant that God is in no way debilitated or crippled by passions, as humans are, or as one might see among the gods of the Greek and Roman pantheons.[43] In other words, God is not fickle in his response to his creatures. The doctrines of impassibility and immutability, properly understood, ensure that God remains steadfast in his nature, character, and responses to his creatures. Furthermore, impassibility does not mean that God is unresponsive. He is not apathetic as the Stoics believed. God is really related.[44] There is genuine love, long-suffering, compassion, and so forth. The doctrine of impassability, then, in the words of Thomas McCall, "*safeguards* and *protects* the fact that holy love is the essence of the triune God."[45] He continues, "Rather than a denial of the love of God, it resoundingly affirms that holy love."[46] Perhaps a better understanding of the concepts of divine immutability and impassibility is Karl Barth's emphasis on "constancy"—God is constant in his nature, character, and responses to his creatures:

> The immutable is the fact that this God is as the One He is, gracious and holy, merciful and righteous, patient and wise. The immutable is the fact that He is the Creator, Reconciler, Redeemer and Lord. This immutability includes rather than excludes life. ... God's constancy—which is a better word than the suspiciously negative word "immutability"—is the constancy of His knowing, willing and acting

---

43. Thomas H. McCall, *Forsaken: The Trinity and the Cross, and Why It Matters* (Downers Grove, IL: InterVarsity Press, 2012), 68. For an excellent discussion on the patristic understanding of divine impassibility, see Paul Gavrilyuk, *The Suffering of the Impassible God: The Dialectics of Patristic Thought* (Oxford: Oxford University Press, 2004).

44. Thomas Aquinas argued that there was no real relation between God and his creatures. Consider the following:

> Therefore, there is no real relation in God to His creature, whereas in creatures there is a real relation to God, because creatures are contained under the divine order, and their very nature entails dependence on God. On the other hand, the divine processions are in the same nature. Hence no parallel exists. (Aquinas, *Summa Theologica* Part I of I, Q. 28. Art. 1.)

45. McCall, *Forsaken*, 68.

46. Ibid.

and therefore of His person. It is the continuity, undivertability and indefatigableness in which God both is Himself and also performs His work, ... It is the self-assurance in which God moves in Himself and in all His works and in which He is rich in Himself and in all His works without either losing Himself or (for fear of this loss) having to petrify in Himself and renounce His movement and His riches. The constancy of God is not then the limit and boundary, the death of His life. For this very reason the right understanding of God's constancy must not be limited to His presence with creation, as if God in Himself were after all naked "immutability" and there-fore in the last analysis death. On the contrary it is in and by virtue of His constancy that God is alive in Himself and in all His works.[47]

But how, then, does God experience the full effects of evil? *Pace* McCall, there is a sense in which God, in the divine nature, experienced evil through the incarnation. Following Aquinas and others, McCall believes that one must maintain a clear "distinction between the humanity and the divinity of Christ."[48] Failure to do so, says McCall, may lead to Docetism, that is, it only seemed as though Christ suffered in the flesh. On this I agree. But I would also agree with Erickson that to deny that God was somehow affected by the evil that Christ experienced may just as easily lead to some form of Nestorianism, or in other words, a separation of the two natures. Perhaps the solution is in holding to something like Thomas Morris's two-minds view of Christ. According to Morris there are two distinct centers of consciousness—the divine mind and the human mind. The eternal divine mind of the Son "encompasses the full scope of omniscience."[49] The human mind, however, came into existence at a finite time in the past. "The earthly range of consciousness, and self-consciousness," says Morris, "was thor-oughly human, Jewish, and first-century Palestinian in nature."[50] It would be impossible for the earthly mind to contain the divine mind; rather, what

47. Karl Barth, *The Doctrine of God*, vol. 2.1 of *The Church Dogmatics*, ed. G. W. Bromiley and T. F. Torrance, 1st pbk. ed. (London: T&T Clark, 2000), 495.

48. McCall, *Forsaken*, 69.

49. Thomas V. Morris, *The Logic of God Incarnate* (1986; repr., Eugene, OR: Wipf & Stock, 2001), 102–3.

50. Ibid., 103.

we see is that the divine mind contained the earthly mind. There was an "asymmetric accessing relation between the two minds."[51] Morris goes on to explain:

> The divine mind had full and direct access to the earthly, human experience resulting from the Incarnation, but the earthly consciousness did not have such full and direct access to the content of the overarching omniscience proper to the Logos, but only such access, on occasion, as the divine mind allowed it to have. There thus was a metaphysical and personal depth to the man Jesus lacking in the case of every individual who is merely human.[52]

Morris believes that this solution allows for, on the one hand, the human growth and development of Jesus, and, yet, on the other, his cry of dereliction.[53] If Morris is correct, and something like the two-minds view of Christ is correct, it would mean that the divine mind of the Son had full access to all the emotions, experiences, pains, and horrors felt by the human nature of Christ. It would go to stand that, though there is a distinction within the persons of the Trinity, and though it was Christ alone who suffered on the cross (on pain of the heresy of patripassianism), nevertheless, given that the Father, Son, and Spirit share divine omniscience, it would seem that each of the divine persons of the Trinity have access to the horrors that Christ suffered and faced through his work and his death in the human nature. In this sense, via divine omniscience, the divine Trinity can relate to the various horrors that people in the world face because of the tragedies that Christ went through on the cross.

Yet, there is another way to think of the divine experience of evil. Having an experience of evil against you is not the same thing as experiencing suffering from the evil. We can make such a distinction in our everyday human experiences. We can imagine cases where a person hurls insults at another, but the person receiving the insults is in no way fazed by the insults, perhaps, because this person has a strong and immovable character when it comes to such things as being insulted. Nevertheless, though not

---

51. Ibid.
52. Ibid.
53. Ibid.

fazed by the insults, the person may take the right steps to reconcile with the one doing the insulting. In this case, the person receiving the insults could retaliate, but, instead, absorbs any effects of evil against themselves, and then seeks to reconcile with the other. But let us suppose further that some deep pain is involved. The person receiving the insults feels pain, perhaps even deep mental anguish, from the insults, but nevertheless remains steadfast in character and immovable in resolve. Here, again, the person absorbs the effects of evil—pain in this instance—and, yet, does the good despite the evil. In the same way, perhaps God experiences the effects of evil, even if the deliverance of such evils causes deep mental pain, and, yet, he can respond to them without being affected by the evil, so as to debilitate him or to change his metaphysical stature in anyway. God can absorb any pain—the deepest levels of pain—brought against him because of his infinite love, goodness, resolve, and long-suffering toward his creatures.

Finally, because of divine omnipresence, omniscience, and love, God isn't some mere transcendent deity, as one might find in deism, who is unaware of and unresponsive to his creatures; rather, God is immanent and near to each of them. Jesus tells us that not one sparrow falls to the ground apart from God's knowledge and concern (Matt 10:29). Consider also the words of the psalmist:

> Where can I go from Your Spirit?
>> Or where can I flee from Your presence?
>
> If I ascend to heaven, You are there,
>> If I make my bed in Sheol, behold, You are there.
>
> If I take the wings of the dawn,
>> If I dwell in the remotest part of the sea,
>
> Even there Your hand will lead me,
>> And Your right hand will lay hold of me
>
> If I say, "Surely the darkness will overwhelm me,
>> And the light around me will be night,"
>
> Even the darkness is not dark to You,
>> And the night is as bright as the day.
>> Darkness and light are alike to You (Ps 139:7–12, NASB)

God is fully present (omnipresent) to all created reality, even to those within Sheol. The Christian doctrine of omnipresence shouldn't be confused with some form of pantheism or panentheism, whereby God is enmeshed with or permeates all of creation. God is fully present to his creatures through divine causality and divine omniscience. God continually sustains the entirety of the four-dimensional space-time universe, along with any other created reality that exists. It is because of God's love and goodness and because of this divine awareness and presence to every creature—through omniscience and omnipresence—that we can take comfort in knowing that God is genuinely aware of and has deep concern for our pain and suffering.

EVIL AND DIVINE ACTION

As noted from the above discussion, there is a sense, particularly through the incarnation, that God knows what it means to suffer and to experience the tremendous horrors of the world. Not only does God know these things, there is a real sense in which God is active in defeating evil. In order to see this more clearly, it would be helpful to consider a passage from the book of Job.

In Job 41, we see God answering Job out of the windstorm. Job has asked for his day in court with God, and he gets his wish. Rather than Job questioning God, however, it is the Lord who questions Job. The standard reading of this passage takes it that God reminds Job who is in charge and that Job has no right to question him on these matters. In the end, Job is silenced and realizes his folly. But there is much more to the passage than this. Often, readers fail to recognize the use of Job's allusions to the ancient Near Eastern mythic tradition throughout in his complaints. As John R. Schneider explains:

> In his very first oration, Job uses the mythic tradition to curse the night he was conceived. The anti-cosmic symbolism is powerful: "let those curse it who curse the day, who are skilled to rouse up Leviathan, let the stars of its dawn be dark" (Job 3:8-9). In his second oration he ironically equates himself with chaos. "Am I the sea, or a sea monster, that thou that set guard over me?" (Job 7:12). His personal complaint is expanding swiftly to become global—better

no world at all than one in which chaos lives. His distress over the injustice of history reaches its peak when Job considers God's power over chaos. "By his power he stilled the sea, by his understanding he smote Rahab, by his wind the heavens were made fair, *his hand pierced the fleeing serpent*" (Job 27:12–13, [his italics]. But this of course is no more the triumphant declaration of praise, as it functions in the tradition. In view of what has happened, and in light of what Job now realizes about the world, it has become an ironic lament, the confession of a bitter, broken and thoroughly bewildered man.[54]

In the ancient Near East, the sea is often understood as chaos. It is the unknown and often symbolizes evil. It is also the place where Leviathan—the chaos monster—dwells. Psalms 74 and 83, along with Isaiah 51, provide images of God's victory over the various manifestations of chaos. Job's complaint was that the chaos had not died but was still very much a part of the world.[55] It is no wonder that in Job 41 God begins his divine speech with the Leviathan. God asks Job, "Can you draw out Leviathan with a fishhook or press down his tongue with a cord?" (Job 41:1) Then a few verses later we read:

No one is so fierce that he dares to stir him up.
Who then is he who can stand before me?
Who has first given to me, that I should repay him?
Whatever is under the whole heaven is mine. (Job 41:10–11)

In other words, God is affirming to Job that the chaos monster is still very much a part of this world. No human can think of stopping or resisting him. But, despite this, God is very much in the midst of the chaos. Rather than the chaos monster being in control, it is God who can lead the chaos monster around, as imaged, by a hook. On this point, Schneider provides helpful insight:

---

54. John R. Schneider, "Seeing God Where the Wild Things Are: An Essay on the Defeat of Horrendous Evil," in *Christian Faith and the Problem of Evil*, ed. Peter van Inwagen (Grand Rapids: Eerdmans, 2004), 251.

55. Ibid., 252, 254.

God acknowledges the reality of the chaos, but he now reveals, and Job now sees, that he is in complete control of events. The relationship between God and Leviathan is not friendly, but rather one of grudging domestication.[56]

From this reading of Job, we see that God is in the midst of the evil that is taking place in the world, and he is doing something about it. In dealing with evil, it takes, in the words of N. T. Wright, God getting his "boots muddy" and "his hands bloody" in order "to put the world back to rights."[57] This is most clearly seen in the life and person of Jesus of Nazareth. As Wright explains,

> Jesus on the cross towers over the whole scene as Israel in person, as YHWH in person, as the point where the evil of the world does all that it can and where the Creator of the world does all that he can. Jesus suffers the full consequences of evil: evil from the political, social, cultural, personal, moral, religious and spiritual angles all rolled into one; evil in the downward spiral hurtling toward the pit of destruction and despair. And he does so precisely as the act of redemption, of taking that downward fall and exhausting it, so that there may be new creation, new covenant, forgiveness, freedom and hope. ... What the Gospels offer is not a philosophical explanation of evil, what it is or why it's there, nor a set of suggestions for how we might adjust our lifestyles so that evil will mysteriously disappear from the world, but the story of an *event* in which the living God *deals with it*.[58]

The work of God in the defeat of evil is connected with our future hope. As we'll consider below, God, through Christ's work on the cross, has defeated death, and the ramifications for this will ultimately come to fruition in the eschaton.

---

56. Ibid., 255.

57. N. T. Wright, *Evil and the Justice of God* (Downers Grove, IL: InterVarsity Press, 2006), 59.

58. Ibid., 92–93.

EVIL AND THE CHURCH

Having seen God's work in defeating evil through Christ, there is another area to consider. God has called the church to action in defeating evil in the world. As we begin to think about the church's response to the existential problem from evil (EPE), there are several important things that we must keep in mind. To begin with, in answering EPE, it is precisely at this point that our theology comes together with our praxis. How we respond to EPE is ultimately grounded in what we believe, particularly about God, people, sin, salvation, hope, and so on. In other words, our theology should ground our response to the problem of existential suffering.

In chapter 6 I defended the doctrine of the Trinity, arguing that at the center of all reality is this interpenetrating, dynamic, and self-giving love relationship between the persons of the Trinity. The doctrine of the Trinity should have significant implications for our understanding of human nature and the life of the church. Moreover, at the beginning of this chapter, I argued that God is light and God is love, both of which provide the framework and grounding for ethics. Now we can take into consideration the church's role in what God is doing to defeat evil in the world.

In creating humans, it may be suggested, what God wanted to do was to bring about in his creatures what we see in the perichoretic relationship of the divine persons. God wanted to create individuals who could, in a very real sense, share in the same kind of or similar capacity for, what I shall call, *deep love*, as exemplified within the interpenetrating life of the persons within the tri-unity of God. This deep love is like God's own love. At its heart, deep love is active movement toward the other. It is not the kind of love that is self-seeking or boastful (1 Cor 13:4–7), nor is it passive sympathetic response; rather, it is self-giving in nature, seeking out union with and what's best and good for the other. Human persons, as creatures, then, were created with the ability to relate with and love other persons on the deepest levels possible. It is this capacity for deep love and relationality that separates humans from all other created beings.

From a Trinitarian grounding, then, this means that humans not only have certain qualities (structure) like God, and that they can perform certain tasks (function) like him, but that they are also created to be relational like God. The very notion of relationality like God's own—relationality that can demonstrate itself in deep love for another—can only be so if the human person is freely capable of being relational, that is, if the person is capable of freely reciprocating or not reciprocating love. Humans, then, who were created in God's image and likeness, were not only capable of receiving love from God, but also capable of reciprocating such love. As Marilyn Adams suggests, "God made human beings to enter into nonmanipulative relationships of self-surrendering love with himself and relationships of self-giving love with others."[59]

If humans have the capacity for loving God, then it would also imply that the opposite is true. From the biblical narrative we see that is what happened with humans. Rather than choosing to love God, humans sinned and rebelled against him. Christians typically define sin as disobedience to or rebellion against God's law or commands. Sin is surely that, but this definition does not go far enough. It does not capture the nature or essence of just what sin is. At its core, sin is violence and opposed to love. It is violence because, rather than looking out for what's best for the other, it exalts the self at the expense of the other. All sin, whether intentional or unintentional, brings division, separation, and alienation. It is violent in that it breaks harmony between humans and God, humans and other humans, and humans and nature. Thus, such a rift finds its way throughout all sociological, cultural, and ecological structures. But God does not leave it at that. As Stephen Davis suggests:

> Cosmically, the relationship between God and human beings was severed by the entrance of sin into the world. Personally, it is broken whenever we separate ourselves from God by sin. All of God's actions in history are expressions of the personal relationship that is at the center of reality. God is attempting redemptively to restore human beings to the splendor of that relationship. Christians affirm that the relationship is fully restored through the action of God in the world and preeminently through God's action in Jesus Christ. Its essence is summed up sublimely by the prophet Jeremiah: "I will be

---

59. Marilyn McCord Adams, "Redemptive Suffering: A Christian Solution to the Problem of Evil," in *The Problem of Evil: Selected Readings*, ed. Michael L. Peterson (Notre Dame, IN: University of Notre Dame Press, 1992), 173.

your God, and you shall be my people" (Jer 7:23). At the center of the universe is a personal relationship and a God who acts on its behalf.[60]

According to Christian theism, God's desire is for humans to have abundant life. The very essence of such life is in knowing God[61] and living in accordance to his own being. Yet, because of sin, this life can only come about through the work of the death and resurrection of Jesus, and through the power and work of the Holy Spirit in the life of those who believe. Because of God's own work in human history, and by means of his own love toward us, humans can be set free from the power, corruption, and effects of sin—such freedom overturns sin that brings about alienation from God, alienation with other people, and alienation with creation.

When thinking about our response to EPE, it should be one of self-giving deep love. In other words, our response should be that of care. This response is not merely sympathy toward the other; rather, a deep care that is ultimately self-giving and other-centered. Often, many of the existential sufferings that we see taking place in the world are a direct result of sin. Yet, through the good news of the gospel (the work of God in and through Christ's death and resurrection to restore humanity), we see God's response to evil and sin in the world. It was through Christ's broken body and resurrection that God defeated death.

Nevertheless, we live in an already/not yet realization of the defeat of evil. As noted above, and as we'll consider more expansively below, Christians have hope that because of Christ's work in the world a day will come when there will be no more suffering, pain, and sorrow. Death will be no more (Rev 21:4). Yet, we still live in a world where pain, death, and suffering are very much reality. But the gospel does not stop with the reality that death has been defeated through Christ; sin, too, along with its effects, has been defeated. God, through the gospel, offers new life—eternal life. This life is not something that begins in the future; rather, it begins now. It was through Christ that God defeated death and sin, but it is through the Spirit that God brings new life to the world. As the redeemed community of Christ, then, it is the Spirit who is the agent of change, and it is he who

---

60. Davis, "God's Action," 177.
61. John 17:3.

provides the church with the power to make a difference and to confront the evil in the world. Through the Spirit, God has supplied all the power and energy needed to truly be agents and ambassadors of reconciliation. The church never replaces his work; rather, it is the church in and through the power of the Holy Spirit that God has chosen to confront evils in the world. Therefore, the church should be on the front lines confronting sin, particularly the many social injustices that we see taking place in the world today, as well as bridging the gap of broken relationships through the preaching and proclamation of the gospel. Social justice and the gospel are not opposed to one another. Rather, both have at their center the care and concern for the other.

As we reflect on the mission of the church, God has called it to love its neighbors (Mark 12:31); to help widows and orphans in their distress (Jas 1:27); to love enemies and to make peace so much as it is within its power (Matt 5:44; Rom 12:14, 16, 18); to forgive unconditionally and to reconcile with those who sin against it (Matt 5:44; 18:15, 21-22); to turn the other cheek (Matt 5:39) and not seek revenge (Rom 12:19); to give of its material possessions to those in need (Ps 82; Mark 12:31; Luke 10:25-37; Rom 1:13, 20; Jas 1:27; 2:14-17; 1 John 3:16-18). The church of God has been called to a life of self-giving love—a love that does not retaliate when wronged or seek revenge. The kind of life that the church has been called to is a kingdom life. Such a life represents God's intentions all along in creating. This self-lessness and self-giving is the very life that we see in the interpenetrating relationship of the divine persons of Trinity and demonstrated in God's selfless actions toward his creation through the Son and Spirit. Lastly, the church has been called to be a part of God's work in building his kingdom. When the church accepts its call, it becomes a part of what God is doing (and has been doing throughout the entirety of human history) to confront the evils and horrors in the world. Shall we now turn to the problem of hell and the Christian understanding of final hope?

THE PROBLEM OF HELL

Christians hold to a variety of different eschatological views. There are many points about the future on which they disagree. Despite these dis-agreements, all Christians agree that in the end God wins—God ultimately defeats evil. Central to Christian eschatology and the defeat of evil is the doctrine of the resurrection from the dead. Christians (as do Jews) believe that all people will eventually be raised, including unbelievers. Take Jesus' own words:

> Do not marvel at this, for an hour is coming when all who are in the tombs will hear his voice and come out, those who have done good to the resurrection of life, and those who have done evil to the resurrection of judgment. (John 5:28–29)

From this passage we see a central truth regarding the Christian view on the resurrection: two groups are raised—one group raised to life and the other raised to judgment. It is here that many have a difficulty with the Christian view of the afterlife. Those who are raised to life are raised to be with God in his presence forever, while those who are raised to judgment are raised to eternal separation from God in hell or, as it is called in book of Revelation, "the lake of fire" (Rev 20:10–11).[62] Some doubt whether God is just in assigning eternal or unending punishment to individuals who sin against him. They question whether the punishment fits the crime. How is it that a good and loving God assigns some people to unending punishment for a crime that is only temporal in nature? This has come to be known as (or is at least one version of) the problem of hell. In the *Problem of Pain*, C. S. Lewis surely captures the attitude of many Christians when thinking on hell:

> There is no doctrine which I would more willingly remove from Christianity than this, if lay in my power. But it has the full support of Scripture and, specially, of Our Lord's own words; it has always been held by Christendom; and it has the support of reason.[63]

Christians have generally responded in one of three ways. The first view is called the traditional view. This view has been the historic understanding of the church and takes hell to be a real place of eternal conscious torment. The second view is annihilationism. Annihilationists believe that hell is only temporary. Eventually, people in hell will cease to exist. The

---

62. The Bible seems to make a distinction between "hell" and "the lake of fire," but for our purposes, we will only focus on the point of final judgment.

63. Lewis, *The Problem of Pain*, 119–20.

third view is universalism, which teaches that, even if there is a place for hell, in the end everyone will be saved. Let's take each of these views in reverse order, beginning with universalism. The German theologian Jürgen Moltmann, who understands the importance of the last judgment, yet, who believes all will in the end be saved, writes:

> The eschatological point of the proclamation of "the Last Judgment" is the redeeming kingdom of God. Judgment is the side of the eternal kingdom that is turned towards history. In the Judgment all sins, every wickedness and every act of violence, the whole injustice of this murderous and suffering world, will be condemned and annihilated, because God's verdict effects what it pronounces. In the divine Judgment all sinners, the wicked and the violent, the murderers and the children of Satan, the Devil and the fallen angels will be liberated and saved from their deadly perdition through transformation into their true, created being, because God remains true to himself, and does not give up what he has once created and affirmed, or allow it to be lost.[64]

The eschatological picture that Moltmann paints is certainly one that is hopeful, in that even the devil himself is liberated and restored back to God into "true, created being," and this because of the work of Christ. Yet, Moltmann doesn't seem to take the words of Jesus seriously enough. It is not "every wickedness and every act of violence, the whole injustice of the murderous and suffering world" that's condemned at the judgment, but "those who have done evil." Jesus' words are sharp. Individuals themselves will be judged for their actions. Furthermore, in the book of Revelation, it isn't the acts of the wicked that suffer punishment or the judgment to come but individuals (Rev 20:11–15).

Christian universalists often take passages such as 2 Peter 3:9 and 1 Timothy 2:4, which speak of God's desire for all people in the end to be saved, in conjunction with passages that expect universal reconciliation (Col 1:20; Eph 1:10). But, as J. P. Moreland and Gary Habermas point out, such passages often used in support of universalism

---

64. Jürgen Moltmann, *The Coming of God: Christian Eschatology*, trans. Margaret Kohl (Minneapolis: Fortress, 1996), 255.

should be understood as doing one of two things. Either they are teaching what God's desire is without affirming what will happen, or they are describing, not the ultimate reconciliation of all fallen humanity, but a restoration of divine order and rule over creation taken as a whole.[65]

Surely, passages such as 2 Peter 3:9 and 1 Timothy 2:4 tell us of God's desire for all to be saved, but these passages give no indication that all will in the end be saved. Passages such as Colossians 1:20 and Ephesians 1:10 speak of universal reconciliation, but the emphasis is on the restoration of God's dominion over all things within the created order, as Moreland and Habermas rightly point out. As a matter of fact, when Colossians speaks of individual and personal reconciliation to God, it is conditioned upon faith (Col 1:23).

But what of annihilationism? Annihilationists seem to be on firmer ground biblically than universalists. Passages from the Old Testament often speak of the wicked perishing (Prov 11:10; 37:9-10, 20) or being destroyed (Ps 143:12) or that their names have been blotted out of the "book of the living" (Ps 69:28) "for ever and ever" (Ps 9:5). In the New Testament, we're told that believers are not the ones who perish (John 3:16; 2 Cor 2:15-16). Moreover, Jesus warns: "Do not fear those who kill the body but cannot kill the soul. Rather, fear him who can destroy both soul and body in hell" (Matt 10:28). Unfortunately, such passages only give a partial view of the evidence.[66] Take, for example, the following passage:

> Then he will say to those on his left, "Depart from me, you cursed, into the eternal fire prepared for the devil and his angels. ... And these will go away into eternal punishment, but the righteous into eternal life." (Matt 25:41, 46)

Here, we see those who are "cursed" go to the "eternal fire" and the "righteous" enter into "eternal life." Why is this significant? Annihilationists often suggest that the word "eternal" (*aiōnios*) in such passages refers more to the quality of the judgment than an unending time of duration. This

---

65. Habermas and Moreland, *Beyond Death*, 300.
66. Evans, *The Problem of Evil*, 94.

understanding of *aiōios* certainly fits within the semantic range of the word. But given the above passage, it would be inconsistent to speak of "eternal" as unending when it comes to the life of the believer, and, yet, take it to mean only qualitatively in regard to the unbeliever.[67]

Finally, we are left with the traditional view. How can we defend the traditional understanding of hell and maintain the goodness and justice of God? First, it's important to realize that as awful of a reality as hell is, it is part of what God is doing in defeating evil. This may sound strange but bear with me. God did not originally create hell for humanity; rather, it was prepared for "the devil and his angels" (Matt 25:41). Perhaps, this may not bring much comfort to some, but it shows, at least in part, that hell was not the way things were supposed to be for humanity. As noted earlier, I take it that what God wanted to do in bringing about humans was to create beings, made in his image and likeness, who could demonstrate deep love toward one another, while also reciprocating love back toward God. But as was argued, deep love takes a certain kind of freedom—the kind of freedom that lies at the very heart of who God is in the perichoretic relationship of the Godhead. Each of the persons of the Trinity are self-giving in love and fully open to the other persons. But such freedom means that God's creatures could choose to do otherwise. They could choose freely to rebel against him and not to reciprocate his love and be loving toward others.

Freedom is precisely the problem that lies at our second point. People who are in hell are there by their own choices. To flesh this out, it would be helpful to consider the words of C. S. Lewis:

> If a game is played, it must be possible to lose it. If the happiness of creatures lies in self-surrender, no one can make that surrender but himself (though many can help him to make it) and he may refuse. I would pay any price to be able to say truthfully "All will be saved." But my reason retorts "Without their will, or with it?" If I say "Without their will" I at once perceive a contradiction; how can the supreme voluntary act of self-surrender be involuntary? If I say "With their will," my reason replies "How if they *will not* give in?"[68]

---

67. Other passages that indicate the everlasting nature of punishment include Mark 9:47–48; Rev 14:9–11; 20:10.

68. Lewis, *The Problem of Pain*, 120.

Though responding to universalists, Lewis' insight is important for understanding why God does not save all and why hell is itself just punishment. Christians take it that God is himself the source of life, not merely biological life, but a qualitative kind of existence that is meaningful, purposeful, and good, or as Scripture calls it, "abundant life." Abundant life is ultimately found in conforming to God's ways. To have this abundant life requires self-denial on the part of the individual. It means that she is following God's ways and not her own. As has been argued throughout this chapter, not only is God love, but God is also light. There is no darkness at all in God. God is good, pure, and holy, and this is the path that God expects of us. Entering into a relationship with the Triune God is the way to ultimate salvation and eternal life (John 17:3), and this is why Jesus himself, the incarnate Son of God, claims to be "the way, and the truth, and the life" (John 14:6). Throughout salvation history, God has offered his perfect love to his creatures, inviting them into abundant life, and even providing the means for them to live a life of holiness. But as the gospel writer tells us, people love "darkness rather than the light" (John 3:19). People are ensnared by their sins and refuse to embrace God's way for them.[69] They would rather be ruled by their vices than to repent and surrender them over to God. Jerry Walls sums this up well.

> As astounding as this is to contemplate, some human beings may refuse the gift of perfect love. They may choose not to welcome God into their lives. They may choose to reject the Trinitarian God of eternal love, the Creator of the universe who gave his Son in order to give us eternal life with him.[70]

This is what makes the connection with hell obvious. Those who choose not to love God and invite him into their lives have chosen to exclude themselves from heaven by that very choice. Remember, heaven is the ultimate experience of "God with us." Because of God's goodness, he desires and seeks out our best. God wants all to repent and be saved (1 Tim 2:4; 2 Pet 3:9),

---

69. To see this, I would highly recommend C. S. Lewis' fictional work *The Great Divorce* (New York: HarperOne, 2001). On multiple occasions Lewis gives insight on how people might psychologically become ensnared by their vices.

70. Jerry L. Walls, *Heaven, Hell, and Purgatory: A Protestant View of the Cosmic Drama* (Grand Rapids: Brazos, 2015), 72–73.

but the reality is that some fail to see that God has their best interest in mind.

Third, in choosing to go their own way, straying from God's original intention for them, God's human creatures become less than what he intended for them as his image bearers. Again, Lewis provides deep insight on this point:

> Destruction, we should naturally assume, means the unmaking, or cessation, of the destroyed. And people often talk as if the "annihilation" of a soul were intrinsically possible. In all our experience, however, the destruction of one thing means the emergence of something else. Burn a log, and you have gases, heat and ash. To *have been* a log means now being those three things. If souls can be destroyed, must there not be a state of *having been* a human soul? And is not that, perhaps, the state which is equally well described as torment, destruction, and privation? You will remember that in the parable, the saved to a place prepared for *them*, while the damned go to a place never made for men at all. To enter heaven is to become more human than you ever succeeded in being on earth; to enter hell, is to be banished from humanity. What is cast (or casts itself) into hell is not a man; it is "remains". To be a complete man means to have the passions obedient to the will and the will offered to God: to *have been* a man—to be an ex-man or "damned ghost"—would presumably mean to consist of a will utterly centered in its self and passions utterly uncontrolled by the will.[71]

If Lewis is right, this turns the annihilationist's understanding of "destruction" on its head. Destruction, then, has less to do with one's ceasing to exist and more to do with the person shrinking back from what it means to be truly human.

Fourth, it would be unjust for God to allow unrepentant sinners into heaven. As Lewis rightly points out,

---

71. Lewis, *The Problem of Pain*, 127–28.

To condone an evil is simply to ignore it, to treat it as if it were good. But forgiveness needs to be accepted as well as offered if it is to be complete: and a man who admits no guilt can accept no forgiveness.[72]

But someone might object: despite peoples' unwillingness to give and receive forgiveness, wouldn't it still be unloving for God to send them to hell, especially if he seeks their best? It's not an issue of God's love. It is a misconception to think that God ceases to love those in hell. Rather, it is precisely because God loves that he doesn't allow just anyone to enter heaven. People who refuse to repent and to be reconciled to God refuse the kind of life God offers. Rather than living in abundant life, they choose to remain in death. It's not the individual or particular sins that send people to hell. Christians readily recognize, and the Bible affirms, redeemed people still sin. What separates people from God is a continual state of sinfulness, whereby sinners refuse God's offer of eternal life, to be cleansed of unrighteousness, and to be made new. Because they refuse reconciliation and God's work in making them new, they remain in death. Perhaps, this is the reason that the book of Revelation calls being thrown into the lake of fire the "second death" (Rev 21:8).

THE DEFEAT OF EVIL

Many believe that Christian hope lies in going to heaven when we die. On the one hand, there is some truth to this. Heaven is ultimately about being in the presence of God, which fulfills our deepest longings and desires. But as N. T. Wright has shown in his numerous works, Christian hope is ultimately found in the resurrection of Jesus. On this, he says:

> The first Christians did not simply believe in life after death; they virtually never spoke simply of going to heaven when they died. … When they did speak of heaven as a postmortem destination, they seemed to regard this heavenly life as a temporary stage on the way to the eventual resurrection of the body. … the early Christians hold firmly to a two-step belief about the future: first, death and

---

72. Ibid., 124.

whatever lies immediately beyond; second, a new bodily existence in the newly made world.[73]

This is certainly the message the Bible paints for us. It is because of the death and resurrection of the Son of God that we now have hope that our lowly bodies will one day be transformed into his glorious likeness (Col 3:4; 1 John 3:2). We were once alienated from God because of our sinfulness, but through the death of Christ, we have found peace and have been reconciled back to God (Col 1:21-22). But not only will God's human creatures be restored, all of creation will eventually be reconciled back to God through Christ's work on the cross (Col 1:19-20; cf. Rom 8:18-21). Through Christ's work on the cross and through his bodily resurrection, God has defeated death. As Paul reminds us in his first letter to the Corinthians:

Death is swallowed up in victory.
O death, where is your victory?
O death, where is your sting? (1 Cor 15:55)

Paul isn't waxing eloquent; he's taunting death! Paul knows that death no longer holds power over us. The Bible points to a time when God will restore the created order and make all things new. Consider the words of the author of Revelation.

Then I saw a new heaven and a new earth, for the first heaven and the first earth had passed away, and the sea was no more. And I saw the holy city, new Jerusalem, coming down out of heaven from God, prepared as a bride adorned for her husband. And I heard a loud voice from the throne saying, "Behold, the dwelling place of God is with man. He will dwell with them, and they will be his people, and God himself will be with them as their God. He will wipe away every tear from their eyes, and death shall be no more, neither shall there be mourning, nor crying, nor pain anymore, for the former things have passed away." (Rev 21:1-4)

---

73. N. T. Wright, *Surprised by Hope: Rethinking Heaven, the Resurrection, and the Mission of the Church* (New York: HarperOne, 2008), 41.

One day God will bring it about that all sin, death, and evil will be overcome. Just as God has redeemed his human creatures, reconciling them to himself, he will also restore all of creation. In reconciling all things to himself, God will bring about his kingdom, which was his intention from the beginning. It will be a kingdom of peace where there will be no more pain, suffering, violence, or hurt. God's human creatures will demonstrate God's deep love, reciprocating it not only to God but to one another and to creation. This kingdom will be a kingdom of flourishing and life, whereby God's creatures will live to their fullest. In this kingdom, God's righteousness, holiness, and love will reign supreme. Through the indwelling Spirit, God's people will be united to Christ and to the Father, and all of creation, full of God's presence, will rejoice in the greatness of God for its redemption. It is in this way, when all of God's enemies have been defeated, and when all things have been brought into proper subjection to him, God will be all and in all (1 Cor 15:28).

Because God is that which nothing greater can be conceived, God is the ultimate Good—a good incommensurate to all of the created goods and temporal evils found in this world.[74] In contrast to other worldviews, in which the joys we experience are destined for extinction, the incommensurate good relation of the Triune God of Christian theism defeats any of the sufferings that may be endured in this life, including those horrific evils that rob us of any meaning, turning our deepest tragedies into victories and our greatest sorrows into joys.

---

74. Marilyn McCord Adams, "Horrendous Evils and the Goodness of God," in *The Problem of Evil*, ed. Marilyn McCord Adams and Robert Merrihew Adams (Oxford: Oxford University Press, 1990), 218.

GLOSSARY

actual entities/occasions—A term in process theology used to describe events or "drops of experience" considered to be the basic constituents that stand behind reality.

animism—The view that a living soul or life spirit is behind the organization and animation of various phenomena in the world, including plants, trees, and certain inanimate objects (e.g., stones)

anthropic principle—A scientific principle stating that the universe has certain fundamental features or cosmological constants within it that are necessary if there is to be life within the universe.

aseity—Coming from the Latin terms *a* (from) and *se* (oneself), aseity is a term that refers to God's self-existence.

concrescence—A feature of process philosophy whereby an entity/occasion becomes a unified subject by integrating feelings brought on through the reception of data from a previous actual occasion.

contingent —Refers to any object, proposition, or state of affairs that is both possible and non-necessary; to say that something could have been other than it is.

cosmic dualism —A metaphysical theory that suggests that all of reality consists of two opposing principles or forces.

cosmological argument —A family of arguments for the existence of God that attempt to demonstrate the universe has a "sufficient reason" or "first cause" for its existence.

creation *ex nihilo* —A view on creation suggesting that God created out of nothing, using no pre-existing matter.

creation *ex materia* —A view on creation suggesting that God used pre-existing matter in forming the universe.

creativity —A metaphysical principle within process philosophy whereby the many (the constituent parts of the universe) become one actual occasion (the conjunction of all things within the universe).

defense —An argumentative strategy employed by theists to show that the arguments from evil—whether the logical or evidential argument—are unsuccessful according to their own terms.

dharma —A cosmic law or principle often found in Hinduism, Buddhism, and other eastern religions that either makes life possible and/or grounds duties and laws for right living, in order to maintain social order.

divine command theory —An ethical theory that suggests morality is grounded in God or the divine, and that moral obligation rests in obedience to God's commands.

emanation —The view that creation is a flowing forth from God, rather than God, in some sense, making, forming, or fashioning the world.

Five Ways —Refers to five arguments or proofs for God's existence (from motion, from causation, from contingency, from degrees, from final causes) developed by the medieval philosopher, Thomas Aquinas (1225-1274).

gratuitous evil —Those severe (or horrendous) evils that have no underlying reason, warrant, or justification as to why God allows them to exist, that is to say, such evils produce no greater good, nor do they keep at bay some worse evil; rather, they are pointless and/or meaningless.

horrendous evil —Those evils that go beyond physical or mental pain, producing deep suffering, whereby the individual becomes devalued and degraded, engulfing any positive value in his or her life.

initial aim—A term used in process theology to describe God's attempt at persuading a subject toward choosing a possibility that is in its best interest.

kalam cosmological argument—A version of the cosmological argument for the existence of God, first used by Islamic thinkers, that seeks to show that the universe had a beginning and is not eternal in itself.

karma—A view often found in Indian and New Age religions that suggests a cosmic force either punishes or rewards a person, presently or in the future, based on his or her right or wrong actions.

libertarian freedom—This view, also known as libertarian free will or libertarian free choice, expresses a genuine ability within an individual to abstain from or to perform some morally significant action, apart from any kind of determination or coercion.

metaphysical naturalism—The belief that physical reality is all that exists and that there is no God, miraculous intervention, or afterlife.

metaphysics—That discipline of philosophy that seeks to describe how things are in reality but may also refer to systems that seek to explain reality.

methodological naturalism—Refers to an epistemological approach to science, whereby the individual examines the world from the assumption that there is no God, even if he or she believes that such a being exists.

mind-body dualism—The metaphysical view that suggests human nature consists of two, irreducible, but interrelated features—a mind and a body.

Monism - A philosophical view, held by such philosophers as Parmenides (c. 515-492 BC) and Spinoza (1632-1677), that stands in contrast to dualism and pluralism, suggesting that all of reality consists of a singular substance or one kind of thing.

monolatry—The view that worship belongs exclusively to one god, even if other deities exist. This contrasts with monotheism in that the existence of other gods is not denied in monolatry.

moral evil—Refers to those kinds of evil that are the result of a moral agent or agents (e.g., rape, murder, genocide, infanticide, etc.).

moral supervenience—An ethical theory that suggests moral truths in some sense supervene on conscious intelligent moral creatures.

natura naturans—The pantheistic view that nature, which is both eternal and self-renewing, creates itself from or out of itself, apart from any external creator.

natura naturata—A concept within pantheistic thought referring to those orders within nature, some of which bring about experiences of the sacred or numinous.

natural evil—Refers to those kinds of evil brought about through natural means, apart from any action of a moral agent or agents (e.g., disease, suffering due to natural disasters)

necessary being—A being whose existence is neither contingent nor through accident, but who exists necessarily.

ontology—A branch of metaphysics that studies being.

open theism—A theological perspective that reinterprets or dismisses certain attributes classically attributed to God (e.g., divine timelessness, simplicity, and immutability), but centrally for this view, God does not have exhaustive foreknowledge of the future.

panexperientialism—Process theologies view that actual occasions (the basic constituents of reality) have a mental pole and are capable of experience.

panentheism—A metaphysical view whereby God is not identical to the world (as in pantheism), nor is God fully transcendent (as in theism); rather much like the soul relates to the body, God, who is deeply immanent to the world, also transcends it.

pantheism—The metaphysical view that God is identical to the world.

panpsychism—The view that all things, even those most basic constituents of reality, are not merely physical, but have an element of mental or consciousness with them.

perichoresis—A term employed by John of Damascus (676-749) to describe the "mutual indwelling" or "mutual interpenetration" between the Father, Son, and Holy Spirit of the Trinity.

prehension—A term used in process theology to describe when an actual occasion feels a previous occasion.

problem of evil—Generally refers not to one objection but a family of objections raised against Christian theism due the nature, kinds, and intensity of evil in the world.

process panentheism—A view, also known as "process theism" or "process theology," originally developed by Alfred North Whitehead (1861-1947), but later expanded upon by Charles Hartshorne (1897-2000), that teaches that process is fundamental to all of reality, and that all things within reality are in process and are changing, including God.

subjective aim—A term used in process theology to describe whether a subject chooses to actualize an initial aim sent by God.

theism—The metaphysical view that exactly one God exists who is non-physical, possesses perfect moral goodness, is omnipotent, omniscient, eternal, and necessary, and is the creator of all things.

theodicy—An attempt by theists to provide a positive explanation for why God allows evil in the world.

Thomistic Cosmological Argument—A version of the cosmological argument for the existence of God, developed by medieval philosopher, Thomas Aquinas (1225-1274), that seeks to demonstrate the contingency and causal dependency of the universe upon a necessary being.

transition—A term used in process theology to express when actual occasions transmit feelings to subsequent occasions.

ultimate—For process theology, "creativity," "the many," and the "one" all make up ultimate reality, whereas in theism and naturalism, ultimate reality consists of one thing—either God or nature.

worldview—A conceptual system, or a particular way of looking at the world, by which a person or group of people understand(s) and engage(s) life.

BIBLIOGRAPHY

Adams, Marilyn McCord. "Horrendous Evils and the Goodness of God." In *The Problem of Evil*, edited by Marilyn McCord Adams and Robert Merrihew Adams, 209-21. Oxford: Oxford University Press, 1990.

———. "Redemptive Suffering: A Christian Solution to the Problem of Evil." In *The Problem of Evil: Selected Readings*, edited by Michael L. Peterson, 248-67. Notre Dame, IN: University of Notre Dame Press, 1992.

Adams, Robert Merrihew. *Finite and Infinite Goods: A Framework for Ethics.* Oxford: Oxford University Press, 1999.

Akin, Daniel L. *1, 2, 3 John.* Nashville, TN: Broadman & Holman, 2001.

Allen, Diogenes. "Natural Evil and the Love of God." In *The Problem of Evil*, edited by Marilyn McCord Adams and Robert Merrihew Adams, 189-208. Oxford: Oxford University Press, 1990.

Alston, William P. "The Inductive Argument from Evil and the Human Cognitive Condition." In *The Evidential Argument from Evil*, edited by Daniel Howard-Snyder, 97-125. Bloomington, IN: Indiana University Press, 1996.

Anglin, Bill, and Steward Goetz. "Evil Is Privation." *International Journal for Philosophy of Religion* 13, no. 1 (1982): 3-12.

Anselm, "Proslogium." In *Anselm of Canterbury: The Major Works*, edited by Brian Davies and G. R. Evans, 82-104. New York: Oxford University Press, 1998.

Applegate, Kathryn. "A Defense of Methodological Naturalism." *Perspectives on Science and Christian Faith* 65, no. 1 (2013): 37-45.

Aquinas, Thomas. *Summa Theologica*. Vol. 1. Part 1. Translated by the Fathers of the Dominican Province. 1912. Reprint, New York: Cosimo Classics, 2007.

Athanasius. *On the Incarnation*. Translated by D. Nutt. Edited by Cliff Lee. Lexington, KY: Createspace Independent Publishing, 2007.

Augustine. *The Confessions*. Translated by Maria Boulding. Hyde Park, NY: New City Press, 1997.

———. *Enchiridion*. Translated by J. F. Shaw. Nicene and Post-Nicene Fathers: A Select Library of the Christian Church. Series One. Vol. 3. Edited by Philip Schaff. Peabody, MA: Hendrickson Publishers, 2004.

Baggett, David, and Ronnie Campbell. "Omnibenevolence, Moral Apologetics, and Doubly Ramified Natural Theology." *Philosophia Christi* 15, no. 2 (2013): 337–52.

Baggett, David, and Jerry L. Walls. *God and Cosmos: Moral Truth and Human Meaning*. New York: Oxford University Press, 2016.

———. *Good God: The Theistic Foundations of Morality*. Oxford: Oxford University Press, 2011.

Barrow, John D., and Frank J. Tipler. *The Anthropic Cosmological Principle*. Oxford: Oxford University Press, 1986.

Barth, Karl. *The Church Dogmatics*. Vol. 1.1, *The Doctrine of the Word of God*. Edited by G. W. Bromiley and T. F. Torrance. 1st pbk. ed. London: T&T Clark, 2004.

———. *The Church Dogmatics*. Vol. 2.1, *The Doctrine of God*. Edited by G. W. Bromiley and T. F. Torrance. 1st pbk. ed. London: T&T Clark, 2004.

Bauckham, Richard. *God Crucified: Monotheism and Christology in the New Testament*. Grand Rapids: Eerdmans, 1998.

———. *Jesus and the God of Israel: God Crucified and Other Studies on the New Testament's Christology of Divine Identity*. Grand Rapids: Eerdmans, 2008.

———. "Monotheism and Christology in the Gospel of John." In *Contours of Christology in the New Testament*, edited by Richard N. Longenecker, 148–66. Grand Rapids: Eerdmans, 2005.

———. "The Worship of Jesus in Philippians 2:9–11." In *Where Christology Began: Essays on Philippians 2*, edited by Ralph P. Martin and Brian J. Dodd, 128–39. Louisville, KY: Westminster John Knox, 1998.

Beck, W. David, and Max Andrews. "God and the Multiverse: A Thomistic Modal Realism." *Philosophia Christi* 16, no. 1 (2014): 101–15.

Beilby, James. "Divine Aseity, Divine Freedom: A Conceptual Problem for Edwardsian-Calvinism." *Journal of the Evangelical Theological Society* 47, no. 4 (2004): 647–58.

Berlinski, David. *The Devil's Delusion: Atheism and Its Scientific Pretensions.* New York: Crown Forum, 2008.

Boyd, Gregory A. *God of the Possible: A Biblical Introduction to the Open View of God.* Grand Rapids: Baker, 2000.

———. *Satan and the Problem of Evil.* Downers Grove, IL: InterVarsity Press, 2001.

Brand, Paul, and Philip Yancey. *The Gift of Pain: Why We Hurt and What We Can Do About It.* Grand Rapids: Zondervan, 1997.

Broad, C. D. "Phantasms of the Living and of the Dead." *Proceedings of the Society for Psychical Research* 50, no. 183 (1953): 51–67.

Budziszewski, J. "Phillip Johnson Was Right: The Rivalry of Naturalism and Natural Law." In *Darwin's Nemesis: Phillip Johnson and the Intelligent Design Movement,* edited by William A. Dembski, 244–60. Downers Grove, IL: InterVarsity Press, 2006.

Campbell, Ronnie P., Jr. "The Eternality of the Immutable God in the Thought of Paul Helm." Master's thesis, Liberty University, 2008.

Clark, David K., and Norman L. Geisler. *Apologetics in the New Age: A Christian Critique of Pantheism.* 1990. Reprint, Eugene, OR: Wipf & Stock, 2004.

Clarke, D. S. "Panpsychism and the Philosophy of Charles Hartshorne." *Journal of Speculative Philosophy* 16.3, no. 2 (2002): 151–66.

Clarke, W. Norris. *Explorations in Metaphysics: Being, God, and Person.* Notre Dame, IN: University of Notre Dame Press, 2008.

———. *The Philosophical Approach to God: A New Thomistic Perspective.* 2nd rev. ed. New York: Fordham University Press, 2007.

Cobb, John B., and David Ray Griffin. *Process Theology: An Introductory Exposition.* Louisville, KY: Westminster John Knox, 1976.

Collins, Robin. "A Scientific Argument for the Existence of God." In *Reason for the Hope Within,* edited by Michael J. Murray, 47–75. Grand Rapids: Eerdmans, 1999.

———. "The Teleological Argument." In *The Blackwell Companion to Natural Theology*, edited by William Lane Craig and J. P. Moreland, 202-81. Oxford: Wiley-Blackwell, 2009.

Cooper, John W. *Panentheism—The Other God of the Philosophers: From Plato to the Present*. Grand Rapids: Baker Academic, 2006.

Corrington, Robert S. "Deep Pantheism." *Journal for the Study of Religion* 1, no. 4 (2007): 503-7.

Craig, William Lane. *God, Time, and Eternity*. Dordrecht: Kluwer Academic, 2001.

———. "A Middle Knowledge Response." In *Divine Foreknowledge: Four Views*, edited by James K. Beilby and Paul R. Eddy, 55-60. Downers Grove, IL: InterVarsity Press, 2001.

———. "The Middle Knowledge View." In *Divine Foreknowledge: Four Views*, edited by James K. Beilby and Paul R. Eddy, 119-43. Downers Grove, IL: InterVarsity Press, 2001.

———. *The Only Wise God: The Compatibility of Divine Foreknowledge and Human Freedom*. 1987. Reprint, Eugene, OR: Wipf & Stock, 1999.

———. *Reasonable Faith: Christian Truth and Apologetics*. 3rd ed. Wheaton, IL: Crossway, 2008.

———. *Time and Eternity: Exploring God's Relationship to Time*. Wheaton, IL: Crossway, 2001.

Craig, William Lane, and Paul Copan. *Creation Out of Nothing: A Biblical, Philosophical, and Scientific Exploration*. Grand Rapids: Baker Academic, 2005.

Craig, William Lane, and James D. Sinclair. "The Kalam Cosmological Argument." In *The Blackwell Companion to Natural Theology*, edited by William Lane Craig and J. P. Moreland, 101-201. Oxford: Wiley-Blackwell, 2009.

Creel, Richard E. *Divine Impassibility: An Essay in Philosophical Theology*. New York: Cambridge University Press, 1986.

Cullmann, Oscar. *The Earliest Christian Confessions*. Translated by J. K. S. Reid. London: Lutterworth Press, 1949.

Davies, Brian. "Reply to Mark Robson on Evil as Privation." *New Blackfriars* 94, no. 1053 (September 2013): 565-68.

Davies, Paul. *The Cosmic Jackpot: Why Our Universe is Just Right for Life*. New York: Houghton Mifflin, 2007.

————. *God and the New Physics*. New York: Simon and Schuster, 1983.

————. *The Mind of God*. New York: Touchstone, 1992.

Davis, Stephen T. *Christian Philosophical Theology*. Oxford: Oxford University Press, 2006.

————. *God, Reason and Theistic Proofs*. Grand Rapids: Eerdmans, 1997.

————. "God the Mad Scientist: Process Theology on God and Evil." *Themelios* 5, no. 1 (1979): 18–23.

————. "God's Action." In *Defense of Miracles*, edited by R. Douglas Geivett and Gary Habermas, 163–77. Downers Grove, IL: InterVarsity Press, 1997.

————. "Is the God of Process Theology a Valid Option?" In *Disputed Issues: Contending for Christian Faith in Today's Academic Setting*, 121–31. Waco, TX: Baylor University Press, 2009.

————. "Three Views of God, Which is Correct?" In *Disputed Issues: Contending for Christian Faith in Today's Academic Setting*, 205–22. Waco, TX: Baylor University Press, 2009.

Dawkins, Richard. *The God Delusion*. New York: Mariner Books, 2006.

————. *River Out of Eden: A Darwinian View of Life*. New York: Basic Books, 1995.

————. *The Selfish Gene*. 30th Anniversary Edition. New York: Oxford University Press, 2006.

Dell'Olio, Andrew J. "Do Near-Death Experiences Provide a Rational Basis for Belief in Life After Death?" *Sophia* 10 (2010): 113–28.

Dennett, Daniel C. *Breaking the Spell: Religion as a Natural Phenomenon*. New York: Viking, 2006.

DeWeese, Garrett J. *God and the Nature of Time*. Burlington, VT: Ashgate Publishing Company, 2004.

————. "Natural Evil: A 'Free Process' Defense." In *God and Evil: The Case for God in a World Filled with Pain*, edited by Chad Meister and James K. Dew Jr., 53–64. Downers Grove, IL: InterVarsity Press, 2013.

Dilley, Stephen C. "Philosophical Naturalism and Methodological Naturalism: Strange Bedfellows?" *Philosophia Christi* 12, no. 1 (2010): 118–41.

Dodds, Michael J. *The Unchanging God of Love: Thomas Aquinas and Contemporary Theology on Divine Immutability*. 2nd ed. Washington, D.C.: The Catholic University American Press, 2008.

Dorner, Issac August. *Divine Immutability: A Critical Reconsideration*. Minneapolis: Fortress, 1994.

Dougherty, Trent. *The Problem of Animal Pain: Theodicy for All Creatures Great and Small*. New York: Palgrave Macmillan, 2014.

D'Souza, Dinesh. "Why We Need Earthquakes." *Christianity Today* 53, no. 5, May 2009, 58.

Dunn, James D. G. *Did the Early Christians Worship Jesus?: The New Testament Evidence*. Louisville, KY: Westminster John Knox, 2010.

Easwaran, Eknath, trans. *The Bhagavad Gita*. 2nd ed. Tomales, CA: Nilgiri Press, 2007.

Erickson, Millard J. *Christian Theology*. 2nd ed. Grand Rapids: Baker, 1999.

———. *The Word Became Flesh: A Contemporary Incarnational Christology*. Grand Rapids: Baker, 2000.

———. *What Does God Know and When Does He Know It?: The Current Controversy Over Divine Foreknowledge*. Grand Rapids: Zondervan, 2003.

Evans, C. Stephen. *God and Moral Obligations*. Oxford: Oxford University Press, 2013.

Evans, C. Stephen, and R. Zachary Manis. *Philosophy of Religion*. 2nd ed. Downers Grove, IL: InterVarsity Press, 2009.

Evans, Jeremy. *The Problem of Evil: The Challenge to Essential Christian Beliefs*. Nashville, TN: B&H Academic, 2013.

Evans, Hilary. *Seeing Ghosts: Experiences of the Paranormal*. London: John Murray, 2002.

Feinberg, John S. *The Many Faces of Evil: Theological Systems and the Problems of Evil*. Rev. and exp. ed. Wheaton, IL: Crossway, 2004.

———. *No One Like Him: The Doctrine of God*. Wheaton, IL: Crossway, 2001.

———. "Theism." *The Evangelical Dictionary of Theology*, 2nd ed., edited by Walter A. Elwell, 1182–83. Grand Rapids: Baker Academic, 2001.

Folger, Tim. "Will Indonesia Be Ready for the Next Tsunami?" National Geographic (website). Updated September 28, 2018. http://news.nationalgeographic.com/news/2014/12/141226-tsunami-indonesia-catastrophe-banda-aceh-warning-science/

Fracasso, Cheryl, and Harris Friedman. "Near-Death Experiences and the Possibility of Disembodied Consciousness: Challenges to Prevailing Neurobiological and Psychosocial Theories." *NeuroQuantology* 9, no. 1 (2011): 41–53.

Franks, W. Paul, ed. *Explaining Evil: Four Views.* London: Bloomsbury Academic, 2019.

Fretheim, Terence E. *The Suffering of God: An Old Testament Perspective.* Philadelphia: Fortress, 1984.

Gavrilyuk, Paul. *The Suffering of the Impassible God: The Dialectics of Patristic Thought.* Oxford: Oxford University Press, 2004.

Geisler, Norman. *Systematic Theology, Volume 2: God, Creation.* Minneapolis: Bethany House, 2003.

Geisler, Norman, and William Watkins. *Perspectives: Understanding and Evaluating Today's World Views.* San Bernardino, CA: Here's Life Publishers, 1984.

———. "Process Theology: A Survey and an Appraisal." *Themelios* 11, no. 1 (1986): 15–22.

Glynn, Patrick. *God the Evidence: The Reconciliation of Faith and Reason in a Postsecular World.* Rocklin, CA: Forum, 1997.

Goetz, Stewart, and Charles Taliaferro. *Naturalism.* Grand Rapids: Eerdmans, 2008.

Gregersen, Niels Henrik. "Three Varieties of Panentheism." In *In Whom We Live and Move and Have Our Being*, edited by Philip Clayton and Arthur Peacocke, 19–35. Grand Rapids: Eerdmans, 2004.

Greyson, Bruce. "Near-Death Experiences and Spirituality." *Zygon* 41, no. 2 (2006): 393–414.

———. "Seeing Dead People Not Known to Have Died: 'Peak in Darien' Experiences." *Anthropology and Humanism* 35, no. 2 (2010): 159–71.

Griffin, David Ray. *A Process Christology.* Philadelphia: Westminster Press, 1973.

———. *Evil Revisited: Responses and Reconsiderations.* Albany, NY: State University of New York Press, 1991.

———. *God, Power, and Evil: A Process Theodicy.* Louisville, KY: Westminster John Knox, 2004.

———. "Panentheism: A Postmodern Revelation." In *In Whom We Live and Move and Have Our Being*, edited by Philip Clayton and Arthur Peacocke, 36–47. Grand Rapids: Eerdmans, 2004.

———. *Religion and Scientific Naturalism: Overcoming the Conflicts*. Albany, NY: State University of New York Press, 2000.

———. *Unsnarling the World-Knot: Consciousness, Freedom, and the Mind-body Problem*. Berkeley, CA: University of California Press, 1998.

———. *Whitehead's Radically Different Postmodern Philosophy: An Argument for Its Contemporary Relevance*. New York: State University of New York Press, 2007.

Grudem, Wayne. *Systematic Theology: An Introduction to Biblical Doctrine*. Grand Rapids: Zondervan, 1994.

Grula, John W. "Pantheism Reconsidered: Ecotheology as a Successor to the Judeo-Christian, Enlightenment, and Postmodernist Paradigms." *Zygon* 43, no. 1 (2008): 159–80.

Habermas, Gary. *The Historical Jesus: Ancient Evidence for the Life of Christ*. Joplin, MS: College Press, 1996.

———. *The Risen Jesus and Future Hope*. Lanham, MD: Rowman & Littlefield, 2003.

Habermas, Gary R., and J. P. Moreland. *Beyond Death: Exploring the Evidence for Immortality*. 1998. Reprint, Eugene, OR: Wipf & Stock, 2004.

Habermas, Jürgen. *Time of Transitions*. Edited and translated by Ciaran Cronin and Max Pensky. Cambridge: Polity, 2006.

Haraldsson, Erlendur. "Alleged Encounters with the Dead: The Importance of Violent Death in 337 Cases." *Journal of Parapsychology* 73, no. 1 (2009): 91–118.

———. "Survey of Claimed Encounters with the Dead." *Omega* 19, no. 2 (1988–9): 103–13.

———. "The Iyengar-kirti Case: An Apparitional Case of the Bystander Type." *Journal of the Society for Psychical Research* 54, no. 806 (1987): 64–67.

Harris, Sam. *Waking Up: A Guide to Spirituality without Religion*. New York: Simon & Schuster, 2014.

Harrison, Paul. *Elements of Pantheism: A Spirituality of Nature and the Universe*. 3rd ed. Lexington, KY: CreateSpace Independent Publishing Platform, 2013.

Harrison, Verna. "Perichoresis in the Greek Fathers." *St. Vladimir's Theological Quarterly* 35, no. 1 (1991): 53–65.

Hart, David Bentley. *The Experience of God: Being, Consciousness, and Bliss*. New Haven, CT: Yale University Press, 2013.

Hartshorne, Charles. *Aquinas to Whitehead: Seven Centuries of Metaphysics of Religion: The Aquinas Lecture, 1976*. Milwaukee, WI: Marquette University Publications, 1976.

Hartshorne, Charles, and W. Creighton Peden. *Whitehead's View of Reality*. New York: The Pilgrim Press, 1981.

Hasker, William. *Metaphysics: Constructing a World View*. Downers Grove, IL: InterVarsity Press, 1984.

———. *Metaphysics and the Tri-Personal God*. Oxford: Oxford University Press, 2013.

———. "Persons and the Unity of Consciousness." In *The Waning of Materialism*, edited by Robert C. Koons and George Bealer, 175–90. Oxford: Oxford University Press, 2010.

———. *The Emergent Self*. Ithaca, NY: Cornell University Press, 1999.

———. *The Triumph of God over Evil: Theodicy for a World of Suffering*. Downers Grove, IL: InterVarsity Press, 2008.

Hawking, Stephen. *A Brief History of Time*. Updated and Expanded Tenth Anniversary Edition. New York: Bantam Books, 1996.

Hayman, Peter. "Monotheism—A Misused Word in Jewish Studies?" *Journal of Jewish Studies* 42, no. 1 (1991): 1–15.

Hedley, Douglas. "Pantheism, Trinitarian Theism and the Idea of Unity: Reflections on the Christian Concept of God." *Religious Studies* 32, no. 1 (1996): 61–77.

Heiser, Michael S. "Monotheism, Polytheism, Monolatry, or Henotheism: Toward an Assessment of Divine Plurality in the Hebrew Bible." *Bulletin for Biblical Research* 18, no. 1 (2008): 2–4.

Helm, Paul. "Divine Timeless Eternity." In *God and Time: Four Views*, edited by Gregory Ganssle, 28–60. Downers Grove, IL: InterVarsity Press, 2001.

———. *Eternal God: A Study of God without Time*. New York: Oxford University Press, 1988.

———. *The Providence of God*. Downers Grove, IL: InterVarsity Press, 1993.

Hick, John. *Evil and the God of Love*. Reissue. New York: Palgrave Macmillan, 2007.

Holmes, Arthur F. *Ethics: Approaching Moral Decisions*. 2nd ed. Downers Grove, IL: InterVarsity Press, 2007.

Horrell, J. Scott. "In the Name of the Father, Son, and Holy Spirit: Toward a Trinitarian Worldview." *Bibliotheca Sacra* 166 (2008): 131–46.

———. "Toward a Biblical Model of the Social Trinity: Avoiding Equivocation of Nature and Order." *Journal of the Evangelical Theological Society* 47, no. 3 (2004): 399–421.

Howard-Snyder, Daniel, ed. *The Evidential Argument from Evil*. Bloomington, IN: Indiana University Press, 1996.

Howard-Snyder, Frances. "Christianity and Ethics." In *Reasons for the Hope Within*, edited by Michael J. Murray, 375–98. Grand Rapids: Eerdmans, 1999.

Hunt, David. "The Simple-Foreknowledge View." In *Divine Foreknowledge: Four Views*, edited by James K. Beilby and Paul R. Eddy, 65–103. Downers Grove, IL: InterVarsity Press, 2001.

Hurtado, Larry W. "First-Century Jewish Monotheism." *Journal for the Study of the New Testament* 71 (1998): 3–26.

———. *God In New Testament Theology*. Nashville, TN: Abingdon Press, 2010.

———. *How on Earth Did Jesus Become God? Historical Questions about Earliest Christian Devotion*. Grand Rapids: Eerdmans, 2005.

———. *Lord Jesus Christ: Devotion to Jesus in Earliest Christianity*. Grand Rapids: Eerdmans, 2003.

———. *One Lord, One God: Early Christian Devotion and Ancient Jewish Monotheism*. Philadelphia: Fortress, 1988.

International Association for Near Death Studies, Inc. [IANDS]. "Key Facts about Near-Death Experiences." About NDEs. Last updated August 29, 2017. Accessed January 28, 2019. https://iands.org/ndes/about-ndes/key-nde-facts21.html?start=2

James, William. *Principles of Psychology.* Vol. 1. New York: Henry Holt and Co., 1890.

Keating, James F., and Thomas Joseph White, eds. *Divine Impassibility and the Mystery of Human Suffering.* Grand Rapids: Eerdmans, 2009.

Keener, Craig S. *Miracles: The Credibility of the New Testament Account.* 2 vols. Grand Rapids: Baker Academic, 2011.

Kelly, J. N. D. *Early Christian Creeds.* 3rd ed. Burnt Mill, UK: Longman Group Ltd., 1972.

Kemp, John. "Pain and Evil." *Philosophy* 29, no. 108 (1954): 13-26.

Köstenberger, Andreas J. *John.* Grand Rapids: Baker Academic, 2004.

Kruse, Colin G. *The Letters of John.* Grand Rapids: Eerdmans, 2000.

Layman, C. Stephen. "A Moral Argument for the Existence of God." In *Is Goodness without God Good Enough? A Debate on Faith, Secularism, and Ethics,* edited by Robert K. Garcia and Nathan L. King, 49-65. Lanham, MD: Rowman & Littlefield, 2009.

———. "Moral Evil: The Comparative Response." *International Journal for Philosophy of Religion* 53 (2003): 1-23.

———. "Natural Evil: The Comparative Response." *International Journal for Philosophy of Religion* 54 (2003): 1-31.

Leftow, Brian. *Time and Eternity.* Ithaca, NY: Cornell University Press, 1991.

Lennon, John. "Imagine." Track 1 on *Imagine.* Apple Records, 1971.

Levine, Michael P. *Pantheism: A Non-theistic Concept of Deity.* London: Routledge, 1994.

———. "Pantheism, Substance and Unity." *International Journal of Philosophy of Religion* 32, no. 1 (1992): 1-23.

Lewis, C. S. *The Great Divorce.* New York: HarperOne, 2001.

———. *Mere Christianity.* New York: HarperSanFrancisco, 1980.

———. *Perelandra.* New York: Scribner, 1996.

———. *The Problem of Pain.* New York: HarperSanFrancisco, 1996.

Licona, Michael R. *The Resurrection of Jesus: A New Historiographical Approach.* Downers Grove, IL: InterVarsity Press, 2010.

Lister, Rob. *God is Impassible and Impassioned: Toward a Theology of Divine Emotion.* Wheaton, IL: Crossway, 2013.

Little, Bruce A. *A Creation-Order Theodicy: God and Gratuitous Evil.* Lanham, MD: University Press of America, 2005.

———. *God, Why This Evil?* Lanham, MD: Hamilton Books, 2010.

Lommel, Pim van, Ruud van Wees, Vincent Meyers, and Ingrid Elfferich. "Near-Death Experience in Survivors of Cardiac Arrest: A Prospective Study in the Netherlands." *The Lancet* 358 (December 15, 2001): 2039–45.

Long, Jeffery, and Paul Perry. *Evidence of the Afterlife: The Science of Near-Death Experiences.* New York: HarperCollins, 2010.

Longenecker, Richard N. "Christological Materials in the Early Christian Communities." In *Contours of Christology in the New Testament*, edited by Richard Longenecker, 68–74. Grand Rapids: Eerdmans, 2005.

Lovett, Richard. "Unknown Earth: Why is Earth's Climate so Stable?" *New Scientist* 199, no. 2675, September 2008, 34. https://www .newscientist.com/article/mg19926751-900-unknown-earth-why -is-earths-climate-so-stable/.

Lowe, Victor. "Whitehead's Metaphysical System." In *Process Philosophy and Christian Thought*, edited by Delwin Brown, Ralph E. James, Jr, and Gene Reeves, 1–22. Indianapolis, IN: Bobbs-Merrill Educational Publishing, 1971.

MacGregor, Kirk. "The Existence and Irrelevance of Gratuitous Evil." *Philosophia Christi* 14, no. 1 (2012): 165–80.

Mackie, J. L. "Evil and Omnipotence." In *The Problem of Evil*, edited by Marilyn McCord Adams and Robert Merrihew Adams, 25–37. Oxford: Oxford University Press, 1990.

Marsh, Michael N. "The Phenomenology of the Near-Death Experience (NDE): An Encounter with Eternity—or Simply an Aberrant Brain State?" *Modern Believing* 52, no. 2 (2011): 38–47.

Marshall, I. Howard. *The Epistles of John.* Grand Rapids: Eerdmans, 1978.

Martin, Ralph P. *Worship in the Early Church.* Grand Rapids: Eerdmans, 1974.

Mattessich, Richard. "No Substance without Process, No Process without Substance, and Neither without Energy: Some Thoughts and Extensions on Whitehead and the Endurants (Continuants) v. Perdurants (Occurrents) Controversy." *Process Studies Supplement* 19 (2014): 1–36.

McCall, Thomas H. *Forsaken: The Trinity and the Cross, and Why It Matters.* Downers Grove, IL: InterVarsity Press, 2012.

McTaggart, J. M. "Time: An Excerpt from *The Nature of Existence.*" In *Metaphysics: The Big Questions*, edited by Peter van Inwagen and Dean W. Zimmerman, 67–74. Malden, MA: Blackwell, 2004.

Mitchell, Basil. *The Justification of Religious Belief.* New York: Oxford University Press, 1981.

Moltmann, Jürgen. *The Coming of God: Eschatology.* Translated by Margaret Kohl. Minneapolis: Fortress, 1996.

———. *God in Creation.* Translated by Margaret Kohl. Minneapolis: Fortress, 1993.

———. *The Trinity and the Kingdom.* 1st Fortress Press ed. Translated by Margaret Kohl. Minneapolis: Fortress, 1993.

Moody, Raymond A., Jr. *Life after Life.* Harrisburg, PA: StackPole Books, 1976.

Moreland, J. P. *Consciousness and the Existence of God: A Theistic Argument.* New York: Routledge, 2008.

———. *Kingdom Triangle.* Grand Rapids: Zondervan, 2007.

———. "The Ontological Status of Properties." In *Naturalism: A Critical Analysis*, edited by William Lane Craig and J. P. Moreland, 67–109. New York: Routledge, 2000.

Moreland, J. P., and William Lane Craig. *Philosophical Foundations for a Christian Worldview.* Downers Grove, IL: InterVarsity Press, 2003.

Moreland, J. P., and Scott B. Rae. *Body and Soul: Human Nature and the Crisis in Ethics.* Downers Grove, IL: InterVarsity Press, 2000.

Morris, Leon. *The Gospel According to John.* Grand Rapids: Eerdmans, 1995.

Morris, Thomas V. *Our Idea of God: An Introduction to Philosophical Theology.* Vancouver: Regent College Publishing, 2002.

———. *The Logic of God Incarnate.* 1986. Reprint, Eugene, OR: Wipf & Stock, 2001.

Morse, Melvin, and Paul Perry. *Transformed by the Light: The Powerful Effect of Near-Death Experiences on People's Lives.* New York: Villard Books, 1992.

Nagel, Thomas. *Mind and Cosmos: Why the Materialist Neo-Darwinian Conception of Nature is Almost Certainly False.* Oxford: Oxford University Press, 2012.

Nash, Ronald H. *The Concept of God: An Exploration of Contemporary Difficulties with the Attributes of God.* Grand Rapids: Zondervan, 1983.

———. *Faith and Reason: Searching for a Rational Faith.* Grand Rapids: Zondervan, 1988.

Neiman, Susan. *Evil in Modern Thought: An Alternative History of Philosophy.* Princeton: Princeton University Press, 2002.

Neufeld, Vernon H. *The Earliest Christian Confessions.* Grand Rapids: Eerdmans, 1963.

Neusner, Jacob. "Divine Love in Classical Judaism." *Review of Rabbinic Judaism* 17 (2014): 121-44.

Nichols, Terrance. *Death and Afterlife: A Theological Introduction.* Grand Rapids: Brazos Press, 2010.

O'Connor, David. *God, Evil, and Design: An Introduction to the Philosophical Issues.* Malden, MA: Blackwell, 2008.

Osborn, Ronald E. *Death Before the Fall: Biblical Literalism and the Problem of Animal Suffering.* Downers Grove, IL: InterVarsity Press, 2014.

Owen, H. P. *Concepts of Deity.* New York: Herder and Herder, 1971.

Padgett, Alan G. "Divine Foreknowledge and the Arrow of Time: On the Impossibility of Retrocausation." In *God and Time: Essays on the Divine Nature,* edited by Gregory E. Ganssle and David M. Woodruff, 65-74. Oxford: Oxford University Press, 2002.

———. *God, Eternity and the Nature of Time.* 1992. Reprint, Eugene, OR: Wipf & Stock, 2000.

———. "God and Timelessness." In *Philosophy of Religion: A Reader and Guide,* edited by William Lane Craig, 230-45. New Brunswick, NJ: Rutgers University Press, 2002.

———. "God and Time: Toward a Doctrine of Divine Timeless Eternity." *Religious Studies* 25, no. 2 (1989): 209-15.

———. *Science and the Study of God.* Grand Rapids: Eerdmans, 2003.

Peckham, John C. *Theodicy of Love: Cosmic Conflict and the Problem of Evil.* Grand Rapids: Baker Academic, 2018.

Peterson, Michael L. *God and Evil: An Introduction to the Issues.* Boulder, CO: Westview Press, 1998.

———. "God and Evil in Process Theology." In *Process Theology,* edited by Ronald Nash, 117-40. Grand Rapids: Baker, 1987.

Peterson, Michael, William Hasker, Bruce Reichenbach, and David
    Basinger. *Reason and Religious Belief: An Introduction to the
    Philosophy of Religion.* Oxford: Oxford University Press, 2009.
Pinnock, Clark. *The Most Moved Mover: A Theology of God's Openness.*
    Grand Rapids: Baker Academic, 2001.
———. "Systematic Theology." In *The Openness of God: A Biblical Challenge
    to the Traditional Understanding of God*, 101–25. Downers Grove, IL:
    InterVarsity Press, 1994.
Pinnock, Clark, Richard Rice, John Sanders, William Hasker, and
    David Basinger. *The Openness of God: A Biblical Challenge to the
    Traditional Understanding of God.* Downers Grove, IL: InterVarsity
    Press, 1994.
Plantinga, Alvin. "Essence and Essentialism." In *A Companion to
    Metaphysics*, edited by Jaegwon Kim, Ernest Sosa, and Gary S.
    Rosenkranz, 232–33. Oxford: Blackwell, 2009.
———. "Does God Have a Nature?" In *The Analytic Theist: An Alvin
    Plantinga Reader*, edited by James F. Sennet, 225–57. Grand Rapids:
    Eerdmans, 1998.
———. *God, Freedom, and Evil.* Grand Rapids: Eerdmans, 1977.
———. "Is Naturalism Irrational?" In *The Analytic Theist: An Alvin
    Plantinga Reader*, edited by James F. Sennett, 72–96. Grand Rapids:
    Eerdmans, 1998.
———. "Self-Profile," in *Alvin Plantinga*, edited by James Tomberlin and
    Peter van Inwagen, 3–97. Dordrecht: Kluwer Academic, 1986.
———. *The Nature of Necessity.* Oxford: Oxford University Press, 1982.
———. *Where the Conflict Really Lies: Science, Religion, and Naturalism.*
    Oxford: Oxford University Press, 2011.
Polkinghorne, John. "Time in Physics and Theology." In *What God Knows:
    Time, Eternity, and Divine Knowledge*, edited by Harry Lee Poe and J.
    Stanley Mattson, 61–74. Waco, TX: Baylor University Press, 2005.
Post, John F. *Metaphysics: A Contemporary Introduction.* New York:
    Paragon, 1991.
Pruss, Alexander R. "One Body: Reflections on Christian Sexual Ethics."
    Accessed November 12, 2012. http://bearspace.baylor.edu/
    Alexander_Pruss/www/papers/OneBody-talk.html.

Purkayastha, Moushumi, and Kanchan Kumar Mukherjee. "Three Cases of Near Death Experience: Is it Physiology, Physics or Philosophy?" *Annals of Neurosciences* 19, no. 3 (2013): 104–6.

Rainbow, Paul A. "Jewish Monotheism as the Matrix for New Testament Christology: A Review Article." *Novum Testamentum* 33, no. 1 (1991): 17–91.

Reichenbach, Bruce R. *Evil and a Good God.* New York: Fordham University Press, 1986.

Richards, Jay Wesley. *The Untamed God: A Philosophical Exploration of Divine Perfection, Simplicity and Immutability.* Downers Gove, IL: InterVarsity Press, 2003.

Richard of St. Victor. "Of the Trinity." In *The Christian Theology Reader*, 4th ed., edited by Alister E. McGrath, 177–78. Malden, MA: Blackwell, 2011.

Ross, Hugh. *The Creator and the Cosmos: How the Greatest Scientific Discoveries of The Century Reveal God.* Colorado Springs, CO: NavPress, 1995.

Rowe, William L. "The Evidential Argument from Evil: A Second Look." In *The Evidential Argument from Evil*, edited by Daniel Howard-Snyder, 262–85. Bloomington, IN: Indiana University Press, 1996.

———. "The Problem of Evil and Some Varieties of Atheism." In *The Evidential Argument from Evil*, edited by Daniel Howard-Snyder, 1–11. Bloomington, IN: Indiana University Press, 1996.

Rue, Loyal. *Nature is Enough: Religious Naturalism and the Meaning of Life.* Albany, NY: State University of New York Press, 2011.

Russell, Bertrand. "Why I Am Not a Christian." In *Why I Am Not a Christian*, edited by Paul Edwards, 3–23. New York: Touchstone, 1957.

Sabom, Michael. *Light and Death: One Doctor's Fascinating Account of Near-Death Experiences.* Grand Rapids: Zondervan, 1998.

Schneider, John R. "Seeing God Where the Wild Things Are: An Essay on the Defeat of Horrendous Evil." In *Christian Faith and the Problem of Evil*, edited by Peter van Inwagen, 226–62. Grand Rapids: Eerdmans, 2004.

Searle, John. *Mind: A Brief Introduction.* Oxford: Oxford University Press, 2004.

Segal, Alan. *Two Powers in Heaven: Early Rabbinic Reports about Christianity and Gnosticism*. Leiden: Brill, 2002.

Senor, Thomas D. "The Incarnation and the Trinity." In *Reason for the Hope Within*, edited by Michael J. Murray, 238–60. Grand Rapids: Eerdmans, 1999.

Shermer, Michael. "The Great Afterlife Debate: Michael Shermer v. Deepak Chopra." *Skeptic* 13, no. 4 (2008): 53.

Smart, J. J. C. "Laws of Nature and Cosmic Coincidences." *Philosophical Quarterly* 35, no. 140 (1985): 272–80.

Smart, Ninian. *Worldviews: Crosscultural Explorations of Human Beliefs*. 3rd ed. Upper Saddle River, NJ: Prentice Hall, 2000.

Smith, S. M. "Perichoresis." In *Evangelical Dictionary of Theology*, 2nd ed., edited by Walter A. Elwell, 906–7. Grand Rapids: Baker Academic, 2001.

Southgate, Christopher. *The Groaning of Creation: God, Evolution, and the Problem of Evil*. Louisville, KY: Westminster John Knox, 2008.

Spinoza, Benedict de. *Ethics: Part I*. Chicago: The Great Books Foundation, 1956.

Sprigge, T. L. S. *The God of Metaphysics*. Oxford: Oxford University Press, 2008.

Stannard, Russell. "On the Developing Scientific Understanding of Time." In *What God Knows: Time, Eternity, and Divine Knowledge*, edited by Harry Lee Poe and J. Stanley Mattson, 47–60. Waco, TX: Baylor University Press, 2005.

Steinhart, Erick. "Pantheism and Current Ontology." *Religious Studies* 40 (2004): 63–80.

Stenger, Victor J. *God: The Failed Hypothesis: How Science Shows that God Does Not Exist*. Amherst, NY: Prometheus Books, 2007.

Stevenson, Ian. "The Contribution of Apparitions to the Evidence for Survival." *Journal of the American Society for Psychical Research* 76 (1982): 341–58.

Stump, Eleonore. *Wandering in Darkness: Narrative and the Problem of Suffering*. Oxford: Oxford University Press, 2010.

Stump, Eleonore, and Norman Kretzmann. "Eternity." *Journal of Philosophy* 78, no. 8 (1981): 429–58.

Swinburne, Richard. *The Christian God*. Oxford: Oxford University Press, 1994.

———. *The Coherence of Theism*. Oxford: Oxford University Press, 1986.

———. "A Defense of the Doctrine of the Trinity." In *Philosophy of Religion: A Reader and Guide*, edited by William Lane Craig, 556–67. New Brunswick, NJ: Rutgers University Press, 2002.

———. "Natural Theology, Its 'Dwindling Probabilities' and 'Lack of Rapport.'" *Faith and Philosophy* 21 (2004): 533–46.

———. "Some Major Strands of Theodicy." In *The Evidential Argument from Evil*, edited by Daniel Howard-Snyder, 30–48. Bloomington, IN: Indiana University Press, 1996.

Theisen, Henry C., and Vernon D. Doerksen. *Lectures in Systematic Theology*. Rev. ed. Grand Rapids: Eerdmans, 2000.

Tillich, Paul. *Systematic Theology*. Vol. 2. Chicago: Chicago University Press, 1957.

Torrance, Thomas F. *The Christian Doctrine of God: One Being Three Persons*. London: T&T Clark, 1996.

Tuggy, Dale. "On the Possibility of a Single Perfect Person." In *Christian Philosophy of Religion: Essays in Honor of Stephen T. Davis*, edited by C. P. Ruloff, 128–48. Notre Dame, IN: University of Notre Dame Press, 2015.

van Inwagen, Peter. "The Argument from Evil." In *Christian Faith and the Problem of Evil*, edited by Peter van Inwagen, 55–73. Grand Rapids: Eerdmans, 2004.

———. *The Problem of Evil*. Oxford: Oxford University Press, 2008.

———. "The Problem of Evil, the Problem of Air, and the Problem of Silence." In *The Evidential Argument from Evil*, edited by Daniel Howard-Snyder, 151–74. Bloomington, IN: Indiana University Press, 1996.

van Inwagen, Peter, and Dean W. Zimmerman. "Introduction: What is Metaphysics?" In *Metaphysics: The Big Questions*, edited by Peter van Inwagen and Dean W. Zimmerman, 1–13. Malden, MA: Blackwell, 2004.

Walls, Jerry L. *Heaven: The Logic of Eternal Joy*. Oxford: Oxford University Press, 2002.

———. *Heaven, Hell, and Purgatory: A Protestant View of the Cosmic Drama.* Grand Rapids: Brazos Press, 2015.

Walton, Douglas. *Abductive Reasoning.* Tuscaloosa, AL: University of Alabama Press, 2013.

Walton, John H. *The Lost World of Genesis One: Ancient Cosmology and the Origins Debate.* Downers Grove, IL: InterVarsity Press, 2009.

Ware, Bruce A. "An Evangelical Reformulation of the Doctrine of the Immutability of God." *Journal of the Evangelical Theological Society* 29, no. 4 (1986): 431–46.

Ward, Keith. *God: A Guide for the Perplexed.* London: Oneworld, 2002.

Welty, Greg. *Why Is There Evil in the World (And So Much of It?)* Fearn, Ross-shire: Christian Focus, 2018.

Whitehead, Alfred North. *Process and Reality.* Corrected ed. Edited by David Ray Griffin and Donald W. Sherburne. New York: The Free Press, 1978.

Wierenga, Edward R. *The Nature of God: An Inquiry into Divine Attributes.* Ithaca, NY: Cornell University Press, 1989.

Williams, Bryan J. Review of *Phantasms of the Living* (2 Vols) by Edmund Gurney, Fredric W. H. Myers, and Frand Podmore. *Journal of Scientific Explorations* 25, no. 2 (2011): 367–424.

Wolterstorff, Nicholas. "God Everlasting." In *Contemporary Philosophy of Religion,* edited by Steven M. Cahn and David Shatz, 77–98. Oxford: Oxford University Press, 1982.

Wright, N. T. *Evil and the Justice of God.* Downers Grove, IL: InterVarsity Press, 2006.

———. *Surprised by Hope: Rethinking Heaven, the Resurrection, and the Mission of the Church.* New York: HarperOne, 2008.

———. *The Resurrection of the Son of God.* Minneapolis: Fortress, 2003.

Wykstra, Stephen J. "The Humean Obstacle to Evidential Arguments from Suffering: On Avoiding the Evils of 'Appearance.'" In *The Problem of Evil,* edited by Marilyn McCord Adams and Robert Merrihew Adams, 138–60. Oxford: Oxford University Press, 1990.

Yandell, Keith. *Philosophy of Religion: A Contemporary Introduction.* New York: Routledge, 1999.

Yarbrough, Robert. W. *1–3 John.* Grand Rapids: Baker Academic, 2008.

Zagzebski, Linda. "Omnisubjectivity," in *Oxford Studies in Philosophy of Religion*, vol. 1, edited by Jonathan L. Kvanvig, 231–48. Oxford: Oxford University Press, 2008.

SUBJECT INDEX